LANDSCAPES WITH FIGURES

Landscapes with Figures

*People, Culture and Art in Ireland
and the Modern World*

Liam de Paor

FOUR COURTS PRESS

This book was set in 10.5 on 12 point Ehrhardt
by Woodcote Typesetters for
FOUR COURTS PRESS LTD
Fumbally Court, Fumbally Lane, Dublin, Ireland
e-mail: info@four-courts-press.ie
and in North America for
FOUR COURTS PRESS
c/o ISBS, 5804 NE Hassalo Street, Portland, OR 97213.

A catalogue record for this title
is available from the British Library.

ISBN 1-85182-384-0 hbk
ISBN 1-85182-385-9 pbk

This book is printed on an acid-free paper.

Printed in Ireland
by Colour Books Ltd.

For Colin

Contents

Preface

When Michael Adams, of Four Courts Press, first discussed with me the idea of publishing a collection of essays and occasional writings, I made a selection of unpublished as well as previously published pieces dealing with two or three themes that have interested me. It was soon clear that they fell into two groups and that the simplest way of dividing them was chronological. We decided to make two collections, not one, and the essays dealing with early and medieval topics, and mainly with early Ireland's dealings with the outside world, were published in April 1997 under the title *Ireland and Early Europe*.

The present collection deals, not directly with Ireland's relations with the modern world, but with aspects of that modern world both within and without Ireland. Of the 33 pieces printed here, 12 previously appeared in my 'Roots' column in the *Irish Times*, a few of the others also appeared in the *Irish Times* in different forms, and several appeared in other journals or were given as lectures or broadcast. Ten, mainly of the longer pieces, have not appeared in print before.

I wish to thank my wife Deirdre, who gave me a great deal of help in preparing this matter for publication, and to thank also Michael Adams for his friendly cooperation and advice. Acknowledgments are due to the *Irish Times*, the UCC Folk Music Society, RTÉ, the BBC and the *Recorder* (New York), under whose auspices some of this material originally was prepared.

Introduction

This is the companion to the collection published (also by Four Courts Press) in April 1997, entitled *Ireland and Early Europe*. The essays in that volume dealt with Ireland's cultural interactions with Britain and Continental Europe from prehistory through into the Middle Ages. Again, here, I have drawn on previously published items, including contributions to the 'Roots' column in the *Irish Times* in the 1970s, Thomas Davis Lectures, other lectures and articles written for various journals; and again, there are included here essays not previously published.

The material in this collection, however, deals with the modern world and embraces contemporary concerns. It is written from an Irish perspective, and has a central theme; not, this time, the theme of Ireland's external cultural relations so much as that of Ireland's place in the 'New World Order'. When President Bush used the phrase after the collapse of the political system that had been dominated by the Soviet Union, he was addressing the problems that would face the United States and the world in the aftermath of the Cold War. But it is arguable that the end of the Cold War was not nearly so significant an epoch as it seemed at the time to those who were anxiously concerned in waging that War (which, after all, was not a real war but a metaphor). And the President was signifying perhaps that the end of the Cold War was *not* the end of history, in spite of the brief fashion for believing that it was – that what Benedetto Croce called *History as the Study of Liberty* (a concept also cherished by Lord Acton) had worked its way to a *finis*.

A 'New World Order' came into being several centuries ago. The United States of America is part of it. A metamorphosed Ireland was reborn into it and has played its part in shaping the new order – under the leadership of O'Connell, for example, administering the shock of democracy to that British social and political system which was based on an older, deferential, order. The new order, which has often appeared to be rather a disorder, derives from a conscious rejection of many of the values and beliefs of medieval Europe while at the same time an unconscious acceptance of the substance of those values and beliefs has persisted. The 'Enlightenment' embodied both the rejection and the acceptance. This contradiction has generated a dynamic in Western culture whose energy is far from spent, although old oppositions of social and political thought may have lost much of their force.

Growing up in twentieth-century Ireland, the country of Swift, of Burke, of

Wellington, of Grattan, of O'Connell, of Yeats, of Joyce, of Shaw, of Pearse, of Paisley, of Beckett, of Jack B. Yeats and Brendan Behan and U2, has forced me, and my friends and neighbours, to come to grips with the new order, with imperialism, war, modern art, science, technology and the fading of religion. To be Irish born and based in this century was to be, at once a member of a marginalized community, and at the centre of things – in a potato patch whose suburbs were London, New York, Berlin, Paris and Brussels. The observations on the new world order gathered here are made from that perspective.

Ireland and the British Empire

The first Tudor king of England, Henry VII (who reigned from 1485 to 1509) worked to enrich the crown and enlarge its power. He forbade merchants to use foreign ships when English ones were available, he encouraged shipbuilding and trade (from which the monarchy benefited through customs duties), and he directed John and Sebastian Cabot to seek a sea route to the oriental sources of spices and 'to sail to all parts, regions and coasts of the eastern, western and northern sea'. In 1495, through his deputy, Sir Edward Poynings, he brought the English colony in his lordship of Ireland more firmly under the crown's control, while trying to strengthen its defences against the Irish.

In the reign of his son, Henry VIII (1509–47), a new definition of the nature of the king's *imperium* rose from two issues. One was the need for reform in the English church. The other was Henry VIII's wish to marry Anne Boleyn while his wife, Catherine of Aragon (his brother's widow), still lived. Pope Clement VII ruled that the marriage to Catherine was valid and that to wed Anne would be unlawful. In challenging this, Henry and his advisers in effect denied that the king should be subordinate, even theoretically, to any outside power. In secular matters he was independent of all; in spiritual matters the English church should be independent of 'the bishop of Rome, by some men called the pope'. The Act of Appeals (1533) declared 'that this realm of England is an empire, and so hath been accepted in the world, governed by one supreme head and king having the dignity and royal estate of the imperial crown of the same'.

This declaration of more than mere independence, followed by the Act of Supremacy (1534), led to the need for further definition of the king's right in Ireland. Henry's style and title 'lord of Ireland' derived from the grant *Laudabiliter* made in 1155 by Pope Hadrian IV to King Henry II instructing the king to reform the church in Ireland and correct the morals of its people. Henry II bestowed the lordship on his youngest son, John, who, as it happened, ultimately succeeded to the throne of England. The pope claimed full secular as well as spiritual jurisdiction over islands of the ocean. In the now dawning age of European discovery, this claim led to the papal division of undiscovered parts, all that lay west of an arbitrary longitude in the Atlantic going to the Spanish crown, all to the east of the same line going to the Portuguese. A kingship of Ireland had existed before

Previously unpublished.

the advent of the Anglo-Normans in the twelfth century, and the Irish continued to rule extensive parts of the island. Brian Bóroimhe had styled himself 'Emperor of the Irish' at the beginning of the eleventh century, apparently asserting a full sovereignty embodying the right and duty of quasi-divine governance. This kingship was remembered and its revival occasionally contemplated. When Edward Bruce landed at Larne in 1315 he was acknowledged at Dundalk as king, and Domhnall O'Neill, on behalf of a number of Irish chiefs, submitted a 'remonstrance' to Pope John XXII, justifying the transfer of allegiance from King Edward II on the grounds of the ancient right of the native kings of Ireland, the unworthy motivation of *Laudabiliter*, the failure of Henry II and his successors to act in accordance with the papal directions in that grant, and the denial of law to the Irish lords.

There was great incompatibility in economy, property-holding and criminal procedures between Irish society and Norman; and the Irish, especially in the border zones between the two systems, were denied not only English law but also the security of their own law. An imperialist relationship was already established by the thirteenth century. It was maintained by a series of enactments designed to preserve the separateness of the settlers in law, language and custom.

After his breach with Rome, Henry VIII proceeded, as part of his assertion of imperial right, to an arbitrary assumption of the kingship of Ireland. He had the colonial Irish parliament pass a declaratory act in 1541 acknowledging his kingship, and went on to deal with the native Irish rulers through the policy known as 'Surrender and Regrant,' by which the chiefs (in contravention of Irish law) surrendered their territories, abandoned their Irish titles, disowned the pope and acknowledged Henry as their king, in return for which he granted their lands back to them (within the context of English feudal law) and bestowed English titles of nobility on them. The title claimed thereafter by the English monarchs in Ireland was fully and absolutely imperial. In this it differed from the title claimed by the rulers of Spain and Portugal both in the New World and in the Orient in the sixteenth century. Their claims derived from an equivalent of *Laudabiliter*: the papal division of the world between them, which gave rise to the treaty of Tordesillas in 1494. In the reign of Mary Tudor (1553–58), who was married to Philip II of Spain, the conquest of Ireland began to take on the full character of an imperialist enterprise with the attempted 'plantation' of the south midlands. It was proposed to displace the native Irish landholders and their tenants and to 'plant' loyal English colonies in their stead, in territory that was divided into 'King's County' (now Offaly) and 'Queen's County' (now Laois).

Plantation in several variations was attempted in the ensuing conquest of Ireland, in the reign of Elizabeth (1558-1603), and involved a combination of public and private enterprise. The state made grants of confiscated land to privileged persons who undertook to settle new proprietors and frequently also to plant a loyal tenantry. The queen herself was a joint shareholder with the earl of Essex in one such venture in Ulster, which was unsuccessful. After the final suppression of the Desmond rebellion in 1583, the vast area in Munster that had been declared forfeit to the crown was planted. Huge lots were granted to those prepared to settle them with new tenants, and towards the end of the century the colonists numbered about ten thousand. This plantation failed, however, partly because the area was devastated in the warfare of the end of the century.

The Portuguese, the Spaniards and the Dutch established trading stations, 'factories' and small colonies, both in the East and in the New World that was being revealed to Europeans beyond the Atlantic. In the overseas empire so being created the English first appeared as parasites – as slave-traders to the Spaniards or as licensed pirates raiding and attacking the fleets and bases of the European imperialists. But around the middle of the century the English began to compete, attempting to find a northern passage to the East (the southern passages were the monopoly of the Spaniards and the Portuguese).

Sir Walter Raleigh was given a patent in 1584 to found a colony in America, and in 1585 he established the first settlement on Roanoke Island and named it 'Virginia' in honour of the queen. Raleigh was also prominently involved in the Munster plantation, which began in the same year. The American colony failed, but a parallel was established between plantation in Ireland and plantation in America. Such attempts continued in Ireland and were most successful in the plantation of Ulster, by which, in the seventeenth century, a substantial colony was established in six north-western counties through state-supported enterprise. Private enterprise was even more successful in establishing colonies, partly on depopulated land, in Antrim and Down.

Meantime the East India Company received its charter from Queen Elizabeth on 31 December 1600, and began attempts to win a share of the trade of the East. The English established stations at several places on the coasts of the Indian subcontinent. Following the track of the Spaniards, they also made westward endeavours across the Atlantic, attempting to colonize the eastern coasts and islands of North America. Colonies which were initially rather more successful were founded in Bermuda and the West Indies in the seventeenth century. But the first substantial coastal settlements had been associated with the cod fishery on the Grand Bank (*Talamh an Éisc* – 'the fishing grounds' – to the Irish fishermen), developed since the fifteenth century by the Portuguese and the Bretons. From an early date the ports of south-western England and south-eastern Ireland were sending fleets westward to hunt the cod. The Irish established small settlements on the southern shores of Newfoundland, while the more numerous English fishermen at first tended to winter at home. This was the beginning of the considerable contribution to be made by the Irish to the European colonization of North America.

The settlements made under the Stuarts in New England, Virginia and Maryland were English. The Irish contributed, largely involuntarily, to the repopulation of the West Indies. When Cromwell decided to make an example of Drogheda after its garrison surrendered, we are told that 'every tenth man was knocked on the head and the rest shipped to the Barbados'. They went as indentured servants – slaves for a fixed term of years. This method of populating the colonies was further developed in the seventeenth and eighteenth centuries, accounting not only for much of the early Irish migration across the Atlantic but for much English, Scottish and Welsh migration too. The West Indian and Bermudan settlements were initially attempts at full colonization, and the same methods of dealing with the natives were employed as in North America: forced labour, treacherous dealings and massacre. But the importation of slaves from Africa – to both the mainland and the islands – soon greatly altered the balance in the West Indies, where plantation economies developed in which the imported slaves greatly outnumbered the colonial masters. In some places Irish and African slaves mixed to produce a 'black Irish' people, as most notably on Montserrat.

In their dealings with Ireland itself, English governments of the late sixteenth and seventeenth centuries contemplated from time to time a policy of full colonization and total replacement of the natives – the policy that was to be followed in North America. Genocide and transplantation of the native population were both considered several times but were, in the case of Ireland, beyond the means of government. Instead a more limited policy of plantation was pursued. Policy, which was variable and erratic, was greatly affected by the revolutionary upheavals of seventeenth-century England. The conquest of Ireland took on a religious or ideological as well as a political, social and cultural complexion. It involved ultimately the confiscation of most of the landed estates of Ireland and a redistribution of the land to a newly installed Protestant colonial class, which rapidly developed creole characteristics – English to the Irish, Irish to the English. In response the Catholic landowners and burghers of Ireland developed a constitutional theory, later to be adopted by the colonial ascendancy. This theory asserted that Ireland was an independently distinct nation under the same crown as England, sharing the common law but to be bound otherwise only by its own statutes, enacted by its own parliament. The proposition contained the germ of a significant theory of empire. An opposed theory held that Ireland had been conquered by the English and was thereafter at their disposal for settlement or other purposes.

In the meantime the colony in Ireland encountered competition from English merchants and producers and chafed under Navigation Acts and other restrictive English legislation. The Navigation Acts were instruments of mercantilism, designed to secure England's commerce and wealth through monopolistic restrictions. The first of these Acts, in 1651 and 1660, treated Ireland similarly to England: the Irish were free to trade with the colonies and Irish ships had the same status as English ships. In 1663, however, direct Irish exports to the colonies were prohibited, except for provisions, servants and horses, and in 1667 the import of Irish cattle into England was prohibited. An Act of 1671 listed commodities, including sugar, tobacco and indigo, that must be shipped directly from the colonies to England. In 1696 *all* articles from the colonies were required to be shipped directly to England. And in 1696 an Act prohibited Irish woollen exports to the colonies or any foreign countries: Irish wool and woollens might be shipped to England only.

Ireland therefore occupied an ambiguous position in the growing empire. On the one hand it was a colony, like the American colonies, occupied by descendants of settlers from Great Britain who – after the wars of the seventeenth century – concentrated power and property in their hands and held the country for the English crown. In many ways Ireland could be regarded as the earliest colony of England's empire. On the other hand Ireland was a distinct kingdom with its own Lords and Commons, courts and institutions, whose colonial parliament, although subordinate since the time of Henry VII to the king in council in England, was of considerable antiquity and had had a development in some respects similar to that of the English parliament. But apart from constitutional relationships Ireland was a special case because it was geographically so close to England and closer still to Scotland. For England's defence against invasion by Continental powers such as Spain or France, control of Ireland was of great strategic importance.

The Stuart succession had produced a union of the English and Scottish crowns, and the monarchs of the dynasty ruled three kingdoms: England, Scotland and Ireland. The legislative union of England and Scotland in 1707, which created the United Kingdom of Great Britain, was followed by the Declaratory Act (1719), which asserted the British parliament's ultimate control of Irish legislation. This declaration was an imperial instrument that was to be used again in the dispute with the American colonies: part of its wording is repeated in the (American) Declaratory Act of 1766.

In the matter of restrictions on trade, British governments in the eighteenth century by and large tried to moderate the pressure from British productive and mercantile interests but were regularly constrained to yield to such pressures. These governments tried to exercise their real power over the Irish parliament (as over other colonial assemblies) without making too much show of it. But through the eighteenth century the independence of the Irish parliament tended to grow slowly and erratically (notably in the voting of monies), and this placed an increasing strain on the British system of parliamentary manipulation. This is broadly true too of the colonial assemblies in America and the West Indies. But a sharp distinction remained. Ireland's proximity to Great Britain meant that there was both the need for and the possibility of an exercise of tighter control over the country. On the other hand Ireland's status was superior to that of the other colonies: the country had a true parliament – unlike the colonial assemblies, although these, paradoxically, being remote, had more freedom – and it was itself a kingdom. So there were fundamental differences between the development of the transatlantic colonies and that of Ireland, in spite of striking parallels. There were two circumstances to inhibit colonial Ireland from moving to full economic and political independence. One was the size and character of the Catholic population of native origin: in face of this the colonial ascendancy needed British backing to maintain its power and privilege. The other, perhaps of greater importance, was Britain's strategic need to keep a firm grip on the island.

The British overseas imperial situation was drastically changed by the conflict known in England as the Seven Years War (1756–63) (in America the 'French and Indian War'). This was fought on the European Continent and in India, the West Indies and North America. The British and their allies prevailed, and after the peace settlement, what is known retrospectively as 'the old empire' briefly reached its greatest extent. The British gained New France, or Canada, a vast territory to the north of their American colonies. The British East India Company, with the support of imperial forces, had overcome the rival French company in India, had chastened the decrepit Mogul empire and had occupied the substantial ruins of that Empire's fiscal and administrative system. The Company's servants found themselves able to take over the Mogul communications, collect taxes, discriminate in favour of British traders, usurp the effective government of large territories and hugely enrich themselves in the process. In the West Indies too the British now had the upper hand, but here they allowed the French to retain some possessions.

In spite of this access of territory and power, weaknesses emerged in the imperial system. The defeat of the Jacobite cause at Culloden in 1746 removed a potential danger to the Irish colonials that had made them highly dependent on Britain for their security. Within the next generation some began to revive arguments put forward by the Catholics in the middle of the seventeenth century and by colonial writers like Molyneaux at the turn of the century, for the autonomy and independence of the kingdom of Ireland. 'Patriots' argued this case, which produced a loosely grouped but increasingly effective faction in the Irish parliament. In America, similarly, the British acquisition of Canada in 1763 relieved the colonials of the French threat and made them accordingly less dependent on British imperial military support.

By this time an Irish pattern of transatlantic migration was established. Emigration often meant an escape from religious discrimination and economic hardship. A large part of the movement to the colonies was of Ulster Presbyterians – the 'Scotch Irish' of somewhat later nomenclature---who soon came to form a considerable part of the colonial population of British North America, especially on the frontiers of settlement. A sizeable Catholic migration also took place, from all parts of Ireland.

The first great crisis of the British overseas empire occurred with the War of the American Revolution. It was a crisis not only in America but also in Great Britain itself – and in Ireland. It arose from issues concerning the mercantilist imperial system. Then relations between the colonies and Great Britain ran aground on reefs of constitutional theory. The colonial assemblies controlled their own affairs to a large extent. They had been, and continued to a late hour to be, loyal to the British crown. But were the colonials equal in status to Englishmen in England? Might the government in London tax them for British purposes? What if these purposes involved imperial defence – the costs of the Royal Navy and of imperial military expeditions where the protection of the colonies was involved? The colonials put forward radical propositions about the nature of government and politics, derived from ideas of the European Enlightenment, idealizing the freedoms theoretically enjoyed under the British Constitution.

When the dispute came to war, the American colonials found it expedient to engage the help of the French, now separated by three thousand miles of ocean, whom the Americans had dreaded when they had solid bases of their own in the New World. The colony in Ireland had many grievances that paralleled those of the Americans; but in Ireland the French remained a proximate menace. What the Irish colonials did when the American war began was to raise their own force – the Volunteers – to defend Ireland against French invasion but also to force the British government, in its hour of difficulty, to meet their demand for free trade and parliamentary independence. In the imperial emergency of the American war both demands were conceded. Restrictions on Irish trade were lifted first; then in 1782 Ireland embarked on the experiment which anticipated the concept of a British 'dominion'. But the legislative independence achieved did not quite create the constitutional equivalent of the later dominions. The Irish executive, for example, was not responsible to the Irish Parliament; it continued to be a British executive in Ireland. Yet the legislative independence granted to Ireland under pressure opened the possibility of a reorganization of the empire along lines implicit in some of the arguments of the American colonials before their Revolution.

The 'old empire' ended with the American War. Great Britain lost the thirteen colonies but retained Canada. William Pitt the Younger grasped the possibilities of the situation and tried to negotiate a new imperial arrangement with Ireland. The issues now raised were to recur, in various forms, in discussions of the meaning, purpose and character of the British Empire for as long as it continued to endure. Pitt pointed out that with the loss of the American colonies, 'Great Britain and Ireland are now the only considerable members . . .' of '. . . our reduced and shattered empire;' but Ireland through its colonial parliament was asserting with considerable success an independence which required a wholly new framework if the empire was to continue. The chief Irish spokesman and negotiator was Henry Grattan, leader of the opposition in the Irish House of Commons. Pitt endeavoured to work out a kind of constitutional treaty between Great Britain and Ireland that would link the two kingdoms in an imperial partnership. The initial proposal was for a complete freeing of trade between them. As to imperial defence, Pitt insisted that there must be only one imperial navy, the British navy; Ireland therefore should remit taxes to Great Britain for its maintenance. This raised the issue of 'taxation without representation,' which had been to the fore in the dispute with the American colonies, and Grattan insisted on full Irish liberties. However, the two came to an agreement and in 1795 the Irish parliament passed the necessary legislation. But in the British Parliament the free trade proposal roused such a storm of protest from protectionists that the counterpart bill had to be withdrawn. The experiment in imperial redesign failed, and an uncertainty, deemed by Pitt and others to be very dangerous, prevailed in the Anglo-Irish connection.

Meanwhile external events were wholly changing the situation. The French Revolution had immediate effects on the politics of Great Britain and Ireland. It was to inspire republicanism and nationalism in Ireland and to lead to twenty more years of warfare between the United Kingdom and France. It came at a time when negotiations were in progress between colonial Ireland and Great Britain concerning the imperial relationship of the two, and between Great Britain, colonial Ireland and Catholic Ireland concerning the working out of a new polity within Ireland. An easing of the penal laws against Catholics had begun in 1778, and in 1793 a sweeping Relief Act was passed, abolishing many legal disabilities on Catholics and extending the franchise to them; but the Act fell short of admitting Catholics to Parliament. The uprisings of 1798 revealed the great instability of the country. These, together with the failure of the attempt to establish a stable and permanent imperial relationship between the United Kingdom of Great Britain and the Kingdom of Ireland, led to the change in British policy that resulted in the Act of Union of 1800.

With the Union, Ireland for a time ceased to play an independent part in imperial history. In theory it was now simply a constituent part of the United Kingdom of Great Britain and Ireland – a partner in empire. The British ultimately came out on the winning side in the long war against Napoleon, and were in possession of colonial territories around the globe. Throughout the nineteenth century the Royal Navy dominated the world's oceans, safeguarded British trade, and enabled overseas empire to expand continuously.

For the Irish the nineteenth century was a time of mass migration. Millions went to America; and Irish people, along with English, Scottish and Welsh, helped to conquer, defend, administer and populate British possessions around the world. Large numbers of Irish, some of them political offenders, were transported to the penal colonies, and today the population of Australia has a high proportion of people of Irish origin. Irish people of all kinds were to be found at all levels in the societies of the worldwide empire.

Ireland as a nation began to play an independent part again in imperial history with the agitation, first for repeal of the Union, then for Home Rule. For the country to reacquire legislative independence, however limited, would be to raise once more the difficult questions left unresolved at the end of the eighteenth century. But by now the empire was being thought of as two-tiered: the home countries, and 'British possessions': the subordinate colonies and territories constituting the overseas dependent empire. The notion of an imperial federation of equals, or near-equals, was in abeyance, partly because of the great variety of these overseas possessions after the Napoleonic period. Settlement colonies largely populated by people of British origin no longer dominated the scene. In the Indian Empire, now extensive and still expanding, a handful of people from the United Kingdom governed millions of the native people of the subcontinent, by an autocracy exercised until mid-century through the East India Company's governor-general in Council under the regulation of British law and government. Trade and the flag were entering more and more parts of Africa, and again government, by tiny minorities of intruders, was autocratic. Various accommodations were reached in the remnants of the old empire. Slavery was formally abolished relatively early in the century throughout the empire but essentially slave economies continued. New settlement colonies were being created in Australia and New Zealand, where native inhabitants – like the native Americans – endured partly successful attempts at genocide.

Since the eighteenth century there had been lively debates about the value or purpose of colonies. The Scottish economic theorist Adam Smith had opposed them, arguing that trade alone would more efficiently bring such benefits as might be gained by conquest. Many continued to follow his opinion. But others strongly argued that colonies were valuable, as depositories, for example, of surplus population from the home countries. And many mercantile and business interests sought overseas empire as a means of exploiting mineral and other natural resources. They were interested, for example, in land and climate suitable for the cultivation of specialized crops – tea, teak, jute, cotton and opium in the Indian Empire.

The ideology of 'free trade' dominated the middle years of the century, but in spite of Smith's opinion many free-traders found it possible to reconcile their views with the maintenance of a colonial empires. Indeed some saw the empire itself as a working model of the free trade system and held that it would tend towards the ultimate good of all (although in the meantime cheap Manchester piece goods were taking away the livelihood of Indian handweavers).

In the circumstances the efforts of Irish nationalists to separate Ireland from Great Britain again, even if only partly, led to fears that the break-up of the United Kingdom would lead to break-up of the empire. Such fears became acute in the course of the long-drawn-out controversy on Home Rule towards the end of the century. By this time the relatively calm and moderate debate on the empire that had occupied political and economic theorists for decades was giving way to more intemperate and passionately held views. It was the time of the 'new imperialism' of the 1880s and 1890s, when the rulers of Europe (and America) engaged in headlong competition to bring more and more territories around the world under their own countries' flags. The competition was heightened by the spread of social-Darwinian and racialist views among these rulers; by the widely held faith in 'progress,' and by the increasingly intensive search for occasions to invest capital profitably.

Many had convinced themselves that it was, as it were, the natural right – and duty – of 'Britons,' or 'Teutons,' or 'Anglo-Saxons,' to rule over the inferior races of the earth and confer upon them the benefits of civilization. Rudyard Kipling, for example, who had a background in the bureaucratic and military service of the Raj in India, thought of empire as the rightful and just domination by the benevolent imperial power of 'captive peoples, half savage and half child.' But another view was held by some of the most active practitioners of the new imperialism: that the future would belong to a world-wide federation of English-speaking peoples, and that settlement colonies should in due course enjoy the same status as the motherland. Cecil Rhodes, who envisaged a continuous tract under British rule 'from the Cape to Cairo', and who went a long way himself towards achieving it, looked at the matter from the viewpoint of the self-made imperialist on the ground in the colonies and was in favour of some such federation of equals. Joseph Chamberlain, who had begun his career in local government in Birmingham, favoured decentralization at home (although he strongly opposed Home Rule for Ireland) and came to envisage the Empire as an economic community with internal free trade but tariff barriers against the rest of the world.

Rhodes supported Home Rule; Kipling vehemently opposed it. When Gladstone's Liberal Party split on the first Home Rule Bill in 1886, the Liberal Unionists who refused to vote for the Bill were largely the same people who, in the debate on the empire, were Liberal Imperialists. And Irish unionists, Ulster unionists in particular, were firmly imperialist in sentiment, strongly favouring the 'forward' or 'new imperialist' school. The Ulstermen identified their industrial base in the north-east corner of an otherwise agricultural and pastoral Ireland with 'progress', and 'progress' with the domination of the inferior by the superior races and the clear hegemony of the United Kingdom within the Empire.

On the nationalist side there was much less interest in the Empire as such, but there was more diversity of opinion. The great famine of the 1840s had dispersed hundreds of thousands of people with powerful and bitter nationalist and anti-British sentiments not only to the United States but also to the colonies. Some of them sympathized with other peoples who chafed under British rule throughout the empire. But the racial sentiments of the time prevailed among Irish nationalists too, and their feelings towards Africans, Indians, Maoris and others, however oppressed they might be, were at best ambiguous. The occasional attempts to align Irish nationalism with other nationalisms in the Empire had little consequence. The nascent nationalism of India was influenced by the Home Rule movement and for a time an Indian Home Rule League was in advance, in this respect, of the initially very conservative and cautious Congress movement. In Ireland there were some suggestions of cooperation with Indian nationalism, as when it was proposed that the Irish parliamentary party consider providing representation in Parliament for Indian nationalists by supporting one or two Indian candidates in Irish constituencies for election to the House of Commons. Such efforts came to nothing, but the impulse that led to them lingered on. Major John MacBride, later to be executed for his leading part in the 1916 rising, led an Irish brigade to fight for the Boers against the British in the South African War (while Roger Casement, also to be executed for his 1916 activities, as British consul in Laurenco Marques, was urging firm opposition to the Boers, because of his sympathy for the black population of Southern Africa). Later there was some sympathy and understanding between Éamon de Valéra and Mohandas Gandhi. But most of this had less to do with views of empire than with the common nationalist feeling that England's enemies were *de facto* Ireland's friends.

The policy developed under the leadership of Parnell's successor, John Redmond, in the early twentieth century tended towards something like Grattan's view. Ireland, self-governing under Home Rule (which did *not* involve repeal of the Union) was to be a partner of Great Britain – in imperial as in other matters. Although a Home Rule bill received the support of the House of Commons in 1912, it was negatived by the powerful opposition of Ulster unionism and of the House of Lords, and on its passage into law in 1914 was suspended before it came into effect, because of the outbreak of the Great War. The republican Easter Rising of 1916 and the subsequent swing of nationalist opinion to support Sinn Féin abruptly ended the long Home Rule campaign and the accommodations with Great Britain which had been both implicit and explicit in it. Unmitigated separatism was dominant for a time, and the break-up of the Empire indeed began, as so many unionists had feared it would.

The Government of Ireland Act, 1920, partitioned Ireland and gave the Ulster unionists Home Rule in part of Ulster, 'Northern Ireland.' A similar provision for the rest of the country ('Southern Ireland') was inoperative, because a majority of the Irish had declared and voted for a republic, whose forces were fighting the British in a guerrilla war. After the truce of 1921 a treaty was negotiated between Great Britain and the Irish republicans, establishing, in twenty-six counties, the Irish Free State. This involved the break-up of the United Kingdom and the end of the full Union. The Free State's status was defined as that of a dominion and was declared to be equivalent to Canada's. The term 'dominion' had hitherto remained undefined but it referred to the self-governing settlement colonies: Canada, Australia, New Zealand, South Africa and Newfoundland. These had been pressing towards greater autonomy and freedom from direct British control, and had been discussing common interests in a series of imperial conferences. All five countries had given substantial help to Great Britain in the Great War. When the war ended, Great Britain, weakened by loss of blood and fortune, had to give way to their pressure. They succeeded, for example, in obtaining separate representation at the Peace Conference of 1919. The Irish Free State now joined this club.

The Free State had been forced into this constitutional position through the Treaty of 1921 signed under British pressure in refusing to countenance the Republic. The compromise was resisted by many republicans, and the establishment of the state in 1922 was followed by a bitter civil war in which the opponents of the Treaty were defeated. Irish representatives took part on behalf of the new dominion at the Imperial Conference of 1923. The Irish now proceeded to go beyond the other dominions in interpreting 'dominion status' in favour of greater autonomy. In 1924 the Free State created a precedent by appointing a minister to Washington and the Irish government so arranged matters that the minister was largely independent of the British Ambassador. Canada, which had been working towards some such arrangement, followed the Irish example in Washington in 1927, when the United States reciprocated by appointing ministers to Dublin and Ottawa. It was in 1924 too that the Irish Free State registered the Anglo-Irish Treaty of 1921 with the League of Nations. The British government protested that this was a matter internal to the 'British commonwealth,' not within the purview of the League; but the other dominions tacitly supported the Irish action, and the British were obliged to withdraw. The dominions had already succeeded in having separate representation in the League of Nations. When a British representative, speaking at the League in 1925, claimed that in a matter affecting the vital interests of any one of the 'six equal partners' there had to be solidarity of action by all, the Irish representative denied this, and again the British backed down.

Other difficulties arose in connection with appeals from the dominions to the Privy Council, and with relations between the British and dominion parliaments. Ireland's status had been defined by reference to Canada, but now Canada, as well as the Irish Free State and South Africa, was pressing for a more clearly autonomous status. The British, realizing that this was inevitable, prepared the way for a reorganized empire, and in 1926 separated the Dominions Office from the Colonial Office. A distinction between 'Empire' and 'Commonwealth' was also made at the Imperial Conference of that year, when the British Commonwealth was defined as 'the group of self-governing communities composed of Great Britain and the Dominions', which were 'autonomous Communities within the British Empire, equal in status, in no way subordinate to one another in any aspect of their domestic or external affairs, though united by a common allegiance to the Crown and freely associated as members of the British Commonwealth of Nations'. To meet Irish wishes, through this conference the King's official title was changed, to omit the term 'United Kingdom of Great Britain and Ireland': instead he was styled king 'of Great Britain, Ireland and the British Dominions beyond the seas.' The conference had set up a committee to report on imperial restrictions on dominion legislation and related matters. Legislation based on the report was drafted by the dominions and recommended to the Imperial parliament in Westminster. This led to the passing of the Statute of Westminster of 1931.

In effect the Statute of Westminster freed the dominion parliaments from all Imperial legislative control. It also required the concurrence of all the parliaments in any matter touching royal titles or the succession to the throne. The Irish Free State and South Africa immediately moved to exercise their newly defined autonomy to the full.

In the Irish Free State the government of William Cosgrave gave way after the general election of 1932 to the government of Éamon de Valéra, who had opposed the Treaty. De Valéra's aim was a republic in external association with the Commonwealth, but his immediate concern was to separate the Free State from Great Britain. He proceeded to dismantle the Treaty by obstruction and legalistic devices. For example, he did not attempt to abolish the office of governor-general (the king's representative) but reduced it to a mockery by appointing one of his republican followers – Domhnall Ua Buachalla – who ignored the trappings of the post. In 1936 de Valera made use of the abdication crisis (when the parliaments of all the dominions were required to consent to the royal succession arrangements) to rush through legislation reducing the crown to the merest cipher in Irish affairs. Then in 1937 he submitted a new constitution to the people of the Free State to be enacted through referendum. This was republican in all but name and contained no reference to the crown. The name of the state was changed to 'Ireland'. The crown retained only the most shadowy relation with the state, mainly through the accreditation of diplomatic representatives. In 1939, when the United Kingdom went to war with Germany, the Irish state set a precedent by remaining neutral – the only dominion to do so. And in 1948 the government headed, not by de Valéra but by John A. Costello, leader of Cosgrave's old party, suddenly declared a republic and took the state out of the Commonwealth and Empire.

A curious and interesting connection remained. The British 'Ireland Act, 1949,' recognizing that the 'Republic of Ireland' was a sovereign independent state, also declared that 'notwithstanding that the Republic of Ireland is not a foreign country for the purposes of any law in force in any part of the United Kingdom or in any colony, protectorate or United Kingdom trust territory.' And Northern Ireland continued to be part of the United Kingdom, although it was to lose its Home Rule status in 1972.

2

Before the American Century

The twentieth century, according to Henry Luce (perhaps paraphrasing Tocqueville) was to be 'the American century'; and his prophecy, which required no great perspicacity, has been more than well borne out. It is true that for a period of one or two decades the Soviet Union offered a challenge and embodied (especially under the leadership of Nikita Kruschev) the ambition to make it the Marxist, or the Soviet, or the Russian century; but the challenge failed. The United States, showing itself to be a warlike power which exercised its military strength in all the major conflicts of the time, usually directly, sometimes indirectly, and in many minor ones as well, has been dominant in the world for a hundred years. As I write at the end of the twentieth century, the world order bears an American stamp. American economic, political, military and cultural policies affect us all. The conversion of American public policy to 'the New Imperialism' in 1897–8 may be taken to mark the beginning of that dominance. But the conversion did not signify a sudden deviation of the thrust of American policies and purposes in the world outside the United States; it can be seen as the maturation of attitudes and aspirations developed in the course of the previous two centuries.

When they declared their independence of the British crown in 1776, the American colonials were, in a way, announcing a foreign policy. For example, they were asserting that Great Britain was to be foreign from now on. But more than that, they were, in another sense, setting America against Europe; the Old World as a whole was being rejected in favour of an experiment in the New – where, it soon transpired, Paradise was to be re-created.

The Declaration also recited some grievances of the disaffected colonies in respect of relations with other nations in their adopted continent. Long before the crucial conflict with England began, they had been troubled by events beyond the limits of their own settlements.

The colonies that were to become the United States of America had come into being through migration and settlement from Europe (mainly the British Isles), largely directed and controlled by English governmental policy. Their populations had been greatly augmented by the importation of black slaves from Africa. The colonials thought of themselves as fellow subjects of the crown along with the inhabitants of the British Isles, and saw the colonies in a way as an

Previously unpublished.

extension of Britain overseas – although many of them sought in America freedom from certain constraints (religious and otherwise) that had troubled them 'at home.'

There were however important differences from England, Scotland and Wales (Ireland was then still itself different: a separate kingdom, also dominated by British colonials) which made it impossible to sustain the case that the colonies were simply an overseas version of the home countries. The British settlements came to occupy large areas along the eastern seaboard of the North American continent, but the settlers by no means had these areas to themselves and their slaves. The British settlers, from the very moment of their arrival, were in contact with native American peoples – without whose help many of them would not have survived – and there were also colonists from other European nations. Portuguese and Breton fishermen were familiar with the North Atlantic long before the English ventured out on those waters. Spain was directing colonies in the Americas almost a hundred years before Raleigh attempted his Virginia plantation. Colonization was competitive.

So in the seventeenth century the little pockets of settlement from Europe along the eastern seaboard of the continent included Swedes, Dutch, Portuguese, French, Spaniards, Irish and others as well as English. In most parts the English were comparative latecomers; since command of the sea passage was necessary to the maintenance of a colony, and until the late sixteenth century (virtually until the defeat of the Armada in 1588) Spanish, not English, naval power ruled the Atlantic.

The English colonies in the seventeenth century were of several kinds. Some were essentially commercial ventures set up by joint-stock or similar companies for trading purposes. Some were in effect great proprietary estates granted to favoured adventurers with the intention that they would expand further the power and wealth of England. Others were enterprises set up directly by the crown through royal agents and governors for reasons of public policy.

In the seventeenth century the inhabitants of some parts of Europe could be disposed of by royal governments without reference to their wishes, as if they were tenants on large estates (as Clausewitz put it) – when provinces changed hands as the result of wars or dynastic marriages. The development of English polity, however, had been such that this was not likely to happen to the inhabitants of Yorkshire or Suffolk. But it was possible in the colonies, which were still disposable 'possessions.' It was indeed by such disposal that some of the colonies in America by the century's end had become English – as when the Dutch town of New Amsterdam was ceded to become the English town of New York – and nowhere was the population of an English colony simply of English origin. But there was a widespread feeling among the colonials that they should retain the same rights and privileges in this and in other respects as the inhabitants of Yorkshire or Suffolk.

In the early days of settlement the chief external threat to the colonists arose as a consequence of their own actions. The settlers had not come to an empty land. The native inhabitants – the 'Indians' – had to be displaced by force or fraud or, most commonly, a combination of the two. Understandably, they resented this, and numbers of them combined in several attempts in the seventeenth century to dislodge the intruders who had subjected them to treachery, violence and rapine. The response to such Indian attacks was the creation of temporary warlike unions of groups of colonies (which maintained militias), in spite of the great distances and poor communications between some of the colonial centres.

Later, threats came to the English possessions from the colonial forces of other powers, in particular the French. From 1689 onwards, throughout the eighteenth century, England was intermittently at war with France. The long war, although European in its main theatres, was conducted also in various parts of the world, including America, where the colonials became involved marginally in a conflict whose issues were remote from them at first.

But in the middle of the eighteenth century a renewal of that intermittent conflict gained new significance and became an episode that changed the history of the world. This was what became known in England as the 'Seven Years War' and in America as the 'French and Indian War' (in Prussia, the 'Second Silesian War'). It was different. It has good claim to the description, 'the first world war,' since, not only was it fought in different parts of the world, but it directly involved the interests of people far from European shores—including the West Indies, India and North America. The war began in North America in 1755, a year before it was formally declared in Europe, because of French moves which threatened to cut off the coastal British colonies from westward expansion into the interior of the Continent. The Appalachians are not high mountains but in the eighteenth century they constituted a formidable barrier: a zone, two or three hundred kilometers wide, of parallel ridges and valleys heavily wooded and discouraging to settlement. Beyond the mountains, however, the great broad valleys and plains extended into the heart of America. In the 1750s, the British colonials, having fairly well occupied the good lands of the Atlantic slope, were forming speculative companies to exploit the country beyond the mountains. Already their surveyors (one of whom was the young George Washington) were probing across the ridges and through the Appalachian forests. Then the French, from their bases and settlements in Upper Canada and on the lower Mississippi, began extending a line of forts along the western foothills of the Appalachians: a cordon to contain the expansion of the British colonies and to reserve the exploration and exploitation of the continental heartland to themselves.

The British colonial militias therefore fought with heart and purpose in the French and Indian War and fully enjoyed the satisfaction of British victory at its end. The way to the west was open.

Or was it? For, with the successful end to the Seven Years War in 1763, the British Empire was rounded out with vast new acquisitions, including large tracts of India, islands in the Caribbean and enormous territories in North America, surrendered to Britain by the French. The gaining of Canada, or New France, by the United Kingdom greatly altered the character of British North America, since it took under British rule colonies of French-speaking Roman Catholics, who were by origin, faith, custom and their modes of colonial organization, sharply different from the people of British origin in the thirteen colonies further south. It became a grievance in New England that the British, after some vacillation, decided, for practical reasons, to retain the French system of colonial adminis-tration in New France, including the virtual establishment of the Roman Catho-lic church there. Anti-Catholicism spurred on the recurrent colonial agitations against British policies in British America.

No policy caused more anger and frustration among the colonials than the British decision to set a limit to the expansion of settlement and leave the land west of the Appalachians to its native American inhabitants. A royal proclama-tion in 1763 prohibited settlement beyond the line of the watershed which di-vides waters flowing ultimately into the Atlantic Ocean from those flowing ulti-mately into the Gulf of Mexico. The country west of the 'Proclamation Line' was to be reserved for the Indians. Yet colonial settlement – and most certainly colo-nial aspiration – had already passed this line when the Proclamation was made. The French were established on the lower Mississippi, but the way to the upper Mississippi – 'British territory' now – seemed open.

The colonials' decision to break with the distant royal government in Eng-land derived from an accumulation of grievances and frustrations, all of which had in common that the colonials enjoyed what came to be seen as a thwarted freedom. The system under which they lived encouraged them to express their views, in person or through representative assemblies, on matters concerning them. Yet they were excluded from what they believed to be the most important decisions. They were not represented in the only body that had any effective check on the king and his executive government, namely parliament in Westmin-ster. In particular they were denied profitable control of their own trade and of the disposal of their own production.

Once they decided on the break they had to face the certainty that the British executive would attempt to suppress their declared independence; and they sought external support. In the ensuing episode of the intermittent Anglo–French con-flict of the eighteenth century, the American colonials were allies, not enemies, of the French. Without French help – in particular French naval help – they must have lost to the British. As it was, they won a clearcut victory in the end (in 1781), and their independence was established without further question.

Diplomacy, involving persuasive dealings with the Old World, was therefore essential to the achievement of the independence proclaimed in 1776. Some Americans no longer looked on the French as they or their predecessors had looked on them earlier in the century. French toleration of munitions and arms shipments to the rebels and, later, the active intervention of royal French armies and fleets, had helped the British colonials to become independent Americans. Then, after 1789, France became embroiled in the turmoil we know as 'the French Revolution', while the Americans were devising a republican mode of government for themselves. Soon there was a French Republic, owing something in its declared principles to the propositions enunciated in 1776 by the Americans. The Americans and the French might have seemed natural allies. But the powerful impulse to separation from the Old World that had been part of the driving force of the American Revolution was to prevail over any sense of common cause with the new France – in particular once the French revolutionaries proceeded to the excesses of the Terror. And many of the new Americans preserved enough of their old Englishness to retain that intense dislike of the French which (heartily reciprocated) characterizes English outlook to the present day.

The American Revolution had been essentially conservative, although it involved warfare, violence and a good deal of terrorization of political opponents, and although some of its supporters expressed radical ideas. The colonials had wished rather to preserve rights they believed themselves already to have, than to proclaim any new order in the world. Yet in a way they were forced by their own temerity in breaking with England and its King to devise a new order. What was crucial here was the renunciation of the King's right. Although an American monarchy, elective or otherwise, was suggested and expected by some after the success of the revolution, the logic of the break required a different source of legitimacy in government. A monarch ruled by a right which derived from God, however circumscribed it might be by law and custom. The American government would derive its right to rule from the people. This, however, gave a new and problematic meaning to the concept of sovereignty, and would raise long continuing difficulties concerning the precise nature of the social and political contract into which individual citizens and 'sovereign' States were entering with the formation of the new continental nation. These difficulties were so considerable that they were not resolved finally even by the great and terrible Civil War between the States in the years 1861–5.

In some parts of the country people had become used to a form of communal self-government in colonial affairs – through town meetings and the like. The new federal union of thirteen States, with territories spread out over many hundreds of miles, could not be governed like this, directly by the people. Its common affairs were already being handled by a 'Continental Congress' of delegates from the various colonial (later State) assemblies – representatives who functioned more or less as ambassadors from their homelands.

In their dealings with the outside world, therefore, the people of the farms and towns of the new Republic were involved in trading, political or warlike relations with the native American populations, with the peoples and with the military and other forces of the European powers which continued to maintain colonies on the American continent (including the United Kingdom), with overseas markets and powers, and with the citizens of other States of their newly formed confederation.

The thirteen States which had joined to break the connection with England were New Hampshire, New York, Massachusetts, Rhode Island, Connecticut, Pennsylvania, New Jersey, Delaware, Maryland, Virginia, North Carolina, South

Carolina and Georgia. They were very varied, both in the composition of their populations and in the structure of their societies. Large parts of the populations of New England were of French or Irish, as distinct from English, origin; in the middle States there were considerable admixtures of people of German and Dutch origin, as well as many Irish again; the southern States were more predominantly English in their European origins (although once more with many Irish); while everywhere, besides the native American 'Indians,' there were large numbers of black people of African descent, some of them slaves, some free. The efforts to form a union after the end of the war were hampered by quarrels among some of these varied States, in particular about the claims they took over from the British to the land stretching from the mountains to the Mississippi. However, they reached a compromise in 1781, when the Congress agreed that the vast territory between the Appalachians and the Mississippi would be used 'for the common good.' All thirteen States then signed 'Articles of Confederation'.

The Northwest Ordinance of 1787 set the pattern for expansion beyond the Appalachians. Land claimed by the United States could first be designated a 'Territory', under the direct government of the Confederation. When the settler population of such a designated Territory exceeded 5,000, limited self-government was to be permitted, and when it exceeded 60,000, the local legislature could draft a Constitution and apply for membership of the Confederation as a State, with the same rights as any of the original States.

In the more elaborate compromise embodied in the federal constitution that was signed in 1787 and finally ratified by all the States in 1790, the sovereignty of States of the Union was circumscribed in a number of ways, including dealings with foreign powers.

That Constitution, according to its preamble (which was added as an afterthought) was intended, among other things, to 'provide for the common defence.' It vested all federal legislative powers in a Congress consisting of a Senate and a House of Representatives. The Congress had powers to regulate commerce with foreign nations and trade between the States and with Indian tribes; to define and punish piracies and felonies committed on the high seas, and offenses against the law of nations; to declare war, grant letters of marque and reprisal, and make rules concerning captures on land and water; to raise and support armies – 'but no appropriation of money to that use shall be for a longer term than two years'; to provide and maintain a navy; to make rules for the government and regulation of the land and naval forces; to provide for calling forth the militia to execute the laws of the Union, suppress insurrections and repel invasions. It restricted the rights of the several States:

> No State shall enter into any treaty, alliance, or confederation; [or] grant letters of marque and reprisal ... ; No State shall, without the consent of the Congress, lay any imposts or duties on imports or exports, except what may be absolutely necessary for executing its inspection laws ... ; No State shall, without the consent of Congress, lay any duty or tonnage, keep troops,

> or ships of war in time of peace, enter into any agreement or compact with another State, or with a foreign power, or engage in war, unless actually invaded, or in such imminent danger as will not admit of delay.

The Constitution also provided that:

> The President shall be commander in chief of the army and navy of the United States, and of the militia of the several States, when called into the actual service of the United States ...

and:

> He shall have power, by and with the advice and consent of the Senate, to make treaties, provided two-thirds of the Senators present concur; and he shall nominate, and by and with the advice and consent of the Senate, shall appoint ambassadors, and other public ministers and consuls ...

But perhaps the most important provision of all for these matters was simply that:

> The executive power shall be vested in a President of the United States of America.

In effect this meant that in international affairs the president would deal with other rulers as autonomously as any absolute monarch, being only directly responsible at home to the separate governmental institutions set up to balance and check any tendency towards excess of power (he was not encumbered with a Council of State).

This is an example of the ingenious élitism of the original Constitution which strove, fairly successfully, to remove executive actions from the influence of tumultuous assemblies, and which attempted to set up, as the model of republican government, a system of countervailing forces, so balanced as to keep all in harmonious motion, emulating the gravitational forces and orbits of the Newtonian universe. It was in itself a form of self-sufficiency.

So much for the theory painfully worked out by the Founding Fathers. In practice, it was necessary for the rulers of the new republic to make a fundamental decision in respect of the shifting European alliances and quarrels which had more or less intimately affected the lives of Americans for more than a century. An alliance with France and Spain had enabled the American revolutionaries to fight successfully against the British effort to suppress them. Their own struggle had made allies, on the one hand of men of property who sought liberty from arbitrary rule and from onslaughts on their property by taxation and otherwise that would undermine that liberty (for they understood property to be the basis of liberty, since no one is wholly free who is dependent on another for a living) and, on the other hand, of radical and democratic men and women, often of a puritan mentality, who wanted to turn the world upside down and establish a secular equivalent of the rule of the saints, in which the poor would share dominion with the rich.

The men who drafted the Constitution had no such egalitarian ideas. They had barely completed their work – which was as conservative as was consistent with the drastic breach they had made with their former colonial status – when the overthrow of the French *Ancien Régime* began in 1789 and rapidly developed into the great Revolution. For a time, all the former institutions of church, state and society were overthrown. Once again there was war between England and France. In 1791 the Americans palliated the thwarted egalitarianism of their own radicals by the passage of the first ten amendments to the Constitution – the 'Bill of Rights'. Would the American republic now support the French Republic against the British and other European monarchies who opposed the revolutionaries?

The first President, Washington, gave an answer of enduring significance when he proclaimed neutrality in 1793. He elaborated on this decision and reinforced its meaning at the end of his presidency when, in his farewell address to the people, he advised in effect that the United States should cut free of any involvement in the political affairs of Europe and in 'entangling alliances'. He pointed out that the concept of friendships and enmities between states arose from a false analogy with relations between persons. It was the business of rulers of states to act fairly and in compliance with natural and international law, but to consult the national interest rather than any misplaced sentiment.

This set the tone for America's dealings with the world in the nineteenth century. The second President, John Adams, successfully opposed an agitation for war against France, and although under the fourth President, James Madison, the United States blundered into an inconclusive war against the United Kingdom in 1812, thereafter the republic settled into dealings with European powers which were primarily concerned with its own overseas trade and with its own interests in the American continent.

These interests included initially the securing of scope for expansion beyond the boundaries of the original thirteen States and the devising of a policy or system that would restrict further European colonial interference with American affairs. The State of Kentucky was added to the Union, by expansion of settlement, in 1792, that of Tennessee in 1796 and that of Ohio in 1803, bringing the western boundary of the United States to the middle part of the Mississippi.

The third President, Thomas Jefferson, author of the Declaration of Independence, seized an opportunity in 1803 to buy from Napoleon's France, for $14,500,000, an enormous expanse of land claimed by that country beyond the Mississippi, in 'the Louisiana Purchase'. His purpose was as much to exclude European colonial powers from the borders of the United States – as far as possible – as to open up the interior of the continent to the Americans. The boundaries of the newly acquired unsettled and unconquered land were in dispute but were settled by treaties with Britain in 1818 and Spain in 1819. The fourth President, James Madison, in 1810 annexed the area then known as 'West Florida' (comprising the southern coastal lands of what are now Alabama and Mississippi, and that part of coastal Louisiana east of the Mississippi river), and this territory was finally secured for the United States when American soldiers occupied Mobile in 1813. The fifth President, James Monroe, held Spain responsible for raids on the State of Georgia by Seminole Indians operating from Spain's colony, the coastal land of 'East Florida'. The American general Andrew Jackson invaded East Florida, and eventually in 1819 Spain ceded it to the United States for $5,000,000. In December 1823 Monroe included in a message to congress an enunciation of the 'Doctrine' that bears his name – a central principle of American foreign policy ever since. The Monroe Doctrine was prompted by liberation movements throughout Latin America and parts of the Caribbean and by the setting up of republics in place of Spanish and Portuguese colonial rule. It stated the exclusion of European powers from interfering in the affairs of the republics of the Americas and the closing of the continent to further European colonial ventures to be United States policy.

Disputes with Britain about the northern borders were settled when agreement was reached in 1842 concerning the Maine frontier and in 1846 concerning the Oregon country. Meantime Mexico lost about half of its total territory to the expansionist United States, when US policy began to be as aggressive and ruthless towards other peoples as it had been from the start towards the native Americans. First of all, large numbers from the United States migrated into the northern territories of Mexico, which had won its independence from Spain in 1821. In 1836 these settlers declared their independence from Mexico and established a republic of Texas, under the presidency of Sam Houston. Mexico refused to recognise Texan independence, but was forced into war when the United States supported the extension of the Texan frontier south to the Rio Grande. In two years of fierce fighting Mexico was defeated, and was then compelled to cede Texas, including the disputed southern part, as well as New Mexico, Utah, Nevada, parts of Wyoming and Colorado and the present State of California, to the United States. Some further land was added to California by the 'Gadsden purchase' of 1853. By this stage the present extent of the 48 contiguous States of the Union had come under notional US government, although more than half a century was to pass before all that land was finally organized as States (with the admission to statehood in 1912 of Arizona and New Mexico). Northwest of Canada the huge territory of Alaska, which had been colonized from across the Bering Strait by Russia, was purchased from that country in 1867 for $7,200,000; but Alaska did not become a State of the Union (along with Hawaii) until 1959.

The external relations of the United States throughout a large part of the nineteenth century, therefore, largely involved territories beyond its borders on the American continent itself. 'Manifest destiny' was the phrase that began to be used about the middle of the century to express the view that the republic's westward expansion was inevitable and inexorable. There were some who thought that the Union was destined in time to occupy the whole hemisphere, including

Canada, the West Indies and Latin America: the Monroe Doctrine, followed by the purchase of Alaska seemed to suggest that this might become the shape of American policy.

However, things were not so simple. Mid-nineteenth-century America was a society riddled with contradictions. It was founded on a proclamation of equality and freedom, but the institution of slavery had grown in strength in the southern States, particularly since the invention of the cotton gin made cotton (a labour-intensive crop for which English factories provided a huge demand) a staple of southern economy; while the 'white Anglo-Saxon protestant' (Wasp) groups who dominated the country were coming to think of themselves as a chosen people, elected to rule. Many, especially in the north, found in this a source of guilt and in the institution of slavery a misuse of the trust confided in them by God; but there was fairly general agreement that, in one way or another, the non-elect (or reprobate) were inferior – Blacks, Latin Americans, American Indians, Asians, southern Europeans, all the varied peoples of the outer world. What 'manifest destiny' commanded, as Americans had come to believe, was that expansion must involve political and cultural domination by English-speaking Whites. This conviction was reinforced when waves of new immigration from Europe began to break on American shores about the middle of the century. It was widely held that they should conform to the standard set by one particular group of earlier settlers. The concept of the 'melting pot' implied a mould, and the mould was to turn Irish, Germans, Jews, Italians, Swedes and Slavs into 'Americans': they were to speak English and conform to the secular cults of the American republic, including reverence for the sacred texts of the Declaration and the Constitution, oaths, flag-worship, nationalistic parades and displays and obeisance to the New England puritan mythology in which the nation was imagined to have had its source, with origin legends centred on the voyage of the Mayflower.

In the seventeenth and eighteenth centuries, the indigenous peoples of the continent had been widely regarded as the true Americans, embodying the spirit of the New World. Frontiersmen wore Indian costume, followed Indian practices in hunting and otherwise, and were intermittently respectful of Indian concepts and ideas – as the texts of some of the eighteenth-century treaties with Indian nations show. However, these, like so many later treaties with the Indians, were not honoured for long by the intruders. By the middle of the nineteenth century, not only were the expansionists from the east treacherous in their treaty-making; they came to hate those whom they cheated and robbed, and to fob off their own guilt and dishonour by treating the native Americans as vermin, to be removed by extermination if necessary from the path of 'progress.' 'Indian wars' marked the middle decades of the century, as the citizens of the United States, backed by the armed forces of their country, advanced westward.

And it was in the same middle decades of the century that the hatreds and bitterness fomented by the existence of slavery in the southern States broke the Union (in 1861). The Union was restored after a fashion by the four-year Civil War, which was in many ways redemptive, since not only was it marked by the sacrifice of hundreds of thousands of ordinary people fighting and dying, in a magnificent demonstration of the power of freedom to animate and inform simple men, for causes they believed in; but it also evoked a nobility in the definition of political principles which, in the funeral speech of Lincoln at Gettysburg, surpassed that of the funeral speech of Pericles in Athens.

But, if the Union was restored, the division remained. America – official, ruling, possessing, rooted, self-regarding America – continued to look on a large part of its people, free though they might all now legally be, as a different species. Alienation powerfully coloured American attitudes to America itself in the later nineteenth century; still more it coloured American attitudes to the outside world.

3

The World of Brian Merriman:
County Clare in 1780

The year 1780 was the twentieth of the reign of George III, who had become king in 1760 of Great Britain and Ireland, two distinct kingdoms under one crown. Ireland had its own parliament in Dublin, but it was subordinate to that of Westminster. It was an assembly of the Protestant noblemen, bishops and gentry of the kingdom. These, a colonial establishment, had developed a sense of grievance about their treatment by the English administration.

King George's government, headed by Lord North, was faced with a number of pressing problems. The colonials in North America were at war with the mother country and, four years earlier, in 1776, the representatives of thirteen colonies had declared independence. After some hesitation the French had come to the support of the rebellious colonials, and in 1778 England had declared war on France. Then, in June 1779, Spain also went to war with England. The declarations extended the war to the colonies of England, France and Spain in both hemispheres. Soon a world-wide naval conflict was in progress and was most important for the outcome of the hostilities in general.

However distant some of them may have been, the events of the spreading war had an immediate effect upon Ireland. The British were already over-extended by their efforts to suppress a continental rebellion in America. They sent across the wide Atlantic, in huge fleets of slow sailing-ships, the biggest military expeditions ever to leave British shores. They were faced, in 1780, with a major war in south India, where the prince of Mysore, Hyder Ali, had turned his arms against them. Large parts of India by now were administered by the British East India Company, whose trade was regarded as a vital national interest.

The London government, which had employed German troops for the American war (and had attempted to hire Russians), made strenuous efforts to recruit or press men into its service, as sailors or soldiers, and Ireland in particular was combed for recruits. Very many of the men on the fighting ships were Irishmen, drawn largely from the maritime counties. The coast of Clare undoubtedly contributed a handsome quota.

But the British government was unable to garrison Ireland itself adequately to provide defence against a French invasion. All available men were needed for

Previously unpublished. A shorter version of this was given as a lecture at the Merriman Summer School in Ballyvaughan, Co. Clare, in 1980. Some of the material was used in my introduction to Diarmaid Ó Muirithe, ed., *Tomás Ó Míocháin: Filíocht* (Dublin, 1988).

America. England's colony in Ireland had taken this lack of protection as a further grievance, but resolved to provide for its own defence by raising regiments of Volunteers. The colonials showed that they meant to employ this force, raised from among themselves and soon approaching 100,000 men, not merely for defending Ireland's shores against French attack but as a menacing support for their own demands for freedom from British restrictions on their trade and control of their legislation.

On Tuesday, 16 May 1780, two stands of colours arrived for the Ennis Volunteers. They had been sent by the regiment's colonel, the earl of Inchiquin, and were, as a contemporary account tells us, 'elegantly embroidered.' One bore the earl's arms and motto on a ground of red silk; the other, on a ground of green silk, had the Ennis arms, emblems of agriculture and husbandry and trophies of war, and the motto, *pro rege saepe, pro patria semper* – 'usually for the king, always for our country'. On Tuesday, 23 May, at a field day, the regiment's lieutenant colonel, William Blood, formally handed over the colours.

The British needed the Volunteers against the French, but were being forced by their very existence and their armed threats to make unwilling concessions to the colony in Ireland. At the end of 1779 they began to yield on the first major point of grievance and to end restrictions on Ireland's trade with the other colonies. The Volunteers, as they increased in numbers, began to be used by the colonial ascendancy for a third purpose—as a kind of police force, in efforts to bring under control the alarming disaffection among parts of the mass of the Irish people, whom *they* dominated. Meantime, in the Dublin parliament, what was known as 'the country party' continued to press the supporters and agents of the English administration for various reforms. One of this party's leaders was a Clare member, Sir Lucius O'Brien of Dromoland. Political excitement rose through the year.

In July and August 1779, the French navy, lying off Plymouth, won control of the approaches to the English channel. The West Indies fleet was unable to reach England with its cargoes, and this splendid convoy of West-Indiamen sailed instead into the Shannon mouth and anchored off the Fergus estuary for weeks. They made a great camp on the Clare shore.

The war came even more directly to the seas around Ireland. The American John Paul Jones appeared from beyond the Atlantic in late 1779, and his vessel, the *Serapis*, in September defeated a British warship. In the early months of 1780 he was in action in Irish waters. In the same period an Irish adventurer named Dowling, who held an American commission issued at Dunkerque, began preying on British shipping off the south and east coasts. He had two privateers, the *Black Prince* and the *Black Princess*, mainly Irish manned. When they captured packet boats they threw the mails overboard, so that communications and travel between the two islands became hazardous. News of distant battles however often reached Ireland directly from the south or west, when fast naval vessels put in at Cork or Limerick. This was how, early in the year, news arrived of Admiral Rodney's important victory over the Spanish fleet at Cape St Vincent.

The Irishmen who served between decks on the wooden warships which tossed on the oceans of the world were plunged into an existence where the brutality of eighteenth-century life – together with that naval tradition which Sir Winston Churchill long afterwards was to sum up as 'rum, sodomy and the lash' – would be experienced at its worst. One of them in 1780, pressed into the navy, was the Kerry poet Eoghan Rua Ó Súilleabháin. He gives us a glimpse of the warfare of the time in a ballad he wrote (in English) two years later about another of Rodney's victories:

> Broadside for broadside we let fly,
> Till they in hundreds bleeding lie,
> The seas were all of crimson dye;
> Full deep we stood in human blood,
> Surrounded by a scarlet flood,
> But still we fought courageous ...

The war was being fought to maintain England's empire and her world-wide system of commerce. This part of the empire – Ireland – was held chiefly by a class which had been established in power, privilege and property a few generations back. During the time of revolutionary change in England, in the sixteenth and seventeenth centuries, most of the families of magnates who had dominated medieval Ireland found themselves, on one occasion or another, on the losing side in various conflicts, and lost their lands by confiscation. In general, these lands did not go to other Irish magnates but to Englishmen. In the final major redistribution of land, under the Cromwellian and Williamite settlements, the new class, staunch supporters throughout the eighteenth century of the Protestant constitution founded by the so-called 'Glorious Revolution', was given control of the land, the law and the business of the country. Its members were English in origin and in language, and Protestant in religion; and loyalty to the British constitution was the core of the bargain by which they maintained English rule in Ireland, while British power maintained them in turn in enjoyment of their land and privileges. They were landlords and magistrates, judges and administrators, politicians and soldiers. They formed a world of their own, quite distinct from the more-or-less leaderless mass of the population, who were mostly Irish-speaking and Roman Catholic, and who were regarded as a people excluded by right of conquest from any part in the life of politics or the civil or military affairs of the kingdom.

In County Clare however an unusually high proportion of aristocrats and gentlemen of native Irish or old Hiberno-Norman ancestry survived. More than elsewhere, these families, or branches of them, held on by changing their religion and by making other shrewd judgments as to which side to take in the various wars. The survival of a large proportion of the old stock among the landlords had a pacifying effect on the population as a whole and a Gaelicizing effect – especially in the earlier eighteenth century – on some of the new planters. Clare had about 100 gentlemen's houses in 1780. A list of 84 of these includes about a third where the occupiers had Irish or old Norman names – a remarkably high proportion. These were all Protestants. The other houses were occupied by people with English, Scottish and Dutch names. The list gives the upper layer of late-eighteenth-century society in Clare. It includes the O'Brien earl of Inchiquin, who was governor of the county and as such responsible for law, order and defence. He was therefore the militia commander, as well as being colonel of the Irish Volunteers. The militia had been drawn off by the American war, which was why the Volunteers had come into being in the first place, but a stand of militia arms – five hundred muskets with bayonets – was supplied to Clare by grant from the Royal Office of Ordnance. The garrison was based on the barracks at Clarecastle.

In a number of respects the county was underdeveloped, in terms of the rapidly growing network of administrative institutions which were bringing Ireland more and more firmly under centralized control. For example, while 25 of Ireland's 32 counties had county infirmaries, Clare was one of the 7 counties which had none.

In those days elections were infrequent. The parliament sitting in Dublin in 1780 derived from the election of 1769. The gentlemen then returned from Clare were Sir Lucius O'Brien and Francis Pierpoint Burton for the county and Charles MacDonnell and Crofton Vandaleur for the county borough of Ennis. By far the most active was Sir Lucius, a man of incessant busyness. He was ever being elected to committees of the House of Commons, especially those concerned with procedure or with law and order. He was forever thinking up schemes of improvement, for his estates or the country. He was a great one for surveys and statistics, and it is plain that he could talk and talk. He was an indefatigable traveller on the appalling roads, and as a lobbyist in the courts and chancelleries of the two kingdoms – buttonholing Lord North in London as readily as the functionaries of the Irish government in Dublin. He argued forcefully in parliament for the removal of the English control of Irish affairs, and was one of the effective allies of Henry Grattan.

Since the parliamentary electoral system was corrupt, with a very high proportion of seats filled by patronage, it was normally possible for the government – that is to say, for the British imperial interest through its agents and representatives in College Green – to secure a majority for its measures. Under the pressures of the gathering grievances of the colony and the demands of the war, this system was beginning to break down, and 1780 saw its collapse. Now concessions and reforms began to come, yielding to the force of Volunteer arms.

We have no precise information on the size of Ireland's population at this time. No census in our modern meaning of the word was taken in the eighteenth century. However, working from the best estimates available, we can assume that in 1780 there were approximately four million people in Ireland – considerably less than at present. An overall increase since the beginning of the century had been masked by sharp fluctuations, local aberrations, and a considerable internal redistribution. A sharp growth was to take place from about 1785, which soon became obvious to observers, but it would have been quite possible, down to about 1780, to gain the impression that the population was actually falling. This was a widespread and common error of the time in England, although the English population too, as we now know, was rising fast.

Estimating the population of Clare within the overall figure is more difficult still. The best guess would seem to be that in 1780 there were somewhat less than 100,000 people in the county, possibly as few as 75,000. At most a couple of thousand of these would have belonged by family connection or otherwise to the landowning class which effectively had control of the county. There would have been a larger number involved in services and trade and manufacture – merchants, shopkeepers, shoemakers, saddlers, blacksmiths, and so on. This was the class, under the penal laws, within which some Catholics could prosper, and even become rich. There was a large class of tenant farmers. There were numerous cottiers, starting with the group described by James Caldwell as those who

> hold at will a small take of land, seldom more than an acre, and grass for a couple of cows, at an exorbitant rent which they work out at the small wages of four or five pence a day without diet.

There were also 'persons who have short leases or leases of uncertain tenure at high rents'. There were 'inhabitants of cottages in the neighbourhood of towns and small villages, who hold no land and are supported by daily labour'.

Beyond and below the categories enumerated by Caldwell were the destitute, the sick, the starving, the homeless. These lowest orders of society were Irish-speaking, illiterate, most without a knowledge of English. They were the first victims of the recurrent famines. Already by 1780 the diet of the poorest classes was potatoes and sour milk for three-quarters of the year and potatoes and salt in spring-time – if the potatoes lasted. They lived below any tolerable level of subsistence or consciousness, their nakedness barely covered by a rag or two, their physique undermined by hardship. According to one witness, their appearance contrasted with that of the 'middling class of people who live on potatoes, milk and butter and had a good healthy appearance'. The lowest order suffered commonly from scurvy and skin diseases.

Virtually every visitor who comments on the scene in eighteenth-century Ireland refers to the abject destitution of these people living with hardly the most exiguous clothing or shelter and giving an appalling character to the countryside. Ireland looked as if it had suffered some fearful disaster. It had. The country had been fought over for a century, conquered, and exploited as a source of rents and pensions for a class whose essential purpose was to secure England's strategic security on the west. In England itself, a progressive, extravagant, arrogant, ruthless class was sweeping aside many immemorial customs along with the old common lands, relentlessly changing the face of the countryside, causing unparalleled hardships to the rural poor, and in the process laying the foundation for new and unprecedented industries and new, improved, and vastly more efficient agriculture: making the modern world. In England there was provision by law for the poor: at the very beginning of the revolutionary process, in the sixteenth century, the parishes of the country were charged, each with the maintenance of its own poor. There was no such provision in Ireland. Here starvation was legal, and the more fortunate, who avoided it, maintained their equanimity, like people in Calcutta or Bangladesh today, by becoming blind to the sight of perpetual and irremediable poverty and callous to the sufferings involved. It was the visitors who received the shock.

If we too turn our eyes from these unfortunates and look instead at the middling orders of tenant farmers and the like, we enter in a particular way the world of Brian Merriman, and can well begin with the circumstances and occupation of the man himself. We know a little about him, mainly through enquiries made by early editors of his work from people who knew him or knew his family. In 1780, when he wrote *Cúirt an Mheán Oíche*, he was about thirty years old, a thick-set, stocky, blackhaired man according to report. He was teaching school at Kilclaran, about two miles north of Feakle, and he farmed land at Derryvinna, about a mile south-west of Feakle. He had been in the Feakle neighbourhood since he was a child, having been born, it seems, at Ennistymon, perhaps in 1749.

Kilclaran today is a village so small that it enjoys the distinction of having a church but no pub. Feakle was the largest parish in Clare, but in 1780 there was no Catholic chapel in Feakle itself: there were chapels at Killenana, Cahirmurphy and – Kilclaran. We can take it as certain that it was in Kilclaran chapel that Merriman had his school – this was a common custom of the penal times, and tradition points to a spot in the modern churchyard as the place where he was born – a small confusion. It was still illegal in 1780 for 'persons of the popish religion' to 'publickly teach school' or 'instruct youth in learning in any private popish house within this realm' but this law was not enforced, and indeed was shortly to be repealed.

While a few endowed schools existed – there was, for example, an Erasmus Smith school in Ennis – these were regarded with suspicion by most of the people as prosletysing agencies. There were no state or public schools as we would understand it, although the charter schools, which had indeed been initiated with the 'purpose of trying what may be done with their children to bring them over to our church', as Archbishop Boulter put it in 1730, were subsidized by the Dublin and Westminster parliaments. Here and there a priest provided a little tuition, usually in the chapel. Priests, however, were comparatively few and often had to serve large areas.

The principal way of providing schools was through a form of private enterprise which partly depended upon the patchy survival of an old tradition of patronage of learning and poetry. In the Gaelic system of the Middle Ages, the leaders of society were required by immemorial custom to endow and maintain professional poets and scholars. These underwent a long and rigorous course of training, in history, genealogy, prosody and other matters. They no longer existed by 1780 but there were numbers of men who had picked up something of their teaching and attempted to pass it on.

The true professional tradition lasted in Clare into the early eighteenth century. The MacCruitíns of Kilmurry still retained the ancient distinction and were hereditary *ollúna* of the princes of Thomond. Aindrias, learned in the genealogical lore which his profession required, had produced in 1727 a volume on the Ó Lochlainns of Burren. He had sold part of his parents' property to enable him to prosecute his antiquarian researches. He taught school at Kilmurry, but from there travelled to gather records of Irish antiquity. He was a regular visitor at the houses of Edward O'Brien of Ennistymon and Somhairle MacDonnell of Kilkee. He wrote one of the most ironic of the poems marking the passage of the old order when he addressed the ancient Irish god of the dead (under his local name of *Donn na Duimhche*) and enquired whether the gods too had lost their ancient power, like the society they belonged to. When Aindrias died in 1749, he was succeeded by his cousin Aodh Buí MacCruitín, who composed a *caoine* for his predecessor. He published a work in vindication of the Antiquities of Ireland (a condensation of Keating's *Foras Feasa ar Éirinn*) in 1717 – one of the earliest examples of this politically important species of writing – and he published in Paris in 1732 an English-Irish dictionary and an Irish grammar. He served in Flanders with Lord Clare's regiment of the Irish Brigade, and was apparently introduced by his patron Isabella O'Brien, wife of Somhairle Buí MacDonnell, to the household of the Dauphin of France, where he spent some time as a tutor. Aodh Buí wrote Jacobite poetry of the new style, but he belonged to the old order. With his death in 1755, a long thread was broken.

Those who followed lacked the full specialised training and wrote, if they wrote, in popular metres, but they had some opportunity to learn from people like the MacCruitíns. John Nunan, who was teaching school in the second half of the century, was described by a contemporary as 'the best classical scholar in Munster'. One of his pupils was Theophilus O'Flanagan, who went on to be a scholar of Trinity College, Dublin, and later the author of a number of papers on Irish language and antiquities. O'Flanagan was still a youngster in 1780, but he had begun his antiquarian researches by attempting a decipherment of the curious ogham inscription (a seventeenth-century 'practice' ogham?) on Slieve Callan. He may have been stimulated in this by the poet-schoolmaster John Lloyd, who produced his own version of the ogham. He was certainly encouraged and helped by William Burton of Clifden, high sheriff of the county in 1780, a landlord who had taken over, in part at least, the old tradition of patronage. O'Flanagan's reading of the ogham was to be published a few years later by Rev. William Hamilton in the first volume of the *Transactions of the Royal Irish Academy*. Another schoolmaster, at Carne, near Kilrush, taught O'Flanagan the skills of a scribe of Irish manuscripts. This was Peter O'Connell, then a young man, arguably both the best scribe and the best Irish scholar of his generation in the whole country.

A younger contemporary of Merriman's named Patrick Lynch – in his twenties in 1780 – was to become a polyglot scholar. His schoolmaster was one Donncha

Ó Mathúna, known as Donncha an Chairn (probably from Carn Connachtach just north of Ennistymon) who must have been teaching at Ennistymon just about the time Merriman was born there. Donncha knew no English, but through the medium of Irish taught young Lynch Latin, Greek and Hebrew. He is referred to by Tomás Ó Míocháin of Ennis as 'the star of Ennistymon'.

By 1780 most of the masters offered a much simpler curriculum than Latin, Greek and Hebrew: They were several generations removed from the status and security of the old scholars and from the long and intensive training thereby provided. They offered the rudiments of reading, writing and arithmetic, for which they were reimbursed by their pupils' parents. This yielded a miserable pittance, but some teachers had other means of support – a little land, or occasionally the patronage of a landlord. Many of them hankered for the old training and were, as it were, self-educated in its lore, gathering and copying manuscripts, forming with their colleagues a debased but still faithful order of poets, saving what scraps they could from the wreck of their culture. There was a hierarchy among schoolmasters. Some built their own rough-and-ready schoolhouses (often with the aid of their pupils, as did Merriman when he moved his school later to adjoin his land, at Curragh). Others had to use a makeshift shelter by the side of a field or road: from these, the schools in general were referred to as 'hedge-schools'. There was a sharp distinction, as ever, between the settled and the itinerant. The schoolmasters who taught in a fixed place belonged to a higher order than those who moved about.

Kilclaren chapel, like most in the penal days, would have been a small thatched building not much distinguished from a cottage. The school was probably held only in the good-weather months. Generally the children, boys and girls together, who attended such schools didn't come in the wintertime because the cold in the rough unheated shelters was beyond endurance. So, at the end of summer the school would disperse and the teacher (deprived for half the year of his small income) would have to find somewhere else to pursue his writing if, like so many of them, he wrote poems or transcribed other people's poems and stories into exercise or account books.

This point may be illustrated from the other end of the county. Another schoolmaster, Anthony O'Brien, a Limerick man, was working in the parish of Dunaha, near Loop Head. He spent part of 1780 transcribing – in an awkward and shaky hand – material related to St Senan of Scattery into a paper book. When he came to the end of John Lloyd's translation into English of a *Life* of St Senan, he wrote (also in English):

> Finished the holy life of St Senan by me, Anthony O'Brien, in Dunaha chapel, Aug 23rd 1780.

The chapel was where he taught school. At the end of the manuscript he has:

> Finished by me, Anthony O'Brien, September 25th 1780 at Querrin in

the west of the County Clare, and the parish of Dunaha, it being a wet morning.

Note that by late September he had moved from the chapel to finish his work in another place, probably transferring his scriptorium to winter quarters.

Merriman may have done much the same with his original script of *Cúirt an Mheán Oíche*, perhaps beginning it in the chapel of Kilclaran and finishing it in Derryvinna. This is to infer, from some internal evidence in the poem, that it was begun in the summer and finished just after Christmas in 1780. The winter, incidentally, began early: there was a remarkably severe fall of snow in the west of Ireland at the beginning of November, but then there was an unprecedentedly mild spell.

While Irish was taught in some of the 'hedge schools' and Irish grammars were produced to meet their requirements, their main function was to equip the students for the now dominant English-speaking world. In 1780, Tomas Ó Míocháin described himself as 'teacher of Accompts and Mathematics' in Ennis. 14 years later we find him advertising (*Ennis Chronicle*, 6 January 1794) in similar terms:

> Mr Meehan's school: Opens the 14th instant for the usual reception of grown-up youth who wish for the speedy improvement in Accompts, Use of the globes, and the necessary branches of the Mathematicks.

The schools, in Clare and throughout Ireland, it would seem, made use of a limited range of cheap printed books, which must have helped to form the mind of a considerable part of the Irish people of this class in the eighteenth century. The books were sold chiefly by pedlars, and included in particular a series issued in Dublin, Cork and Limerick called 'Burton books,' printed originally by Nathaniel Crouch in 1706 under the name 'Burton'. Hely Dutton, in his *Statistical Survey of the County of Clare*, of 1808, lists the books which 'for half a century have continued to disgrace and corrupt the children of their persuasion':

> History of the seven champions of Christendom; Montelion, Knight of the Oracle; Parismus and Parismenes; Irish Rogues and Raparees; Freney, a Notorious Robber; the most celebrated pirates; Jack the Bachelor, a noted smuggler; History of Fair Rosamund and Jane Shore, two Prostitutes; Donna Rosita, a Spanish Courtesan; Ovid's Art of Love; History of Witches and Apparitions; the Devil and Dr Faustus; Moll Flanders; New System of Boxing, by Mendoza ...

Wakefield, commenting on this list, reported that he met with a 'nearly similar list in Wicklow'. Mason, in 1816, said that 'the hedge schools are as miserable and the books in them as worthless as they have been observed to be in other parts of Ireland'. A little later, William Carleton, who had first-hand experience, reported on a very similar list, adding however works of religious bent:

... ridicule of the Word of God and a hatred to the Protestant religion in a book called Ward's Cantos, written in Hudibrastic verse; the downfall of the Protestant Establishment and the exaltation of the Roman Church, in Columbkille's Prophecy, and latterly in that of Pastorinus; a belief in every kind of religious imposture in the Lives of the Saints, of St Patrick, of St Columbille, of St Teresa, of St Francis Xavier, the Holy Scapular, and several other works disgraceful to human reason. Political and religious ballads of the vilest doggerel, miraculous legends of holy friars persecuted by Protestants and of signal vengeance inflicted by their divine power on their persecutors were in the hands of young and old, and, of course fixed in their credulity. Their weapons of controversy were drawn from the Fifty Reasons, the doleful Fall of Andrew Sall, the Catholic Christian, the Grounds of Catholic Doctrine, a Net for the Fishers of Men, and several other publications of the same class.

How much exactly of such a mixture of Counter-Reformation apologetics and propaganda may have been in circulation near Feakle when Merriman was teaching there in 1780, it is impossible to know: but the testimony is remarkably uniform as to the general range of titles in Clare and elsewhere.

From the site of Kilclaran chapel the road today leads down a short distance to the Graney stream and crosses it over a bridge. In 1780 neither road nor bridge was there. In the whole huge parish of Feakle there wasn't a road fit for wheeled vehicles. Loads were moved by sled, and even the tracks and paths were so poor that Clare was described as bad country for horses. The wealthiest of the gentry kept four-wheeled carriages, which were rarely used: they braved the muddy tracks on horseback, carrying their wives as pillion passengers and using sure-footed mounts acquired, as a rule, at the famous fair of Spancel Hill. Most people had to walk, as Merriman customarily did for pleasure, if he is to be believed, when he went downhill from Kilclaran in the mornings, following a path or crossing the fields, probably to where there was a ford; then turning to follow the Graney upstream:

> Ba ghnáth mé ag siúl le ciumhais na habhann
> Ar bháinseach úr 'san drúcht go trom
> In aice na gcoillte, I gcoim an tsléibhe ...

The description of the landscape is exact and we can follow his route through the narrowing of the hills to the point where the lake appears shining to the north, just as he describes it. River and meadow are still there. The countryside is still a delight to see; but even in that comparatively unspoilt landscape there have been quite considerable changes since he trod the summer dew two hundred years ago. Elsewhere, the changes have been so profound that continuity is hard to trace: it was another country.

The woods Merriman refers to in the opening lines of his poem were much more extensive then than now along the hills. They were partly virgin forest, partly new plantation. In no part of the country do place-names with the element *derry*, 'oakwood', cluster more thickly than around the Graney. But the survival of the woods down to 1780 was exceptional. In general Clare by then had been denuded of its primeval forest. Down to the late seventeenth century the county had been extensively wooded, oakwoods in particular being numerous. Even in the west and north, wherever there was a little shelter from the Atlantic winds, the ancient oak-forest survived in hollows. But in the course of the eighteenth century, as the new Cromwellian and Williamite proprietors and their descendants settled in, the woods were largely cleared, partly by the landlords making fields, partly by their tenants taking timber. In 1780, there was an old man – approaching his century – living at Ennistymon. His name was Michael Daly and he had been huntsman to O'Brien of Ennistymon. He often said that in his youth almost the entire country about Ennistymon was covered with woods, mostly full-grown oak and ash, and that he frequently shot wild pheasants in those woods. But now the woods of north Clare were completely gone.

There had been other great changes in the space of a generation or two. When Merriman was born about the middle of the century, Ennistymon was not yet a town. It was however the location of a big house, and this, in eighteenth-century terms, implied the existence of out-buildings and of the dwellings of family connections, tenants and hangers-on. It was a fortified tower house – where the Falls Hotel now is – which had been built by Turlough O'Brien in 1588 and was still the seat of one of the main branches of the O'Brien family.

Ten years before Merriman was born this area was one severely affected by a terrible famine. The famine was as bad as that of the 1840s, allowing for the much smaller population of Ireland at the time. Proportionately as many people died, and there were scenes of great suffering:

> The misery of the poor in parts of the county of Clare, and of this county (Galway) is inexpressible, many being obliged by the extreme scarcity of provisions of all kinds to eat horses and dogs, and to steal and kill ewes that are ready to wean, so that their foul feeding has already thrown many of them into fluxes etc. Wheat and oatmeal are excessive dear: potatoes 4*s.* 4*d.* a bushel. Many through want perish daily in the roads and ditches, where they are buried.

Such scenes were commoner in Europe in 1740 than in 1840, and therefore came as less of a shock than the great Irish famine of the mid-nineteenth century. However, it must have been a bitter memory in the minds of many still alive and active in 1780.

Up to and beyond the date of Merriman's birth, the region around Ennistymon was effectively beyond the reach of British eighteenth-century civilization. The roads were next to impossible and the wild coast offered no harbours or jetties. The medieval parishes – Kilmanaheen, Killasboglenane, Kilmacreehy, Kilshannig

– still functioned after a fashion round their ancient centres, and the modern towns and villages, Liscannor, Lehinch, Ennistymon, and so forth, had not yet taken shape. The village of Ballyvaughan, for example, didn't exist, and the local centre was Dromcrehy, about a mile to the east. The organization of Gaelic civilization, however, had been broken by Elizabethan, Cromwellian and Williamite expeditions and by the hangings and confiscations which followed them. The ordinary people had suffered severely, as they always do in wars, no matter who wins. The result of the wars punished the landowners who remained loyal to the Stuarts or to the pope, and enormous tracts of land were confiscated, and came into the hands of newcomers. For example, Lord Clare, of the senior branch of the O'Briens, which remained true to James II, lost 57,000 acres. The last efforts to re-edify the old churches of the west were made by landowners during James II's brief tenure of the throne: these were now in ruin. Other parts of the old order of the Middle Ages were also destroyed. The O'Davorens' school of Irish legal learning, maintained for centuries at Cahermacnaghten, for example, was no more. Many of the castles and tower houses of the old gentry had been slighted. The stone cahers of the Burren were deserted. But the old traditions, though now lacking the framework of a social order and organisation, lived doggedly on into the eighteenth century.

The young men of west and north Clare, until about mid-century, were still going to France and Spain to serve in armies opposed to the Hanoverian dynasty which now reigned in England. Clare had a special place among supporters of the Stuart cause. Daniel O'Brien, third Viscount Clare, had raised in 1689 three regiments for King James, one of dragoons and two of infantry, amounting to just under 2,000 men, not counting officers. These mustered at Carrigaholt. From a county whose total population at the time was perhaps forty or fifty thousand, this was a sizeable contribution.

Clare was one of the counties allowed specially favourable treatment under the terms of the Treaty of Limerick. Although that treaty, notoriously, was refused ratification by the Dublin parliament, some of these provisions were in fact tacitly applied in practice. Besides, some of the old families who themselves accommodated to the changing times and held their patrimony, succeeded in sheltering their people from some of the enactments against the Roman Catholic faith. The friars, to illustrate this point, hung on in parts of Clare, and the parishes and cures seem to have been reasonably manned by priests trained on the Continent. On the whole, Catholics and Protestants rubbed along together in Clare perhaps a little better than in some other places under the penal laws.

The country round Ennistymon up to mid-century was Jacobite; but the failure of Prince Charles Edward Stuart's invasion of England in 1745–6 left that cause little hope. The famine of 1739–41 and the 'Forty-five' are two manifestations of a significant break, which we may place about the middle of the eighteenth century – one of the stages in the long process by which Gaelic Ireland was transformed into the Anglicized Ireland we know today. Merriman's birthplace – if it was Ennistymon – was still a part of the world of Gaelic Ireland in its twilight, at the time he was born. By 1780, when he had long been in east Clare, the finality of the conquest was fully apparent, and by then his birthplace was just beginning to be brought under the full dispensation of Hanoverian rule. To illustrate: the establishment of the Anglican church, other than on paper, proceeded very slowly in Clare. Lecky points out that in the eighteenth century, in 62 of 76 parishes, no Protestant church existed. In 1780, the first Protestant church in Ennistymon was nearing completion, on a grant of £300 from the Board of First Fruits. The Revd James Kenny, archdeacon of Kilfenora, collated to the parish of Kilmanaheen in 1775, was also fining down 40 acres of rough ground, about half a mile from the church, and building on it a glebe house and offices, the first in the county. By 1780 he was making his garden, in which he cultivated balm, sage, thyme, pennyroyal, rosemary, camomile, horehound and other herbs.

To return briefly to the wooded and roadless country around Lough Graney. The scene of Merriman's early morning walks, in which he set the opening of his poem, was in the estate of O'Hara of Cahir. The old style of life partly survived, and we can see through the poet's eyes the huntsmen of his day – the halloo no doubt led by O'Hara – appearing from behind the oaks on the hill over the lake, strung out at the gallop –

> Tréanrith gadhar agus Reynard rómpa ...

The clearance of the virgin forest was proceeding in east as well as west Clare, but 'improvement' didn't consist wholly of the making of enclosed fields for the new agriculture. Here and there the primeval woods which had suited the pastoral-venereal style of medieval Ireland were being replaced or modified by ornamental plantations designed to provide pleasing prospects for the new houses – which we call 'Georgian'. A few miles to the north-west of Lough Graney, for example, Robert Gregory was just commencing his extensive system of plantations:

> Mr Gregory (writes Arthur Young) has a very noble nursery, from which he is making plantations, which will soon be a great ornament to the country.

The woods of Coole were taking their first shape.

In the country along the Shannon, from Mountshannon (then in County Galway, 'Mountshannon Daly', as it was known) down to Killaloe and round past Cratloe and Bunratty to the Fergus and the approaches to Clare and Ennis, the landlords were covering the hills and valleys with elegant arrangements of trees. This was the same country that had been thoroughly Normanized in the thirteenth century until the Norman disaster at the battle of Dysert in 1318 reversed the process; now it was the part of Clare most thoroughly Anglicized. To quote Young again:

> Drommoland has a pleasing variety of grounds about the house: it stands on a hill gently rising from a lake of 24 acres, in the middle of a wood of

oak, ash, poplar, etc., three beautiful hills rise above it, over which the plantations spread in a varied manner; and these hills command very fine views of the great rivers Fergus and Shannon at their junction, being each of them a league wide.

Or, in the more flowery English of John Lloyd, in his *Short Tour in the County Clare in 1780*:

> Behold Paradise, with it's lofty and airy Summit, pleasantly situated and overlooking both Rivers on a Commanding Eminence, which freely af-fords a Romantic Survey of a Part of three or four Counties: This noble Situation is Ornamented with a Charming and Bewildering Shrubbery, beautiful Gardens, Avenues, Lawns and Cascades, which truely contrib-ute to make it a Munster Paradise, and stand Conspicuous among the first and most Eligible Seats in this Kingdom.--This is the Mansion Place and Estate of Richard Henn, Esq; (a Minor) eldest son of the late William Henn Esq. ...

The Henns were patrons of Lloyd, a schoolmaster and poet who, although a Limerick man, spent most of his life in Clare. His most copied poem was an *aisling*, beginning with the words 'Cois leasa dhom go huaigneach', set to the air of 'The Flowers of Edinburgh.' He is said to have been put on his trial when an English version of this Jacobite song – made by Michael Comyn – appeared, but I have not been able to trace a record of this event. Comyn, a Protestant landlord and a Gaelic writer of distinction, died in 1760 when Lloyd was nineteen. One of the manuscripts in which *Cois leasa* appears was copied by the scribe John Sharry about 1790, and was for a time in the possession of William Burton, of Clifden, a considerable patron, as we have seen, of old learning. Sharry tells us how and where the poem was composed – it is the usual vision of Ireland in the form of a woman speaking to the poet about the return of the Stuarts:

> John Lloyd sang it, on a day when the old woman Ireland, the grey-green island, showed herself to him on the pleasant green-sided wave beside the green-dappled Shannon above the house of Tadhg Mac Conmara in Rineanna in Tradree beside a *lios*.

The *lios*, incidentally, was one of those excavated by Professor Rynne when they were to be demolished to make way for jet runways at Shannon.

The German scholar Stern, who published an edition and translation (into German) of *Cúirt an Mheán Oíche*, apparently following an earlier editor, Daly, associates Merriman with other parts of Clare – the baronies of Islands and Bunratty Lower – and makes him an intimate of Lloyd, John Hore and John Tuomy (or Seán Ó Tuama). The intimacy seems unlikely, but these men would all almost certainly have known one another. Lloyd had taught school at Dunaha, and perhaps there made the translation of the *Life* of St Senan, the same that Anthony O'Brien was diligently copying in the summer of 1780. Then he moved to Kilrush, where, according to Henry Henn, he 'became indebted to some publicans.' While there he wrote a somewhat obscure squib in Irish addressed to one Pat O'Connor, a wigmaker of the town whose house had collapsed but without damaging his wig-block. Lloyd provided his own translation, into his own English:

> O charming block my block for comb and carol
> That dared and stood the shock of house and all
> A rock a Block to cover heads from Crime,
> My bosom block thou art to the end of time.

From Kilrush he moved to Kilmihil, where he fell foul of Donncha Ó Mathúna – Donncha an Chairn – who wrote contemptuously of Lloyd's writings. He went to Ennis, where he worked for, or with, Tomás Ó Míocháin in his school. This arrangement, again in Mr Henn's words, 'was soon terminated on account of Lloyd's intemperate habits'. He moved on to Tulla and was living at Toureen when he published his *Tour* of Clare in 1780. He was found dead by the roadside there a few years later.

His friend Ó Míocháin was a Clareman born and bred. His father, a tailor, was buried at Quin, and Tomás placed on his headstone there in the friary the words:

> Here lies, three in one
> A poet, a scholar, and an honest man.

He himself, as we have seen, kept a school at Ennis, and was sufficiently well-to-do to put up money for printing Lloyd's *Tour*, which was advertized as follows:

> This short description may be had from the following, viz. Mr Mat. Kelly, Merchant in Limerick; Mr Pat. Ryan, Merchant in Kilrush; Messrs. John Busteed and Geo. Trinder, in Tralee or Ennis; Mr John Hogan, Instructor, in Change-Lane, Limerick; Mr John Lloyd (the Author thereof) at Tureen; and Mr Tho. Meehan, Teacher of Accompts and Mathematicks in Ennis.

This gives us a network of distribution which was the same as that of writings in Irish of the time, which appeared only in manuscript form. An important link was that from Kilrush to Tarbert in Kerry. Corkery was mistaken when he wrote

> that there was a difference in place, Merriman being of the County Clare, Ó Súilleabháin of the County Kerry, with the Shannon, during their formative years, flowing between. That river prevented the one from being like the other as surely as the river of years hindered Eoghan Ruadh from writing a death-song in the way that Ó Rathaille wrote his.

Differences there were, but the Shannon was not a divide but a highway, and communication across it was much easier than most communication by land. Indeed, without appreciating its significance, Corkery himself quotes a very evocative acount by O'Curry of Anthony O'Brien. O'Curry says that O'Brien was one

> who spent much of his time in my father's house, and who was the best singer of Oisín's poems that his contemporaries had ever heard. He had a rich and powerful voice; and often on a calm summer's day, he would go with a party into a boat on the lower Shannon, at my native place, where the river is eight miles wide; and having rowed to the middle of the river, they used to lie on oars ... on which occasions O'Brien was always prepared to sing his choicest pieces, among which were no greater favourites than Oisín's poems. So powerful was the singer's voice that it often reached the shores at either side of the boat in Clare and Kerry, and often called the labouring men at both sides down to the water's edge to enjoy the strains of the music.

To return to Ó Míocháin: he was a radical. He held political views which were probably much more common than our documentary evidence tells us, since it was dangerous to express them. In a poem beginning, 'Le géagaibh gníomhach Chuinn is Eoghain,' he refers to the world events of 1779-80. A few sample couplets translated roughly in the rhythm of the original give the general sense:

> Although they boast their might at sea,
> Hood under sail and Rodney's squadron,
> They'll all be sunk and shattered soon
> By mighty Grasse the gallant hero ...
>
> West they're chased by Gates and Green,
> East they're thrust by Hyder Ali;
> Nor hills nor woods will shelter Clinton;
> Arnold strikes from every vantage ...
>
> Though warships sail to that New World
> The English are both spent and beaten;
> And Washington relentlessly
> Consigns Cornwallis to the devil.

The two-line refrain of the poem reads:

> Oh Bright the day in Inis Fáil:
> God's friars will soon be in their churches,
> Art and learning free from law;
> And Irish in the foreign houses.

In another poem, written a few years earlier, he had celebrated the British evacuation of Boston in 1776:

> It's with triumphant joy I see
> Howe and the English down forever,
> And stalwart Washington, the brave
> And helpful, governing his realm;
> The hirelings roaring without stores,
> Without an ally, town or navy:
> Indeed, by year's end, British boors
> Will be reduced by French dominion.

These lines may be compared with those of the contemporary Limerick poet William Ó Líonáin, in an *aisling* in which the woman, representing Ireland, who appears to the poet speaks to him not about the forthcoming return of the true prince, but about American triumphs beyond the Atlantic. This is much better written than Ó Míocháin's doggerel, and is worth quoting in Irish:

> Do labhair mé ina dhéidh sin go béasach in nGaoidheilge,
> A's d'aithris dam sgéala do mhéadaigh mo chroidhe-se,
> Go rabhadar béaraibh an Bhéarla go claoidhte,
> Gan armaibh, gan éadach, gan tréadaibh, gan tíorthaibh.
> Táid caithte i gcarcair na ndrongaibh gan treoir
> Faoí fhad-thuirse i nglasaibh ag Washington beo,
> I mairg, gan gradam, gan caraid, gan lón,
> As iad ag sgreadaigh le heasbuidh na feola
> Do chleachtadh na bathlaigh do chaitheamh gan teora.

Ó Líonáin has got some real force of passion into those last two lines:

> As they are roaring for lack of the meat
> That without limit the bastards used eat.

– the true voice of envious hunger. It is not a very noble note, but it is expressive of much of the sentiment of the time.

Another aspect of the same or a similar sentiment may be found in a different kind of Irish poetry of the day with political overtones. John Hore, writing a poem in praise of Charles MacDonnell of Kilkee, praises also O'Brien of Dromoland, Burton and the Hickmanns, but singles out MacDonnell as being of the old true stock, one of the very few from the old Gaelic world who could hold their own in the new order:

> When he sits under powder upon his court-bench
> The foreign dogs whisper in awe of him ...

MacDonnell of course was Protestant. The current of resentment which flows in the writings of the Clare poet-schoolmasters was not religious but cultural or ethnic – virtually racial. Race was not always enough, however. A quatrain addressed to a dead O'Brien of Bunratty says:

> Descendant of the generous unstained O'Briens,
> It's a pity I can't say – 'God be with your soul.'

> A ua na mBrianach fial gan mhasla gan táir,
> as truagh nach fiadaim, 'Dia red tanam,' do rádh.

The MacDonnells, however, were particular favourites among these writers, and among the MacDonnells, Mary Bán, who married Murtagh MacMahon of Clonenagh in 1750. The marriage was in secret, in August; in September Murtough carried her off from Kilkee against her mother's consent. John Hore wrote a mock-heroic poem about the abduction, singling out as the hero in MacMahon's band one Michael Lardner, an ale-seller from Cooraclare. Mary Bán however, was dead by 1780, suitably lamented by the poets. She was buried in Kilmihil churchyard. The MacDonnells by then had their main residence at Killone, south of Ennis, and stayed at Kilkee mainly in the summer. This was becoming a common enough custom among the gentry: we hear of a number who had summer or occasional residences near the sea. The house at Killone was Newhall, a lovely brick building designed about the middle of the century by one of the Clare gentry who was a painter and architect of distinction – Francis Bindon.

Such houses were still not very common in Clare, although there were a few of them, including the early-eighteenth-century Mount Ievers. But many older style houses were still occupied – Bunratty and Lemaneh, for example. The need for defence had not altogether disappeared. Compared with some parts of the country Clare in 1780 was quite peaceful. Whiteboy gangs were so active in parts of the neighbouring county of Tipperary (especially around Killenaule) that the county was virtually in a state of insurrection. Clare had only occasional outbreaks, mainly in the east. On Friday 8 September a 'great number' of Whiteboys armed 'with guns, pistols and bayonets, etc.' attacked the house of Luke Wall at Springmount, near Broadford. According to the report they:

> burned it down with offices, destroyed all furniture, cut and tore to pieces all clothes, books, papers; levelled ditches and inclosures on his land, houghed and killed a great number of cattle; scattered all corn and hay. . .

Wall fled to Ennis, but returned a week later with three friends. They were set upon by a large number of men and he was hacked to pieces. Springmount was never rebuilt.

Such agitations were in large part a reaction against 'improvement', a term which covered enclosure, road-making (the press-ganging of tenants into making landlords' roads had sparked off a series of similar movements earlier in the century in Protestant Ulster), the clearing of estates, and the new methods of cultivation. The enclosure movement, which cut across the whole tangle of medieval custom, common lands, open fields, and communal and cooperative systems, had reached its peak in England in the preceding decade. It wholly changed the landscape, introducing the patchwork of fields that survived into the present century. It had already proceeded far in eastern Ireland, but was only beginning to be effective in the more westerly parts. Sir Lucius O'Brien, at Dromoland, was a keen 'improver', as was Robert Gregory, just across the county boundary at Coole. Gregory, according to Arthur Young, at this time had five or six hundred acres, which he was busy improving. He was building many miles of walls

> Dry, six feet high, 3½ feet thick at bottom, 20 inches on top, cost 2s. 6d. the perch. Piers in mortar with gates and irons complete, £1.14s.

Young goes on:

> He has fixed two English bailiffs on his farm, one for accounts and overlooking his walling and other business; and another from Norfolk, for introducing the turnip husbandry; he has twelve acres this year; and what particularly pleased me, I saw some Irishmen hoeing them; the Norfolk men had taught them ...

Young obtained his general information about agriculture and land-holding in County Clare from Sir Lucius O'Brien – which means that the information was not wholly disinterested: Sir Lucius had many fish to fry, and as a lobbyist and politician was as much a propagandist as he was a statistician. According to his information, the average rent in the county was about 5s. an acre, but there was much bad land in the eastern mountains and parts of the Burren – much of this was let at 'nothing at all.' About 20,000 acres, he estimated, of the corcass lands – rich deep black or blue loam and clay soil around the Fergus – was worth 20s. an acre. The sizes of farms varied widely. Young mentions Captain Timothy MacNamara who farmed 7,000 acres – not all however within the county – and Mr Singleton who farmed 4,000 acres. A stock farm of £300 a year would be regarded as very small, £500 as 'middling'. These were the gentlemen ranchers, and an important distinction must be made. The tillage of the county, according to Young, was carried on 'by little farmers, from £20 to £100 a year, but most of it by the poor labourers, who are generally under-tenants, not holding of the landlords.' This distinction runs back through the eighteenth century. In 1735, the Dublin House of Commons resolved that enforcing the tithe of agistment (tithes on grass lands) was calculated to impair the Protestant interest and cause popery and infidelity to flourish. Afterwards, this tax, nominally at least for the support of the Established church, was borne chiefly by the tenants, who were Catholic, and evaded largely by their landlords, who were Protestant. It reinforced the class distinction between graziers and tillers and for a time led to an agricultural regression.

The sequences of crops sown were said to be: potatoes; bere; wheat; oats; oats; oats; grass; or, alternatively: beans; bere; barley; wheat; oats; oats; oats; grass or beans again.

> They sow 10–15 stone of wheat an acre: the crop in corcass ground is 8 barrels, in other land 5 or 6.

The measure was 20 stone to the barrel. Potatoes were measured by the barrel of 48 stone, and were planted 6 barrels to the acres producing an average of 50. They were never sown on the corcass land as they would not grow there. Mr FitzGerald, of Shapperton, was reported to have had 100 barrels an acre. The favourite types were 'apple, Castania, Buck, being a species of the Howard'. This last type, mentioned in Merriman's *Cuirt*, was used for fattening pigs. Hogs were also fattened on grass – 'as fat as a bullock' – and then put up to beans for three weeks to harden the fat. There is a good deal of further detailed information on crops: barley: bere, or two-rowed barley, locally known as 'English,' and four-rowed barley, known as 'Dutch,' oats and beans. The barley was widely used in producing whiskey, a self-sufficiency in Clare of 1780: the smoke of a thousand stills rose from the hills and valleys of the county. Beans, according to Young, were used for home consumption in dear years and for exportation in cheap.

> The poor people make bread of them, and eat them boiled, and they prefer a bushel of them to a bushel of wheat; but they will not eat them, except in a scarcity.

This information however almost certainly relates, like much of Young's, to the country around the Fergus.

Rape was sown in considerable quantity on mountain or boggy gound, 'both of which,' according to Young, 'are burnt for it'. The crop of seed was pressed into oil at the mills of Sixmilebridge and Scarriff and sold mainly in Limerick. From there the merchants exported it to Holland, or, since the easing of trade restrictions in 1780, to Great Britain.

The cultivation of rape is an indicator of the colonisation of marginal lands, and of an expanding population. There was a complementary development. The British agricultural revolution, intimately associated with the early stages of the industrial revolution, was creating new demands. The average weight of oxen sold at Smithfield in London went from 370 lb. in 1710 to 800 lb. in 1795; of calves from 50 lb. to 150 lb.; of sheep from 38 lb. to 80 lb. This was due to a combination of enclosure, new breeding methods, new intensive feeding, and technical change in general. The demand for oilcake was one side-effect.

The Industrial Revolution – a term, incidentally disliked by some historians, but unavoidable – is conventionally dated from about 1760, an arbitrary enough point like most such. In 1780 informed people knew that it was happening but they didn't know what it was: descriptions like 'industrial revolution' are of course labels applied with hindsight by historians. It must be remembered too that although, looking back, we think of the Industrial Revolution as an urban affair, in fact it would be more correct to call it 'urbanizing': the revolutionary change came first; the towns grew from it. It began in villages in the north of England and on the estates of great landlords who were active in parliament and capable of promoting their own welfare and that of their class by legislation. Irish landlords of a progressive cast, not fully appreciating the extraordinary convergence of circumstances which was producing such remarkable results in Britain, thought to keep up with what was happening there by isolating the one or other technical advance which seemed to them to be the clue to the whole. Sir Lucius O'Brien thought for a while it was canals, and agitated for the cutting of these useful waterways, to give better access to Limerick, or from the Shannon towards Clare and Ennis. Edward FitzGerald thought it was coal, and tried hard to find that valuable substance, sinking shafts north and south of Liscannor Bay. Others, including again Sir Lucius, thought the secret lay in 'the Manchester system'. The production of cheap cottons in the north of England at a time when Irish textile production was in deep depression (the number of looms in the Liberties of Dublin, for example, having gone down in a few years from the hundreds to a couple of dozen in 1780 – these of course were working in wool) had caused great agitation in the previous few years. A boycott of British goods was being attempted. In summer, 1780, 'a number of artificers' from Sheffield and Manchester arrived (at Dublin) for the several new manufactures established at Limerick, Birr, Cork: and Dublin. Sir Lucius was involved in this importation of British skill. The first cotton piece-goods were turned out by the end of the year in Limerick by these experts.

Clare however, in the textile business, depended not on gimmicky innovation, but on sheep, which grazed in large numbers in west Clare and the Burren. Restrictions on the export of Irish wool had been one of the main matters at issue between the Dublin parliament and the English government, and the Clare members took a keen interest in the question. The first triumph of the agitation which had been backed by the force of arms of the Volunteers was the lifting of these restrictions. There had been a brisk smuggling trade, and, since the French and Spanish entered the war, a considerable trade with Portugal, but the Portuguese, prevailed upon by the British, attempted to stop Irish wool imports in 1780, and produced a crisis among the exporters. Prices, in any case, were depressed—part of the general and severe depression of the late 1770s. This indeed may be why some observers noted that the people of the county at this time were better clad than they had been some years earlier. Wool also provided the raw material for the one manufacture which was carried out in north Clare at the time – the knitting of coarse stockings by the local women. 'Here is a large and plentiful Market every Saturday,' wrote John Lloyd of Ennistymon, 'and as well stock'd with Stockings as Killaloe is with Eels.'

Poor communications hampered the development and production of the
county. There was a small harbour on the north coast – just below the present
Bell Harbour – and not another reasonable one between there and Kilrush. Bell
Harbour was much frequented by Galway boats, and from it considerable quantities of seaweed were shipped across the Bay, for use in the manuring of land.
Large quantities were also sent inland. This weed, thrown up by the ton by the
Atlantic storms, was spread on potatoes in November, to rot before the planting
season. (The same was done with fern, cut in autumn and spread on the potatoes.) It was widely used, and very large amounts were also brought by boat up
the Shannon estuary, coming through Kilrush from west Clare to Bunratty (a
very active trading place because of good shelter and anchorages) or up the Fergus
or on to Limerick. By this same route peat came from the west: the smoke of
Limerick's chimneys in 1780 almost all came from the turf of west Clare.

A generation later Hely Dutton was to point out the lack of economy in
Kilrush's relation to Limerick:

> The river Shannon ... enters the Atlantic Ocean between this county and
> Kerry, where it is about five miles broad, and seems intended by Provi-
> dence to carry the produce of Ireland, to supply the wants of our neigh-
> bours through this channel. Of this the merchants of Limerick have availed
> themselves ...If capital was not wanting, Kilrush would long since have
> had a very large share of these advantages; and, as Mr Vandaleur must be
> sensible of the great benefit of a flourishing town to his adjoining estate,
> no doubt can be entertained, that liberal encouragement will be held out
> to improving tenants. When the time lost in working up and down the
> Shannon (a distance of 120 miles) and the expence of shipping and re-
> shipping, (for it will scarcely be believed that many articles are sent up the
> Shannon from Kilrush to Limerick, and there shipped) are considered, it
> must point out Kilrush has a most favourable situation for trade, and must
> eventually contribute to the benefit of a part of the county, that is the least
> improved, and the most favourable to improvement in the county.

This was all broadly true in 1780. Kilrush then, however, was a considerable
town in Clare terms: it had a fleet of a hundred fishing vessels, even if they were
small, and was connected by road with Ennis, Limerick and the rest of the country.

The only other bay of significance, between Loop Head and Galway Bay, was
that of Liscannor – but there was no harbour. Fishermen however, worked out
from this stretch of coast, but they could not use the wooden vessels of Kilrush
or Bell Harbour. They used currachs.

> There is an Artificial Curiosity (writes Lloyd) made use of by certain In-
> dividuals, in the upper Part of this dangerous Coast. It's a kind of Canoe
> or Currach, composed of Wattles, cover'd with Raw Hydes: With this In-

dian-like construction, they Fish successfully in the proper Season, and Paddle some Leagues out in calm Weather; in the month of August there is often a large Squadron of them together, in the Bay of Liscanor, and in this Fishing Posture, they appear like so many Porpoises on the Surface: Each Man carries his Wicker Boat, or Canoe, on his Back, occasionally to and from the Shore.

The people of the coast ate shellfish: limpets, periwinkles, lobsters and crabs; they caught turbot in the summer season, and haddock and cod; in winter they ate ling and cod. Trout and salmon are also mentioned. The main fishery of the larger boats was of herrings. Kilrush had a good herring fleet and herring boats also operated in Galway Bay from the north coast. These participated in April-May in the fishery of 'sun-fish', or basking sharks, off the Connemara coast: 'It is not by shares, but the owners of the boats hire the men for the fishery. One fish is reckoned worth £5 and if a boat takes three fish in a month it is reckoned good luck.' There was competition in the herring fishery, and in 1780 the fishermen of Killybegs and the north-west coasts of Ireland petitioned the Dublin parliament because the mayor and corporation of Limerick had imposed a duty or surcharge on them when they tried to sell their catch in that port.

Clare was perceived by contemporaries to be more populous than neighbouring counties – probably inaccurately. In the early nineteenth century its birth-rate was consistently high – putting Clare among the top two or three counties in this respect – and the birth and marriage rates may also have been high in 1780, in spite of the argument of *Cúirt an Mheán Oíche*. Abduction seems to have been a fairly frequent crime. A young man called Coman or Hurley, was hanged in Ennis in November having been found guilty of this crime: half a dozen others were tried for the offence at the same assizes, but were acquitted. Half a century later, we learn that the reason the great annual pilgrimage or 'patron' on Holy Island in Lough Derg was suppressed by the parochial clergy of Inis Cealtra, was the long established custom of abduction there: young men from the territories around the lake would row to the island in fast boats and make raids on the great throng of pilgrims (10,000 to 15,000 people), carrying off young girls. We learn elsewhere that an event which commonly led to matches was a game of hurling. Great crowds of young men and women would stay all night drinking in the shebeens after a game, and this led to marriages. Indeed, Merriman, in *Cúirt an Mheán Óiche*, acknowledges this as one of the recognised occasions for mate-seeking. I quote from Frank O'Conor's translation:

> I tossed my cap at the crowd at the races
> And I kept my head in the toughest places.
> Am I not always on the watch
> At bonfire, dance, or hurling match,
> Or outside the chapel after Mass
> to coax a smile from the fellows that pass?

> The hurling matches, called goals – writes Hely Dutton – are very injuri-
> ous to the morals and industry of the younger classes; after performing
> feats of activity, that would astonish a bread and cheese Englishman, they
> too often adjourn to the whiskey-house, both men and women, and spend
> the night in dancing, singing and drinking until perhaps morning, and too
> often quarrels and broken heads are the effects of this inebriety; matches
> are often made between the partners at the dance; but it frequently hap-
> pens that they do not wait for the priest's blessing, and the fair one must
> apply to a magistrate who generally obliges the faithless Strephon to make
> an honest woman of her. On the strand of Lehinch races for saddles and
> bridles are run almost every Sunday in summer, and the night generally
> concludes with dancing and drunkenness; they are become a great nui-
> sance to those of the inhabitants, who are Christians.

With all these references to singing and dancing, we are unfortunately very poorly
informed about the music of the people at the time. Seventy years later, however,
when Petrie was completing his collection, it is plain that the musical tradition
was stronger in Clare than, perhaps, anywhere else. He has 43 tunes from Clare,
33 from Aran, 24 from Limerick, 23 from Cork. There is probably some bias in
these figures: Petrie had the convenience of collecting a great deal of the Clare
material in Dublin, from Frank Keane. In spite of this, the weight of material
from Clare, Aran and Limerick shows that the musical tradition must have been
particularly strong in this corner of Ireland. Nor was it all purely traditional:
Petrie's tune No. 871, for example, was a planxty by Carolan, preserved, apparently, in Clare.

Aran, of course, is much nearer to the coast of Clare than to that of Galway,
and there was at least one gathering place where the people of Aran regularly
mixed with those of Clare. This was the patron of St Brigid's well at Derreen and
on the strand at Liscannor – one of the survivals of the ancient Celtic festival of
Lughnasa discussed in great detail by Maire MacNeill.

> The last Sunday in July, according to the Rev. Mr Kenny, is a patron day,
> when a number of people assemble at Lahinchy: they amuse themselves
> with horse-racing on the strand, dancing &c. near it. This Sunday is called
> Garlic Sunday, but for what reason is not known. On Saturday evening
> preceding this Sunday, numbers of people, male and female, assemble at
> St Bridget's Well, and remain there the entire of the night. They first per-
> form their rounds, and then spend a good part of the time in invoking this
> saint Bridget over the well, repeating their prayers and adorations aloud,
> and holding their conversations with the Saint &c. When this ceremony is
> over, they amuse themselves until morning by dancing and singing, &c.
> They then (on Sunday morning) repair to Lehensey, distant from the well
> at least three miles, to conclude their merriment. This well is also re-
> sorted to, on the first of February.

The Lehinch patron was only one of many annual assemblies in eighteenth-century Clare. Scattery, or Inis Cathaigh, off Kilrush was another place with a great annual patron. The island at that time was uninhabited: the rounds were performed among the ruined churches. At the other end of the county very large crowds (more than ten thousand people, it would seem) gathered at Whit for the patron of Holy Island, or Inis Cealtra, in Lough Derg near Mountshannon.

The hurling matches, in those days long before the foundation of the GAA, seem generally to have been played by twenty-one-man teams over large tracts of open ground – one goal deciding the issue. It is interesting to note that, at least in this part of the country, inter-county as well as inter-parish matches were played. P. Ó Caithnia, who has made a thorough study of the history of the game, quotes an account published in *Pue's Occurrences* some twenty-odd years before our date:

> Galway Oct. 8. There was a grand Hurling Match in the neighbourhood of Gort in this County for a considerable sum of Money between the Counties of Clare and Galway; the Hurlers of the latter made a very handsome appearance. They marched from Gort to the Turlagh, two miles distant, preceded by a Band of Musick, a French Horn, a Running Footman and a Fellow in an antick or Harlequin Dress. None of the Hurlers were in the least hurt, the greatest Harmony having subsisted. The county of Clare Hurlers were elegantly entertained at Crushenaire the Night following, and 100 Guineas was proposed to be hurled for, but the Time and Place not yet agreed. The above Procession closed with many Carriages and Horsemen; the numerous Company at Turlough made a fine Appearance.

Sometimes, it seems, on Christmas Day or May Day, much larger teams were fielded in matches – probably more like battles – between neighbouring parishes.

For the general social structure and organisation underlying such events, Merriman's long poem is one of the sources. It paints for us a picture of a class or stratum of society which was not unprosperous and which maintained fairly active and complex social relationships. It was also a society which, at least to some extent, was in tune with the time: Merriman's poem, for example, shows a kind of concern for women which was expressive of a new sensibility just then becoming widely manifest in western Europe. This coincides with what has been called 'the first sexual revolution'. We know too little as yet about the detailed workings of Irish society at the time however, to see quite how Ireland fits into the general European movement of social change. There are three points to bear in mind. The first is that the great change from traditional societies to modern societies in Europe began in the eighteenth century with industrial and political revolutions but appears to stem not from the upper orders of society but from the middle and lower orders and to derive from an awakening of mind. The second is that Clare especially had maintained close contacts with Continental Europe through most of the eighteenth century. The third is that there is much evidence to suggest that attitudes, customs and behaviour which in contemporary Ireland might be regarded as 'traditional' and therefore be assumed to have roots in the distant past were in fact established as recently as the middle of the last century. The rural Ireland of our grandparents' time, in other words, was not the traditional society at all. To point to the contrast between that more recent world and the still deeply rooted tradition of the eighteenth century, it is only necessary to recollect the strong opposition, in our own time and in his own place, to any commemoration of Merriman and his work. That work was a natural, if remarkable, product of his milieu and was received and valued immediately by his contemporaries.

In this respect the 'Hidden Ireland' is doubly hidden. Even those who set out sympathetically to discover it, like Daniel Corkery, or, to take two writers who have discussed Merriman and his work, Risteard Ó Foghlú and Aodh de Blacam, failed to see it clearly because they took it for something which is not quite what it was and their perception suffers, in part, from anachronism. A leaven of what we might call modernization was, it seems, working in Irish Gaelic culture as in other western European cultures in the eighteenth century. This is not quite the same as secularization, although of course it is related to it. Religion was a central and enormously important element in the culture of late-eighteenth-century Irish-speaking Clare. Most of the penal laws were still on the statute book in 1780, although not generally or strictly enforced. There had been some slight easement in the law. It had, for example, been made possible for Roman Catholics to swear allegiance to the king without at the same time forswearing their beliefs, and the Catholic bishop, MacMahon, had led his clergy in so doing. This was a beginning of the formal recognition of the Roman Catholics as a part of the body politic, allowing them to present themselves as loyal subjects with a case to state. The institutional church was building the efficient organization which was to serve it so well in the coming time and, by a paradox, the penal laws in some respects were of benefit to it, especially where they were not stringently enforced: the church retained its autonomy, and was becoming *the* institution of the people as distinct from the institutions of the still-alien state or the institutions of the culture which had been destroyed. Apart from formalities the centrality of religion is apparent, for example, from the manuscripts which were being copied in late-eighteenth-century Clare, containing as they do a great deal of devotional or other religious matter, and from prayers or poems composed at the time by writers such as John Hore. It is plain from the same sources that affection for the friars, in particular, was widespread.

In 1780 a younger contemporary of Merriman's, Robert Burns, who was then just twenty-one, founded a bachelors' drinking club. Six years later he was to write a poem which is worth comparing briefly with Merriman's *Cúirt* for the light shed thereby on the distinction between two societies. (As Burns had a great acquaintance with and affection for the Gaelic-speaking Highlands, there is in fact just a faint possibility that by 1786 he might have come across *Cúirt an Mheán Oíche*.) 'Libel Summons', a poem more or less of the *barántas* type, also concerns a court – the poet himself is the president, as, for example, in Tomás Ó Míocháin's tavern-court of poetry in Ennis.. The court is hearing the cases of women whose seducers have let them down. It concludes with the sentencing of one of the culprits to be beaten:

> Our beadles to the Cross shall take you,
> And there shall mither naked make you.

The poem is a piece of jovial Burnsian bawdry, its theme much simpler than that of the *Cúirt*, its argument much less subtle and sophisticated (it is, of course, much shorter).

Burns's is a voice of the Englightenment. That the middle of the century marks a significant change is surely true. Change shows elsewhere in what has been called 'the first sexual revolution'. This revolution, only beginning to be discerned by the new schools of historians of the people, was marked by a steep rise in illegitimacy in Western Europe in the second half of the eighteenth century. It may seem paradoxical that it was accompanied by a rapid spread of contraceptive practices of different kinds, but the paradox is superficial: what was happening was that young women, predominantly of the growing rural and urban proletariat, were liberating themselves – in a spontaneous movement deriving from currents of perception and of non-philosophical enlightenment much more difficult to document than the teachings of Diderot or Hume, Voltaire or Rousseau – from the tyranny of purely economic status and roles. A degree of 'free love,' within limits, is involved; but the real thrust is towards humanity: people dealing with one another as people, who can relate to each other not merely as economic units but as *sentimental* beings – the Age of Reason was also the Age of Sentiment (not sentimentality). A very complex subject; but one of the first effects of 'improvement' and modernization was this movement, originating with young women who began to liberate themselves, and who speeded an underground current of feeling that is of great importance for the major political revolutions of the late eighteenth century. It is no accident that one of the most explosively revolutionary works of the age of reason was a romance – *La Nouvelle Heloïse*. Merriman reflects these developments: Clare in 1780 belonged to a tradition which had much in common with those of France or Germany; was subject to similar pressures and displays some similar trends. His work, stemming from the native tradition, is in its very frameworks and ironies, a sharp comment on that tradition – saying 'Come off it: liberation from our oppression will come not from the politics of Dublin or America or the Stuart court but from the assertion of humanity.' Sex at this date *is* liberation; Merriman in his vignettes acknowledges the common humanity of the young woman, the old man and the bastard child, and he celebrates *life*. In this his is a voice, not merely of the Hidden Ireland: indeed, thanking Corkery for it, we might now abandon the model of the Hidden Ireland – for that eighteenth-century Ireland is visible to eyes that can see. His voice is a voice of the enlightenment of the people, an assertion of the new democracy that was beginning to rise against absolutist Europe. He speaks for a tradition that has spoken again – for life among the deadly aridities of later times – in the voices of *Cré na Cille*, in Seán Ó Ríordáin's affirmations of the integrity of blood and mind, in Molly Bloom's reiterated 'Yes.'

4

The Voice of Tone

Wolfe Tone is on one level a figure of myth, especially since Pearse established a canon for the Irish 'republican' tradition, in which Tone was the fountainhead for the stream of pure doctrine which flowed down through Davis, Mitchel and Lalor.

This tradition is unhistorical. It places Tone, and the whole tangled episode of Ninety-Eight, in the context not of their own time but of nineteenth-century romantic and conspiratorial nationalism. It absorbs them all indeed into Pearse's own political consciousness and into his *fin-de-siècle* part-literary, part-mystical, fantasy of redemption by blood. The tradition is less republican than nationalist and separatist. It is not an inclusive but an exclusive tradition (as may be seen in the detailed history of recent republican splits), and the unity of minds and hearts it has aimed at has something in common with Roman ecumenism before Vatican II; it involved the acknowledgment of truth by error.

On another level, one which is reached as soon as his own writings are read with a clear mind, Tone is one of the least charismatic, least mythical and mystical of revolutionaries; human, fallible, ambitious but at the same time diffident in a way, pragmatic, imprudent, cheerful and likeable.

'Republicans' in the narrow recent sense can indeed find in Tone's writings what they seek. The sacred texts are there:

> To subvert the tyranny of our execrable Government, to break the connection with England, the never-failing source of all our political evils, and to assert the independence of my country – these were my objects; to unite the whole people of Ireland, to abolish the memory of all past dissensions, and to substitute the common name of Irishman in place of the denominations of Protestant, Catholic, and Dissenter – these were my means.

But there is a contrast between his magnanimous and light-hearted spirit and the puritanical sour self-righteousness of some who proclaim themselves his followers.

Like so many of his fellows in the United Irish clubs, Tone thought as a colonial who, partly from the example of America and partly from the teaching of revolutionary France, 'discovered that he had a country'. The 'execrable govern-

---

This appeared in the 'Roots' column in the *Irish Times*, 2 August 1972

ment' was judged to be so on the basis of its actions rather than its pretensions, and that the connection with England was the 'never-failing source of all our evils' was inferred not from any dogma of Ireland's sacred and separate nation-hood but from observation of current politics. Tone was an eighteenth-century man, living in the Age of Reason. His political ideas, right or wrong, were derived not from a mystique but by rational process.

He moved to a political extreme partly because he lived in terrible times when moderation could find little place. It was a contest, as he saw it and put it, between 'aristocracy' and 'the people': it was in other words the time of the French Revolution, and Tone's principles were Jacobin. His political ideas were not, perhaps, very profound, but they were soundly democratic. He believed in the *independence* of Ireland as a necessary means to achieving the *liberty* of its people, as individuals. He always distinguishes the two words, in this sense: he hardly envisages any abstract of 'Ireland' as distinct from the people of the island, still less any concept of 'Ireland's freedom', and his priority is always for the individual's freedom. Tone was the type of the bourgeois revolutionary, content enough in acceptance of the contemporary values of his class, resentful of aristocratic and unearned privilege, humane and magnanimous, conventional in most of his sentiments.

On the question of property, crucial in examining the thought of any revolutionary, Tone is ambiguous. He writes in his *Journal* on 27 April 1798:

> Why does England so pertinaceously resist our independence? Is it for love of us – is it because *she* thinks *we* are better as we are? That single argument, if it stood alone, should determine every honest Irishman. But, it will be said, the United Irishmen extend their view farther; they go now to a distribution of property, and an agrarian law. I know not whether they do or no. I am sure in June, 1795, when I was forced to leave the country, they entertained no such ideas. If they have since taken root among them, the Irish gentry may accuse themselves ... If such men, in the issue, lose their property, they are themselves alone to blame, by deserting the first and most sacred of duties – the duty to their country. They have incurred a willful forfeiture by disdaining to occupy the station they might have held among the People, and which the People would have been glad to see them fill; they left a vacancy to be seized by those who had more courage, more sense, and more honesty; and not only so, but by this base and interested desertion they furnished their enemies with every argument of justice, policy, and interest, to enforce the system of confiscation.

His view of the Ireland of his time is cool, as set forth in his memoranda to the French government in 1796, proposing an invasion. He estimates the population at about four-and-a-half million persons (about the same as today),

> of whom the Protestants, whose religion is the dominant one, and estab-

lished by law, constitute four hundred and fifty thousand, or one-tenth of the whole; the Dissenters, or Presbyterians, about nine hundred thousand, or one fifth; the Catholics form the remaining three million one hundred and fifty thousand.

Of these he regarded the Protestants, the group which formed his own background, as being, by their interest, 'devoted implicitly to the connection with England', and the Catholics as being, by theirs,

> trained from their infancy in an hereditary hatred and abhorrence of the English name, which conveys to them no ideas but those of blood and pillage and persecution.

Of the three groups it is plain that he most highly esteemed the Dissenters who, he says, 'are, from the genius of their religion, and the spirit of inquiry which it produces, sincere and enlightened republicans,' and who had, he believed, been finally converted by the example of the French Revolution to principles which overcame their distaste for 'the Catholic natives, whom they detested as Papists and despised as slaves'.

While he sincerely hoped for the merging of the distinction between the three groups in 'the common name of Irishman', Tone did, as a matter of practice, envisage an alliance of Catholics and Dissenters against the English government, which meant in effect against the Irish Protestants too – since he had no hope of winning them over in advance of revolution. But after the establishment of independence he aimed at a union of the three in a new Ireland, which would *not* be a revived medieval Gaelic society but a rationalistic secular state on the model of the French Republic. He failed; his failure has not been been diminished by all who claim to be his successors. He is still worth reading.

5

Tom Moore and Modern Ireland

Éamon de Valéra once commended a book on recent political history for which he was writing an introduction by stating that there should be a copy in every Irish home. At one time there was perhaps no book which came closer to such a distribution than the collection – in its various versions and editions – that was commonly and simply known as 'Moore's Melodies'. Like many people of my own and several earlier generations growing up in Dublin I came upon Moore through 'the Melodies' at an early age. My first public performance of any kind indeed was a rendition of 'The Minstrel Boy' offered to the infants' class at St Patrick's School, Drumcondra, when I was six.

The green-bound volume with its slightly tarnished stamped gilt lettering and patriotic devices, seemed in my early childhood to be the very essence of the Irishness of Ireland. It was opened after tea when aunts and uncles came to visit. They gathered round the piano to play and sing – not Moore alone of course, since the repertoire included a variety of popular drawing room songs – and of Moore not the *Irish Melodies* alone ('Oft, in the Stilly Night', for example, was commonly included). One or two of Davis's ballads would be sung ('The West's Awake', regularly), snatches of Balfe, 'Robin Adair', and an odd miscellany of faded ditties such as 'The Old Rustic Bridge by the Mill'. It was rather less genteel, and of course a full thirty years later, than the programme depicted by Joyce in 'The Dead' – but firmly within the same tradition.

Joyce in that marvellous story displays his acute and accurate observation of the accommodations of late colonial Ireland. In the account of the Christmastime evening of dance, song, feasting and conversation in the music teachers' house on Ussher's Island, Moore figures only indirectly – in a passing mention – but, if indirectly, tellingly. When Gabriel Conroy is rehearsing in his mind the speech of thanks he is to make, we are told that:

> He was undecided about the lines from Robert Browning for he feared they would be above the heads of his hearers. Some quotation that they

This was given in Cork as the fourth Ó Riada Memorial Lecture and was published in 1989 by the Irish Traditional Music Society, University College, Cork, as *Tom Moore and Contemporary Ireland*. Parts of the lecture were based on a talk I gave on BBC Radio 3 in 1974 on 'Tom Moore and Irish Nationalism,' published in *The Listener*, 11 April 1974.

> could recognize from Shakespeare or from the Melodies would be better.
> The indelicate clacking of the men's heels and the shuffling of their soles
> reminded him that their grade of culture differed from his. He would
> only make himself ridiculous by quoting poetry to them which they could
> not understand ...

Nothing by Moore is included among the musical pieces mentioned as having
been performed in the course of the evening. A part of that drawing room's culture, but already by the turn of the century beginning to be devalued, 'the Melodies' are thus shown very subtly to be regarded by the company as provincial, out
of tune with the participation in the cosmopolitan musical world that was being
celebrated. Gabriel's shame at his wife's origin in a more degrading provincial-
ism – peasant Connacht – is also tellingly indicated. Then, piercing the tissue of
shallow and hesitant snobberies, we receive the first intimation of 'The Dead':
the half-heard, half-finished, half-sung song, 'The Lass of Aughrim', which
'seemed to be in the old Irish tonality and the singer seemed uncertain both of
his words and of his voice.'

Joyce's story has a meaning which goes deeper than social history; but it is
also superb social history. I return, with much diffidence in this context, to my
personal commonplace reminiscence only to introduce a theme. My father pri-
vately played on the concertina mainly hornpipes and reels – but this was a domestic matter within his small household and was not for social occasions when
the extended family was present (he had come from County Waterford and married into Dublin). His father, a stonemason, had had a reputation as a dancer.
And when my only sister died at the age of nineteen my father never played traditional music again, although he occasionally performed beside the piano, singing
'The moon hath raised her lamp above' in duet with a musical uncle. Different
kinds of music answered different affinities of the soul.

Being neither a musician nor a musicologist (my career in this respect has
been in steady decline since 1932), I responded with trepidation to the invitation
to deliver the 1988 Ó Riada Memorial Lecture. But Seán Ó Riada was a friend,
admired in life; to do his memory honour is a work of *pietas*. And there is a
comparison to be made, even if a remote one, in terms of the social and historical
meaning of musical culture. Moore's medium was words, Ó Riada's music, but
both in their different ways have acted as mediators between the world of the
Gemeinschaft and the world of the *Gesellschaft*.

Two fairly abrupt shifts have taken place in comparatively recent history in
Ireland in the transition from one of those worlds to the other. The first such
shift was accomplished just before the Famine, and clinched by that dreadful
episode. It involved the change from the old Gaelic system which was medieval
and in some respects prehistoric in its character to a traditional system which
was recognisably early modern. The old Ireland to which we in our time can look
back, now across a gulf, was a century and a half ago a newly wrought Ireland –
the Ireland of, for example, late marriages; the Ireland also of intensive angliciza-

tion, of religious puritanism, and to a large extent of social aspiration combined with demoralisation. The second great shift was accomplished round about 1950, when that 'old Ireland' began to disappear into history, as the gombeen man yielded place to the whiz kid.

We have in Ireland remarkable instances of acculturation. For example – to go back to the 1920s – there was a political transition that had its cultural counterpart. The Cosgrave government had begun an attempt to revive Irish, mainly through the schools. The Irish language was only a part, then, of what was thought of as the national consciousness. The effort was assumed to involve areas other than the purely linguistic or political. for example, the new Civic Guard (the Gárda Síochána, the police of the Irish Free State), being stationed like their predecessors the RIC in counties other than those to which they were native, felt a need to connect with their roots, especially after the Civil War. They found it necessary to arrange their own entertainments and, calling on traditional musicians to come on occasion to perform for them they stimulated the first orchestral, or group, performances of instrumental players, such as the Kilfenora band. In 1926, the year of the foundation of Fianna Fáil, the céilí band was born. It gave rise for thirty years or so to a spurious tradition (but what, if not everything, is spurious in modern folk culture?). and there were more calculated and conscious efforts to square the circle and promote 'national culture' in ways that would assimilate it to modern culture (which in practice meant British or sometimes Anglo-American culture): to modernize the essentially archaizing process of cultural revival. There were attempts, for example, to provide competition for English comic papers by making comics in Irish available. On the other hand the schools in trying to carry out their task of restoring the Irish language frequently introduced the language to urban children through texts or spelling primers which set it firmly in a rural setting. And this often reinforced the natural resistance of the children to a task which, without this alienating element, was already hard work.

K.R. Minogue in his little book on nationalism published just over twenty years ago (*Nationalism*, Methuen, London, 1967) described with particular reference to Germany how an acute contradiction developed as nationalism gained force in the nineteenth century. Nationalism by definition was based on the concept of the Nation; the Nation, in the German tradition and commonly enough elsewhere, was based on the *Volk* – on distinctive language, customs, traditions, music, dance, storytelling, costume, religion, myth, and so forth. But nationalism also aimed at the creation of a national State – which must succeed in the modern world of cities, industry, competitiveness and, in a word, departure from tradition. This led to a stage at which, according to Minogue,

> ... nationalism became selfconsciously quaint – with folk dancing and *Lederhosen* – and encouraged superficial national differentiation for which the tourist industry later supplied new motives.

We can see this clearly enough in Ireland of the early twentieth century in the confident, probably over-confident, search for a national identity. What about the Ireland of the beginning of the nineteenth century, when the Union was enacted?

At this much earlier stage of the transition from the traditional to the modern world, from Gaelic Ireland to anglicized Ireland, we yet find many similar features.

Tom Moore is undoubtedly one of the significant figures of the transition at the point where anglicization was beginning to be fully effected. There is hardly an earlier one who will serve to illustrate the cultural process. Edmund Burke's is a figure that might come to mind; but Burke, although he stemmed from an Irish Catholic background, was himself Protestant and, further, he is innocent of any trace of the nationalism that was already existent in his time and was to dominate the times ahead. In those two respects, interesting and attractive though he may be for other reasons of study, Burke fails as an example of certain complex ambiguities than can arise from acculturation.

In Moore the ambiguity is fully evident and he was well aware of it. He gave it expression of regret tinged with guilt.

> Oh! blame not the bard, if he fly to the bowers
> Where Pleasure lies, carelessly smiling at Fame,
> He is born for much more, and in happier hours
> His soul might have burned with a holier flame;
> The string that now languishes loose o'er the lyre,
> Might have bent a proud bow to the warrior's dart;
> And the lip, which now breathes but the song of desire,
> Might have poured the full tide of a patriot's heart.

His appeal to be spared blame for his devotion to pleasure rather than to the lost cause of Erin – as he believed it to be – was made in the knowledge that it was unnecessary. Nobody blamed the bard: on the contrary. In his lifetime he was a fashionable and famous poet in England; from very modest origins he had risen quite rapidly to mingle with the great. He was much more successful, at least in this rapidity, than was Oliver Goldsmith a generation earlier, and if Goldsmith in his days of destitute poverty in London suffered, as he put it himself, from being

> ... without friends, recommendations, money or impudence; and that in a country where being born an Irishman was sufficient to keep me unemployed,

Moore had the greater disadvantage of being the wrong *kind* of Irishman. But he overcame it.

The collection which he published under the title *Irish Melodies* was to make him known wherever romantic nationalism was flourishing and won him an extraordinary esteem in Ireland, which was to endure, slowly fading, until the present century. The slow fading is important, and it is true that later generations of nationalists, if they did not blame the bard, at least treated him with small regard.

But in his own time he was accepted both abroad and at home among those who knew of him as one who gave expression to the true sentiment of Ireland. It was a sentiment which seemed to be as harmless as that of 19th century Jacobitism – a regret for what was irretrievably lost rather than any programme or even aspiration for the return of the old order of things.

> Then vanish'd forever that fair, sunny vision,
> Which, spite of the slavish, the cold heart's derision,
> Shall long be remember'd, pure, bright, and elysian,
> As once it arose, my lost Erin, on thee.

It was antiquarian, as to a large extent was his attitude to traditional music of any kind. This had an element of opportunism in it: the past, whether historical, literary or musical, was a quarry from which he might extract nuggets to be polished as romantic gems. In introducing his international collection of *National Airs*, for example (which he began in 1819), he wrote:

> It is Cicero, I believe, who says '*Natura ad modos ducimur*'; and the abundance of wild indigenous airs which almost every country except England possesses, sufficiently proves the truth of his assertion. The lovers of this simple but interesting kind of music are here presented with the first number of a collection, which I trust their contributions will enable us to continue. A pretty air without words resembles one of those half creatures of Plato, which are described as wandering, in search of the remainder of themselves, through the world. To supply this other half, by uniting with congenial words the many fugitive melodies which have hitherto had none, or only such as are unintelligible to the generality of their hearers, is the object and ambition of the present work. Neither is it our intention to confine ourselves to what are strictly called National Melodies; but wherever we meet with any wandering and beautiful air, to which poetry has not yet assigned a worthy home, we shall venture to claim it as an *estray* swan, and enrich our humble Hippocrene with its song.

He was criticized quite bitterly by Bunting for drawing on traditional Irish airs (in 'the Melodies') but subordinating the music to the words as indeed he believed should be done. Yet Bunting, like everybody else in Moore's day, wanted not to be seen denigrating the national Bard. The words which thus took preeminence were often trivial. For many of the airs in the collections Moore drew on, they served the purpose – which he may in part have sought – of rigidifying the tradition and clamping down on variation, a process on which Breandán Breathnach has commented. It was like writing down an early law text. Once the words are committed to writing they become unalterably sacred and even when their original meaning is forgotten they are preserved as mantras of power unchanging within a thicket of growing commentary.

But it is pointless to take issue with Moore's methods of the best part of two hundred years ago. What is worth doing is to criticize him sympathetically, to try to understand how and why he did what he did, and more importantly perhaps, to understand why what he did was so well and gratefully received by his contemporaries.

He himself was a warm, friendly, sensual, charming man, whom people liked. He was physically small and had a corresponding cockiness and prickliness, feeling called upon to stand up for himself whenever he apprehended a slight. He met the editor of the *Edinburgh Review* to fight a duel because of a severe notice which appeared in that journal. The duel was prevented by the police, who found that neither pistol contained a ball. This nearly led to another duel with Byron, who made a jocose reference to 'leadless pistols' in his *English Bards and Scotch Reviewers*; but characteristically Moore became friendly with both Jeffrey the Scotch reviewer and Byron the English bard.

For he was an ingratiating man; and it was for this that he blamed himself:

> But, alas for his country! – her pride has gone by,
> And that spirit is broken, which never would bend;
> O'er the ruin her children in secret must sigh,
> For 'tis treason to love her, and death to defend.
> Unprized are her sons, till they've learned to betray;
> Undistinguish'd they live, if they shame not their sires;
> And the torch, that would light them through dignity's way,
> Must be caught from the pile where their country expires.

The references to 'treason' and 'death' were not fanciful exaggerations. At Trinity College, Dublin, in the 1790s, Moore had mixed with a group most of whom belonged to the Dublin Society of United Irishmen and had become involved in the planning which led to the widespread and bloody uprising of 1798. He himself underwent interrogation in the Visitation of the College organized by the University's vice-chancellor Lord Clare for the purpose of discovering and expelling undergraduates found to be members of the oath-bound and illegal society; and he saw how some of his companions came forward as informers against their friends. His own close and admired friend Robert Emmet was publicly hanged in front of St Catherine's church in Dublin for organizing the abortive uprising of 1803.

It was only four years after this, in 1807, that the first part of the *Irish Melodies* came out – publication in parts was to continue until 1834. Elsewhere, in London, Edinburgh or America, the sympathy which many young men had felt for the early egalitarian and libertarian ideas of the French Revolution had been repelled in due course by the Terror. In Ireland, the same sympathies, combined with the aspiration for an independent country, had led to the confrontations of 1798, in which tens of thousands were killed and appalling atrocities were committed both by the rebels and by the government. The ruthlessness with which the government suppressed Jacobinism in Ireland gave an air of finality to the settlement of the Irish question, the Act of Union of 1800 by which Ireland was to be incorporated into the United Kingdom. It really seemed settled for a while even if many found the settlement bitter.

Moore's gift was that he did in fact represent the sentiment, if not of Ireland, at least of Irish respectability – the English-speaking aspirant middle class coming up in the world. He was nothing so dangerous as a revolutionary or rebel but he gave an acceptable voice to expressions of carefully modified regret at the suppression of Irish independence, and in the sentimental embroidery which he devised for this regret he contributed to the making of the new nationalist myth. He greatly helped to reconcile Ireland to a slow modernization by glorifying the past while making the changes of the present seem to be of the order of nature.

His own career is full of ambiguity and shows in his development and changing attitude the superficial weakness of character of an affable and complaisant man. But in the long run a strength slowly emerges – and this is an important part of the history of Moore as a person. He toyed with revolution in his youth but, not to put too fine a point on it, he was frightened off it. He toyed anonymously with erotic verse but ran up against the remarkable change of outlook that characterizes the young generation emerging in the time of the Napoleonic wars and – again by the *Edinburgh Review* – he was directed differently and bowed henceforth to the stern moral principles of the new age, at least in his published words. He bobbed up early to the surface in the social swim and as a talented performer made the acquaintance of the Prince Regent, but he suffered real or imaginary slights or rebuffs which set him on a slightly different course.

Making his way by patronage, flattering the mighty, showing a capacity to be bored by routine duties (as when he secured through patronage the job of Admiralty Registrar at Bermuda in 1803, but soon put in a *locum tenens* who fiddled the accounts) showing such fashionable adaptability that on payment of an advance of £3,000 he produced on the basis of library research a long poem (*Lalla Rookh*) in the current Oriental mode – in the long run he nonetheless showed an underlying toughness.

Neither a Whig nor a Tory he launched into political satire which was especially severe on the Whigs – and was unsuccessful on the literary market. He supported the Catholic cause in the Emancipation agitation and he gradually formulated, even if in sentimental drawing-room terms, the mythology of nineteenth-century Irish nationalism and depicted the stage apparatus of shamrocks, stringless harps, round towers and other images of departed glory. Such paraphernalia began to become embarrassing to nationalists by about the end of the century; that is, to the new puritanically earnest nationalists whose cultural aspirations were for a return of the real thing – the Irish language, the Aran Islands, the music, songs and poetry of 'the people' – although their own notions of the real thing were often enough mistaken or misguided.

Tom Moore had not been concerned in this sense with the real thing. He was a performer who wrote his own lines, dealing in sweetly musical words to present an acceptable pastiche of MacPhersonian antiquity to the great real world of London and the Home Counties. He was the public relations man of the movement whose political leader was O'Connell but he was honoured in his day by the leaders of most parties in Ireland.

Moore was born in 1779, in Dublin. He was the son of a Catholic grocer who was reasonably well-to-do and he was sent to the school run by a somewhat eccentric educational reformer, Samuel Whyte, which was quite a famous establishment in late-eighteenth-century Dublin. He was just three years old when the Protestant Ascendancy's Volunteer movement – which had come into being to defend Ireland's shores against the French at the time of the American war – was used to secure parliamentary independence. Moore grew up, in other words, under what is known as 'Grattan's parliament' and like so many others of his time he retained to the end of his days an enormous admiration for Henry Grattan, who had achieved liberal reform without revolution and who had shown a willingness to accept the great suppressed and oppressed Catholic masses as part of the independent Irish nation.

For Moore's Ireland of the late eighteenth century was of course one in which a large distinct minority ruled the majority by right of conquest—a right which was commonly allowed in eighteenth-century thinking. The Glorious Revolution, the Declaration of Rights and the British Constitution, which in England wore the colour of liberty, for the majority in Ireland wore the colour of alien conquest—alien in religion, in language and in culture. The sharp division in that situation was between the Irish-speaking or recently Irish-speaking Catholics of the Gaelic stock and English-speaking Protestants. But the division was not everywhere sharp or clear. The Catholic tradition of the 'Old English,' for example (to use a seventeenth-century term) was different from that of the 'Old Irish' and some areas of the country, whatever the origin of their inhabitants, had been anglicized for centuries. The Presbyterians of the North occupied a third position, less clearly defined. They had to some extent evaded religious discrimination by emigration to America and many of them had favoured both the American and the French revolutions but they were of course, in religious terms, deeply divided from the Catholics.

Moore belonged to the still small group of English-speaking urban Catholics of means, a group whose numbers and significance were to increase rapidly. His schooling placed him on a level with the Dublin middle-class Protestants with whom he mixed at Samuel Whyte's. His religion, however, while the popery laws were in force debarred him from the professions, from the university, from parliament and from the army. This was felt by Moore and others like him as an intolerable humiliation. His reaction to these laws was quite unlike that of the peasants who rose in 1798 in Mayo, Wexford, Meath, Longford and half a dozen other places. His was not the rage against oppression, against the pitch-cap and the whip and the gallows, which drove the Wexfordmen to fury, but the cynicism of one who felt cheated.

Boast on, my friend, while in this humble isle
Where Honour mourns and Freedom fears to smile,
Where the bright light of England's fame is known
but by the baleful shadow she has thrown
On all our fate—where, doom'd to wrongs and slights,
We hear you talk of Britain's glorious rights,
As wretched slaves, that under hatches lie,
Hear those on deck extol the sun and sky!"

Although the native Irish of the old Gaelic-speaking stock to whom Moore belonged by ancestral origin formed the great submerged majority in the eighteenth century, they were socially and culturally maimed and diminished. Most of their own native aristocracy and gentry had gone into exile after the enormous land confiscations of the seventeenth century. The retainers of these old families had lingered on, patronless, giving for a long time the message to the people that the Stuarts would return bringing back the old lords. But this was a dream. The old culture was shattered; the medieval Gaelic world had broken down and was being systematically dismantled by the new order imposed by conquest. The way to survival for the individual was to leave the familiar secure society of ancient custom, tradition and hierarchy; to learn English and come into the world whose capital was London.

Such old families as survived and retained some of their lands – the O'Connells of Kerry for example – had the security of acceptance in the Catholic European *ancien régime*. Their Continental connections through the so-called Wild Geese, the officers serving in the armies of France, Spain or Austria, gave them a place of esteem – although this hardly enabled them to claim such status in Hanoverian Ireland. After the failure of the Forty-Five they accepted the new order of things, and it was only the continuing disabilities on their religion which denied them, as one of them put it, the privilege of shedding their blood for the British rather than a foreign monarch.

But the same psychological security was not enjoyed in this respect by those who were left in Ireland clinging to the wreckage of the world of the Gael—the poets, the harpers, the merchants, the timid and accommodating bishops and clergy. These, when they relinquished their grip on the past, were admitted to the lower orders of the colonial establishment, if at all, only in the guise of refugees from a conquered savagery coming to receive the first benefits of civilization.

Only gradually did they come to find a voice. In the English-speaking as distinct from the Irish-speaking world one of the first publicists for the values of the conquered society was Charles O'Conor of Belnagare whose works on this topic are a form of apologetics. He had one foot in one world, one in the other, as was to be characteristic of the emerging Catholic culture that spoke English. He was a mediator. So we find in late-eighteenth-century Clare the poets praising the MacDonnells of Kilkee and Newhall both because they were of the old true Gaelic blood (they were a Protestant family of Highland Scottish origin) and continued to patronise the Gaelic poets and because –

> ... *nuair a shuíonn tú fé phúdar ar bhinnse na cúirte* ...

– as one poet put it, they could also hold a high place among the colonial establishment where it was expected they would defend their 'own people'.

One of the most influential writers of the time in this matter, the Limerick doctor Sylvester O'Halloran, who produced sustained works of historical apologetics in English, wrote in 1772:

> Having a natural reverence for the dignity and antiquity of my native country, strengthened by education, and confirmed by an intimate knowledge of its history, I could not, without the greatest pain and indignation, behold on the one hand, almost all the writers of England and Scotland (and from them of other parts of Europe) representing the Irish nation as the most brutal and savage of mankind, destitute of arts, letters and legislation; and on the other hand the extreme passiveness and insensibility of the present race of Irish: instances of inattention to their own honour, unexampled in any other civilised nation.

O'Halloran's writings were a great influence on Moore's generation, showing it glimpses of an ancient civilization, to which the young men reacted as Keats did to Chapman's *Homer*. And the model of an ancient Gaelic world of the past—an Orient of time, as it were—suited the Romantic sensibility. Its evidences were seized upon—MacPherson's *Ossian*, the remnants of Irish music, the skill of a few harpers, the ivy-clad ruins of mysterious monuments. As Moore put it:

> On Lough Neagh's bank, as the fisherman strays
> In the calm, cold eve's declining,
> He sees the Round Towers of other days,
> In the wave beneath him shining.
> Thus shall memory often, in dreams sublime,
> Catch a glimpse of the days that are over;
> Thus, sighing, look through the waves of time
> For the long-faded glories they cover.

The image that constantly recurs is that of the harp, an indication that this was a mediating symbol. All groups had some appreciation of Irish music. For there was a fairly general acceptance of the view that, whatever other qualities the old Gaelic culture may have had, it had been musical. The testimony of Giraldus, arriving on the heels of the first Anglo-Norman invaders of the twelfth century, stood. And since the reign of Henry VIII the harp had been the chief device in the arms of Ireland. The famous harp festival of 1792 was organised by a group of people in Belfast who had come to share the interest in the old culture in a partly antiquarian, partly patriotic, spirit. It was not the first such gathering – several had been arranged earlier in the century – but it was the first and indeed the only one to be arranged for antiquarian purposes. Ten harpers attended, survivors of the flood which had swept away the Gaelic world, and Edward Bunting, then a young man, was engaged to write down the music exactly as they played it (which unfortunately he didn't quite do). Wolfe Tone, who attended the concert with his head full of ideas for a new rather than an old Ireland, reacted with an impatient and famous comment – 'Strum, strum and be hanged'. but Bunting's publication of the music had a different effect on others.

In 1793 the Catholic Relief Act among the other changes it brought about opened Trinity College, Dublin, to Catholics and Moore entered the university. There in 1797 he met Robert Emmet, who was senior to him, and tells that Emmet often sat with him while he played the airs from Bunting's collection. And he tells the well-known story of how Emmet started to his feet when he played '*Maldrín Rua*', saying 'Oh! that I were at the head of twenty thousand men marching to that air.' Twenty thousand men, of course, have more than once marched to it long since then, and to Moore's words, 'Let Erin remember the days of old ...' But in 1803, when Emmet was hanged, having marched through Dublin at the head of a much smaller company, Moore had already entered on his career of social success, sailing for Bermuda and from there to the United States, where he met President Jefferson.

Whatever republican ideas he may have picked up in the 1790s, when Trinity was full of French ideas and talk of liberty, seem to have been dissipated at this stage of his life, when his companions were officers of the Royal Navy. The new republic of the West didn't impress him favourably:

> Who can, with patience, for a moment see
> The medley mass of pride and misery,
> Oh whips and charters, manacles and rights,
> Of slaving blacks and democratic whites,
> And all the piebald polity that reigns
> In a free confusion o'er Columbia's plains?
> To think that man, thou just and gentle god,
> Should stand before thee, with a tyrant's rod
> O'er creatures like himself, with soul from thee.
> Yet dare to boast of perfect liberty:
> Away, away – I'd rather hold my neck
> By doubtful tenure from a sultan's beck,
> In climes where liberty has scarce been named,
> Nor any right but that of ruling claimed,
> Than thus to live, where bastard freedom waves
> Her fustian flag in mockery over slaves."

His views here and later were libertarian and impatient of hypocrisy and cant. In the continuing publication of the *Irish Melodies* he gave expression to sentiments which moved a stage beyond mere apologetics. They were different from the sentiments being expressed, in those same years, by the few poets still writing in Irish and from those felt by the sections of the people to whom Moore's language and his writings were unknown, but they were not too far removed. And Moore's sentiments gave a feeling of self-respect to the emerging Catholic middle class while at the same time they were acceptable to other parties and groups in Ireland and England. Even the redoubtable Dr Henry Cooke, the Presbyterian divine who was to bring the Presbyterians into accord with the Anglicans in defence of the Union in Ulster and who was to drive O'Connell from that province knew and quoted from the *Irish Melodies*.

O'Connell himself organised the public dinner at which Moore was entertained in Dublin on 8 June 1818, where politicians and others of all parties, creeds and views gathered to do him honour. At the preliminary meeting O'Connell said that there could not live a single Irishman so lost to every feeling of affection for his country, as not to feel pride and pleasure at hearing the name of Moore. It was a name that raised the fame of Irish talent, and placed the poetic character of his country on the highest pinnacle of literary glory.

In this grandiloquent language O'Connell summarizes Moore's value to that large and increasing part of Ireland which had made its peace with the cultural values of the English-speaking world. He was outstanding among those who made the origins of native Ireland – the old cultural values – respectable. In doing so of course he distorted them. He processed them for his audience, presenting Irish music in a transmuted form and offering a gentrified version of the past and an anodyne anger at what he pronounced to be his country's wrongs. But it was only a short step from this to the assertion of the old values as the political myth of the historic Irish nation, which was to prove a very powerful myth indeed.

Moore belongs to that period in which the balance was finally seen to have tilted against Gaelic Ireland. Anglicization was no longer resisted but was widely welcomed and sought. Irish Ireland was consigned to the past, even if it was yet to take a very long time to die. Although an Irish nationalism was to grow and become dominant in the course of the nineteenth century, it must be distinguished sharply from the parallel nationalism that developed at the same time in Germany. The German nationalists saw the *Volk* as a force for the present and the future and as a source of strength and nourishment to their ideas. While there are elements of this in Irish nationalism, there is a much more powerful anglicizing element. The cultural ambitions of the new Ireland of the nineteenth century were directed toward the values of the European bourgeoisie as mediated by the evangelically Protestant England of the time. Moore just anticipated this, making a considerable contribution to the process of assimilation by his gentrification of the Irish tradition. He helped create a pseudo-tradition, which served very well for a while until a newer nationalism sought ultimately to direct Ireland on a course wholly separate from that of England.

The pseudo-tradition, or intermediate Irish tradition, gradually lost vigour and credibility. The great changes since the Second World War have seen its virtual disappearance, and I doubt if there have been many gatherings round the piano in recent years (except perhaps occasionally in a spirit of camp) to sing 'the Melodies'. The waves of emigration in the forties and fifties and, after a remission, in the eighties, are among the major events that have removed us by now from any but the most tenuous contact with Tom Moore's Ireland. But change is inevitable; the direction of change, however, is set by the past. Moore, coming as he did at a crucial moment, has had a great effect on the developments down to the present day of cultural nationalism and of traditional music. In both, his effect may have been partly by provoking reaction. The reaction, however, came after some interval. In his time, in his way, he led, as best he could and at times bravely enough, and, in his way, he deserves to be reckoned among those who

> rose in dark and evil days
> To right their native land.

6

The Hag and the Queen

There is a theme in Irish literature, not unknown in other traditions but here applied in a particular way, of beauty revealed by embracing ugliness. It is like the theme of the princess and the frog in the German fairy-tale except that in the Irish versions beauty does not take the form of a prince, but of a queen. Or, rather, of sovereignty; for that is the meaning in the earliest recensions.

The theme is exemplified in the story told of Niall of the Nine Hostages, in his youth. His brothers rejected the advances of a hideous old hag whom they met on the way, but he lay with her, at which she was revealed as a beautiful woman who announced to him that she was Sovereignty and that by possessing her he possessed kingship. So he came to rule at Tara. The idea of wedding the sovereignty was apparently embodied in ceremonies connected with early Irish kingship. The *feis* of Tara, for example, as Professor Carney and others have pointed out, probably embodied a symbolic or enacted mating of some kind. A variation is suggested in an account given by Giraldus Cambrensis at the end of the twelfth century of the inauguration ceremony of a local king in the north, who apparently coupled with a mare and then drank broth made from her flesh.

The personification of sovereignty becomes in the tradition something slightly different; the personification of the kingdom. In time the woman whose beauty is revealed to the rightful sovereign becomes Ireland, a powerful myth. In Jacobite verse the beauty is no longer hidden by ugliness, but is seen by the poet in a dream or vision:

> Gile na gile do chonnarc ar slí in uaigneas;
> criostal an chriostail a gormroisc rinnuainne;
> binneas an bhinnis a friotal nár chríonghruama;
> deirge is finne do fionnadh 'na gríosghruanna.

The beautiful woman shows her beauty but laments because she is married to the wrong spouse, the false sovereign; her rights will be restored only when the true king returns from over the water. Sometimes, in the later verse, Ireland (or perhaps the sovereignty) appears in other guise, although still displaying beauty or value – as a brown cow, for example, the finest of the kine, when one myth borrows reinforcement from another.

This appeared in the 'Roots' column in the *Irish Times*.

These images passed into modern romanticism and sentimentality about Ireland. The harsh quality of the early versions, where the young hero, to win kingship, was required to mate with a hag of hideous aspect and unpleasant demeanour, was softened. The hag, insofar as she survived in the tradition, was sentimentalised into the *Seanbhean bhoct*, everybody's poor old granny. The 'Caesar', or hero, coming over the sea lost some of his quality too –

> The French are on the say,
> Says the Shan Van Vocht

Or Ireland became the weeping beauty with the stringless harp, a wolfhound at her feet, a Round Tower behind her, silhouetted against a sunburst in the imagery of the new nationalism which dispensed with the 'rightful king'.

Yet softened and sentimentalized although it was, the image still had potency. It occurs still in one of the favourite songs of present-day northern nationalists, 'The Four Green Fields'. It was this sentimentalized image that Seán Lemass singled out, towards the end of his career, as one to be abandoned. He wanted to see Ireland become a modestly prosperous bourgeois republic – a decent enough ambition – and he realised perhaps that the Poor Old Woman, whom he called on us to forget, not merely concealed the beauty of the goddess whose true name was Sovereignty, but has long been the Irish version of the death goddess.

Others, notably poets, have seen that the ugliness, although suppressed in the modern sentimentalised versions, was as important to the theme as the beauty which it concealed. The transformation served as well with the image of Ireland as with the image of Sovereignty, but it required the perception that Ireland's beauty, if it existed in this sense, was hidden beneath a hideous outer aspect, that Ireland was ugly, 'the sow that eats her farrow'. Nationalists have pretended that the beauty was immediately visible, although sorrowful in bondage. Poets have seen that, as Yeats put it:

> ... All that was sung,
> all that was said in Ireland is a lie
> Bred out of the contagion of the throng,
> saving the rhyme rats hear before they die.

For poets and artists perceive what political nationalists deny, that Ireland is a truly barbarous country, and therefore ugly, its people being, in that other Yeatsian image, the eunuchs who ran through Hell to stare enviously 'upon great Juan riding by'.

Like other symbols and images of the period of romantic nationalism, that of Ireland personified has faded very much in the Republic, where independence gradually brought about concern with everyday and mundane affairs and a diminishing response to the old stimuli of patriotic fervour. It has been otherwise in the North where, among the nationalist part of the population sentimental and romantic imagery, now the cause merely of amusement in the South, still has power to move. The poor old woman lamenting the loss of her fourth green field is not a joke in Creggan, Ardoyne or Derrybeg. She shows her white-haired, sentimental aspect there, in sentimental songs. She seems long removed from the hideous hag whom early kings embraced. But that hag presumably had a good Indo-European ancestry, and her description in the early stories matches well that of another, at the farther end of the Indo-European world, Kali, or Durga, with her necklace of skulls, her lolling red tongue, her carnivorous tusks and her many arms bearing weapons. Kali, the wife of Siva the Destroyer, dances in the North, and has not yet resumed her benevolent aspect as Sati, the Virtuous, or Parvati.

The meanings of old myths have long been pressed unduly into the service of politics. Although the old image of Sovereignty as a woman had, on the face of it, to do with political situations, its meaning was not really concerned with them. It referred rather to the good ordering of the universe.

Kingship, in the early concept, belonged rather to the order of nature than to that of politics. The rightful king was to be recognised and discerned by signs which showed that he was the one fitted and chosen by the gods to act as intermediary between the powers of nature and the world of men. This concept, although diluted, persists right down to the eighteenth-century Jacobite poems. The exile over the water whose return the poems anticipated was still 'the one who is born to be king' – born, not elected. It is only at the point of change when the French fleet is awaited to carry, not the preordained rightful king but the rationalism of a republic that confusion begins; the image is misapplied. But, even yet, it persists, with the hope that the poor old woman will suddenly be seen to be, as in Lady Gregory's play

a young girl, and she with the walk of a queen.

7

Sive Oultach's Children

The IRA is one of our oldest and most enduring institutions. It bears the stigmata of a perverse, exclusive and stubbornly persistent sect. Its members cherish the memory of a time that never was and the hope of a time that will never be.

At the end of his excellent study of the subject (*The Secret Army*, 1970 edition) J. Bowyer Bell remarks that ' . . . what is peculiar to the IRA, by contrast with most revolutionery groups, is persistence in the face of failure'. He attributes an age of 50 years to the organization. That would now be 65; but it can be argued that the IRA, if not quite in its present form, is much older.

It derives, by way of various splits and splinters, from the Volunteers founded in 1913. But the Volunteers in turn came under the auspices of the Irish Republican Brotherhood, which brings us back to the Fenians and, through some of their founder members, to Young Ireland, and then, more sketchily, to 1798 and the United Irishmen.

But there is a different, perhaps more significant, continuity which underlies this. The organizers who gave a political shape to the tradition tapped a reservoir of discontent and grievance that simmered away, decade after decade, in modern Ireland. The United Irishmen, to flesh out the somewhat exiguous membership of their urban revolutionary clubs, turned to the federation of Catholic rural secret societies known as the Defenders. Young Ireland and the Fenians drew on similar support, the support of 'Captain Moonlight' (whose English cousin was known as 'Captain Swing').

There are variations on and exceptions to the pattern. The people who organized the 1916 Rising tried to some extent to fight an orthodox war as if they were the real government of an existing nations state. They tried to be, in their way, respectable: gallant, chivalrous and so forth, according to the conventions of the imperial armies of the day. They tried to behave 'correctly.'

But within a couple of years the old secret society tradition greatly modified the activities of the Volunteers, now more commonly known as the IRA. People like Tom Barry maintained something of the conventions of orthodox, or Great Power, warfare. But Michael Collins, for example, effecively conducted a campaign of assassination and terror much more in line with the precedents set by 'Ribbonmen', 'Whiteboys' and others of the kind.

This appeared in the *Irish Times*, 6 June 1985.

The pattern is basically rural, but in Ireland it has long had an urban development as well. The intimacies, allegiances, hatreds, feuds and religious and class divisions of the countryside were brought, sometimes intact (as in Belfast), into the towns and cities. The urban wing of secret society agitation has from time to time made contact with ideologies whose thoughts were formed on a European or world model rather than on a local grievance. Such people, giving political form or direction to widespread discontent, have also given the millennium a name: the Republic, United Ireland, the Workers' Republic, and so on.

On the one level, in other words, we are dealing with something that is amenable to rational discourse, to planning, negotiation and compromise. The IRA, through its political and propaganda machines, will publish programmes, arrange party conferences, appeal to the principles of law and justice. But that is not its real function. Its real function is to give violent and intimidating expression to the stresses produced at the base of a malfunctioning society. It is the growl – and the bite – of a dog that turns on its master.

This is not peculiar to Ireland. Similar phenomena have occurred in many parts of the world, including England under the stresses of the Industrial revolution. But in Ireland it has been unusually persistent and has continued side by side with the development of modern democracy. And it has been associated, right down to the present, with an ancient and potent symbolism that goes back to the dawn of history.

The Irish Republican Army is not the army of the Irish Republic – or of any Irish republic. It is a closed society of believers, within which, and only within which, salvation is to be found. It is bound together by oath, by obligations similar to the Sicilian *omerta*, by the shedding of blood (of its members or others) and by a fanatical devotion, not to a political programme, but to a mystical cause.

The IRA is nowadays chiefly localized in Ulster, in all nine counties. It is a set of local reactions against Northern Ireland rather than a movement with any real all-Ireland framework. The 12–14 per cent of the vote that the IRA, through its surrogates, commands in Northern Ireland, would diminish to perhaps 3–5 per cent overall in the 32 counties.

In the eighteenth century, the Whiteboys, the centre of whose prolonged uprising was in County Tipperary, called themselves 'Sive Oultach's Children'. Who was Sive Oultach? It is not possible to say with precision: the shifting figures of myth and legend are hard to pin down. Sadb, daughter of Conn of the Hundred Battles, was the legendary ancestress of the early Munster dynasties. We may take her to be a manifestation of the goddess of sovereignty, who appears under many names. She is Medb in Tara and in Cruachain. In Ayrshire Burns called her Coila. She is often unnamed:

> Níl suim ag an spéirbhean i spórt ná i bpléisiúr,
> Ach í ag gol is ag caoineadh 's ag réabadh bos ...
> (The skywoman has no interest in sport or pleasure
> But weeps and laments and tears her hands ...)

says the '98 ballad, 'Sliabh na mBan', of the aftermath of the insurgent defeat at
New Ross.

But that Sive is 'Oultach' suggests something else, since the word seems to be
a variant of *Ultach* ('of Ulster'). It suggests (as Dr P.J. Corish pointed out in a
brief discussion of the matter) the element of darkness and strife associated with
the north in the Irish cosmos. There the war-goddesses prevail. Macha rules in
the centre of ancient Ulaid. Near Beleek, in lower Lough Erne, a strange two-
faced idol may be seen on the island named from Badb (corrupted to 'Boa'), the
raven-goddess of war. Cúchulainn, the defender of Ulster, learned his trade from
the war-goddess on Skye. His image, so often evoked by Pearse in St Enda's, now
in the form of the Sheppard bronze, marks the central event of modern Irish
republican history in the Dublin GPO.

The image of the Ulster champion is increasingly potent in the north today,
not least among loyalists, who find in it a symbol to suit their burgeoning myth. A
fine variation on the theme, for example, by John Behan, in the entrance to the
Armagh Museum, has an appeal across the Ulster divide. The icon of the slain
hero, tied to a pillar-stone, with a raven revealing that he has expired by perching
on his shoulder, can be read in two ways. It is the defeat by death of the warrior.
It is the apotheosis of the raven.

The IRA of today, in spite of the ballot-paper in the hand that doesn't carry
an Armalite, does not communicate with the outside world. It is a society of the
rejected and the elect, with intense dedication, but not to a rational programme
of compromise. Sive Oultach may be forgotten, but equivalent symbols dominate. The black uniforms with their overtones of sado-masochistic gear, the aggressive stance, the defiance of the established world, offer – unlike a football
club – not only an occasion for comradeship and loyalty in spite of the world, but
a justification for violence and a recognition of worth in those dedicated to the
service of death.

8

Finn and the Fairies

Books for children are written by grown-ups and while they may aim to please and to entertain, almost invariably they also set out in some measure to help to mould childish minds, morals and opinions. Even Babar, most innocent of elephants, contrives in his amusing doings to preach little sermons about race, life and politics. The writer for grown-ups may assume a common outlook and shared opinions, but the writer for children is almost always aware, if not of working on a *tabula rasa*, at least of being singularly well placed to persuade to a particular view.

Children's books, in other words, are a part of the education, of the formation, of children, and their authors are usually fully conscious of this. Since one of the chief functions of all our systems of education is the transmission of our own culture, whatever it may be, to the child, there are whole series and classes of children's literature which are overtly and directly devoted to this purpose.

Fortunately perhaps, we are most of us incapable of standing outside our own culture and seeing what it is really like, so that when we make a conscious effort to convey it to a child we tend to show it rather as we would wish it to be, or as we imagine it might ideally be. We teach prayers that we do not pray, truths that we do not tell, deeds that we do not do. But these fond imaginings about our culture are, of course, in themselves part of our culture, the part which is appropriate to innocence.

Such attempts at transmission endeavour to acquaint the child with the heritage of her community and to indicate to her her identity. She is taught the story of Troy, to let her begin to grasp that she belongs to a society which is the intellectual heir of Greece. He is told stories from the Bible, to show him that he belongs to the Judaeo-Christian religious tradition. And in the age of nationalism, the stories, legends, mythology, sagas or other ancient or folk traditions of what was conceived to be the child's own nation, were retold with the intention of making the child conscious and proud of being French, Polish, English, Scottish or Norse, as the case might be. Where necessary, in this age, new 'ancient' nationalities were invented – 'British,' for example.

It was not necessary to invent a nationality for Ireland. This already existed.

This was published in the *Irish Times* on Monday, 18 December 1972. It has been slightly modified for printing here.

But in the great period of romantic archaeology and antiquarianism at the beginning of the nineteenth century Irish nationality was reconstructed in a new way from the discoveries or imaginings of the antiquaries. 'The harp that once through Tara's halls the soul of music shed' (a fairly fabulous instrument) was new-strung. It sounded at a time when romanticism had triumphed over eighteenth-century reason, the gothick barbarisms of the North-European past were being exalted over the restraint and careful taste of the classical tradition, and the deep mysteries of blood and race were beginning to oust the social contract as the basis of national community. MacPherson and Gray had opened a window onto a mythical past of bards and druids, Scott had made medieval antiquarianism a fashion, and Moore had endeavoured to discern from Lough Neagh's banks 'the round towers of other days, in the wave beneath them shining'.

Speculation stimulated research. Old manuscripts were collected and studied; field antiquities were observed and drawn; interest was renewed in the Irish language among a class of people who had formerly regarded it as no more than quaint; Irish records were examined. Research led to renewed speculation when the true shapes of the past were half-discerned and then given the forms of enchanted fancy in the 'Celtic Twilight'. In the middle of the nineteenth century there began a trickle of imaginative works which attempted to encapsulate, in English, although often in an English which attempted to convey the sense of Gaelic exoticism, the mind, literature and culture of Irish autochthony. By the beginning of this century the trickle had become a flood.

A tremendous effort was being made to define the national culture and identity, and there was plainly, at the time of the Literary Revival and the foundation of the Gaelic League, a great demand for books by which children might recover a part of the cultural inheritance of which – by the Union, by the intrusion of English ways and institutions, by the school system, or by whatever – they were seen to have been deprived.

> When I asked the little boy who had shown me the pathway up the Hill of Allen [wrote Yeats in his introduction to Lady Gregory's *Gods and Fighting Men* in 1904] if he knew stories of Finn and Oisin, he said he did not, but that he had often heard his grandmother telling them to his mother in Irish. He did not know Irish, but he was learning it at school, and all the little boys he knew were learning it. In a little while he will know enough stories of Finn and Oisin to tell them to his children some day. It is the owners of the land whose children might never have known what would give them so much happiness. But now they can read this book to their children, and it will make Slieve-na-man, Allen and Benbulben, the great mountain that showed itself before me every day through all my childhood and was yet unpeopled, and half the countrysides of south and west, as populous with memories as are Dundealgan and Emain Macha and Muirthemne, and after a while somebody may even take them to some famous place and say, 'This land where your fathers lived proudly and

finely should be dear and dear and again dear,' and perhaps when many names have grown musical to their ears, a more imaginative love will have taught them a better service.

'A more imaginative love to teach them a better service.' This would seem to me to sum up the purpose of many of those who, in the time of Yeats, produced books for Irish children along the lines of Lady Gregory's. Going back a little in time, it is not always easy to decide which books of legend or folk-tale were specifically designed for children. The Victorian was a period in which many children's books were published, and it was a highly didactic time. But it was also a time when many books were published popularizing the work of scholars, and when there was widespread interest in these themes. Anyway, some of the most durable of children's classics, like many nursery rhymes, *Gulliver's Travels*, or the collections of the brothers Grimm, did not originate as children's literature

One of the early and important works was that of Crofton Croker, who made a collection of legends and fairy tales of Ireland in the first half of the nineteenth century. This was subsequently much drawn on by writers and compilers of the turn of the century who were seeking Irish material of a racy or folkish kind. Crofton Croker's full collection was published towards the end of the century by a New York publishing house. But stories of leprechauns, banshees and rustic enchantments seem to have had their chief vogue before the full Literary Revival, and to have catered for the same taste for Irish quaintness and humour as enjoyed the works of Lover and Lever. Under the more serious and romantic influence of Young Ireland this type of material began to be treated in a different way. Lady Wilde's *Ancient Legends* sees the stories of the people in the light of Victorian pathos and sentiment, and it was not until Letitia Maclintock in Ulster and Douglas Hyde in the West began treating the legendary lore of the countryside with a more matter-of-fact seriousness that publications relatively free from distortion began.

An anthology selected by Yeats and published in London in 1888 with the title *Fairy and Folk Tales of the Irish Peasantry* is a landmark. It draws intelligently on the collections of the previous half-century or so and gives indications of the search for a more formal and literary body of legend to draw on. It seems, however, not to have been intended for children. In the following year Edmund Leamy produced, specifically for children, *Irish Fairy Tales*, drawn from scholarly sources (mainly O'Curry and Joyce) and in 1902 Séamus MacManus published *Donegal Fairy Stories*.

Writers with a more imaginative approach drew on early Irish history, producing historical fictions which were the counterpart of *Hereward the Wake* and similar English works of the time. 'E.A.,' for example, published in Belfast in 1880 *Kathleen, A Tale of the Fifth Century*, a story of an Irish girl carried off by sea-robbers, and Mrs Gay in 1908 published *The Druidess*, the story of a Pictish boy, set in Scotland, Ireland and England in ancient times.

But it was research on early Irish literature, and the publication of texts, that provided the basis for the most important body of material of this general character, produced first in popular form and soon rendered into children's literature of an improving nature. Standish O'Grady may in a sense be said to have begun this process with his two-volume *History of Ireland, the Heroic Period*, of 1878, which was an attempt to produce a kind of literary and legendary history to reduce it to its 'artistic elements.' He followed through with a re-telling of saga stories in a series of publications of the nineties and of the opening years of the present century – *Finn and His Companions, The Coming of Cuchulain, The Gates of the North*.

This was the kind of material which was seized on by the writers of the Revival period, and which formed the main body of what might be called cultural propaganda for children in those crucial years. The collection by Joseph Jacobs published in 1891 with the title *Celtic Fairy Tales* (recently issued in paperback) consists in fact chiefly of hero tales and similar material. In 1896 D. Comyn published *The Youthful Exploits of Finn*. But it is with the opening of the new century that the flood begins, as a short list will indicate: 1899, W.L. O'Byrne, *A Land of Heroes*; 1900, W.L. O'Byrne, *Kings and Vikings*; 1902, Lady Gregory, *Cuchulainn of Muirthemne*; 1904, Ethna Carbery, *In the Celtic Past*; W.L. O'Byrne, *Children of Kings*; 1905, L. Chisholm, *Celtic Tales*; 1906, Lady Gregory, *Gods and Fighting Men*; W.L. O'Byrne, *The Knight of the Cave*; 1907, Lady Gregory, *A Book of Saints and Wonders*; P.W. Joyce, *Old Celtic Romances*; 1908, Standish O'Grady, *The Gates of the North*; E. Grierson, *The Children's Book of Celtic Stories*; M. Bayne, *Fairy Tales from Erin's Isle*; J. Hannon, *The Kings and the Cats*; 1909, A.P. Graves, *The Irish Fairy Book*; Eleanor Hull, *Cuchulainn*; 1910, Lady Gregory, *The Kiltartan Wonder Book*; D.A. Mackenzie, *Finn and his Warrior Band*; 1911, T.W. Rolleston, *Myths and Legends of the Celtic Race*; 1913, V. Russell, *Heroes of the Dawn*; 1914, Alice Milligan, *Sons of the Sea Kings*; 1916, M. Bayne, *Tales of Ireland for Irish Children*; J.M. Flood, *Ireland, Its Myths and Legends*.

Any child who had all those on her bookshelves in 1916 was well indoctrinated in an Irish culture which had been transmitted and transmuted, through romanticism, nationalism, nineteenth-century scholarship, Victorian and Edwardian fashion in children's literature, and the English language, and was probably as much an heir of Thomas Carlyle as of Cúchulainn of Muirtheimhne—was at any rate exposed to the heroic. Some of the books have been forgotten. Many have weathered well, and some, especially those of O'Byrne, are worth reprinting.

Already by this date some imaginative writers were beginning to treat the saga and heroic literature less seriously, or in an indirect way. Pádraig Colum's *A Boy in Eirinn* (1913) has his young nineteenth-century hero learn the old stories and legends on his travels in Ireland. James Stephens in his *The Crock of Gold* (1912) was beginning to play with the legendary material, as others after him were to do.

The effort to acquaint Irish children, through books in English, with the ancient culture of their country, continued in later years, although perhaps in a more detached way, producing further classics of collection, like Eileen O'Faolain's *Irish Sagas and Folk-Tales*, or of imaginative interpretation, like Rosemary Sutcliff's *The Hound of Ulster* (both significantly parts of series which are not confined to Ireland). But the great effort to imagine a past which would liberate Ireland not merely from the influence of England but, one feels, from the greyness of the modern world, has gone. The books however must have had a lasting – and surely on the whole beneficial – effect on the minds of those who read them and enjoyed them when young, and who had their imaginations opened to an Ireland of honour, chivalry and high heroic deeds.

9

The Melancholy of Coole

The woodland paths, in late November, were not dry; the autumn beauty of the trees was fading; there were no swans to be seen on the rain-swollen lake at Coole. There had just been a night's heavy rain when I was there a couple of weeks ago, and everywhere there was the sound of water dripping from leaves and branches. For a while the distant dull sound of an axe came from the damp woods.

This is a melancholy place. In 1930, on the eve of her grandson's twenty-first birthday, Lady Gregory wrote in her journal:

> But it is a contrast to Robert's coming of age, with its gathering of cousins and the big feast and dance for the tenants – Coole no longer ours. But the days of landed property have passed. It is better so. Yet I wish some of our blood would after my death care enough for what has been a home for so long, to keep it open.

Of course, she did not have her wish, and very soon the house was pulled down, a symbol, more poignant than most, of the sour destructiveness that has animated so many of our public gestures since the Treaty. A floor of broken kitchen tiles remains among some fragments of the kitchen walls. The main house has vanished almost as if it had never been, as if indeed the whole Anglo-Irish literary revival had taken place in a Celtic twilit never-never land that disappeared at the first gleam of bleak daylight.

The very tourist signs and trappings (for ravished Coole has been pressed into at least the part-time service of this national industry) add to the bedraggled, put-upon air of the place. The sign on the main Gort road points downward and reads 'OOLE'. The beach tree on which distinguished guests of the house carved their initials has had a somewhat forlorn bare patch created in the growth around it, and has been penned in (for its own protection) in a kind of small monkey-cage – a prisoner of the Irish nation put on show.

> And on the great stem, smooth as parchment, of a copper beech, whose branches sweep the ground as we come near the gate into the woods, many a friend who stayed here has carved the letters of his name, W.B.Y. of course and Jack B.Y. with a graving of the little donkey he loves; and

First published in *The Irish Times*, 12 December 1970.

J.M.Synge and AE and An Craóbhin (Douglas Hyde) and John Masefield
and Sean O'Casey and as it should be a very large G.B.S. And this A.J. was
cut by Augustus John after his descent from the very topmost boughs
where he had left those letters also to astonish the birds of the air.

Lady Gregory, who gave this account of the tree in her little book on Coole published by the Cuala Press, went on to tell how all kinds of other less distinguished
people had contributed inscriptions, and how she had prevented a party of American boy scouts from adding their names. She went on to wonder if she had thus
deprived the tree of the initials of some future President of the United States.
The multiplication of initials has continued – the date 1955 is clearly visible –
and the somewhat unseemly railing had no doubt become necessary.

Coole was frequented by writers and artists, and by some who served Ireland
well, as Lady Gregory herself did. The names on the tree do not seem to include
any that are 'double-barrelled' or that are those of 'belted earls' (to quote Kevin
Boland's description of people like Kevin B. Nowlan, Conn Ó Cléirigh and myself who favoured saving some Dublin buildings from his friends), although the
duke of Marlborough was one of the shooting guests in the 1870s. But Coole was
a landlord's house, and it seems that even down to the present day the feeling of
many Irish people against the landlord class is too strong to be overcome by considerations either of the merit of some of its members or of the merit of some of
their work, whether political or literary service to the country or the creation of
fine architecture. The destruction of that house, which had given hospitality to
Yeats and O'Casey, Shaw and Synge, was an early instance of the desire to erase
the material remains of landlordism from the land, which is still manifest in the
utterances of highly-placed persons today about such matters as the conservation of eighteenth-century Dublin.

As I tried to trace part of the foundations of the razed house at Coole last
month, there came to my mind the memory of an occasion nearly twenty years
ago when I was being driven through the County Louth countryside by the late
Seán P. Ó Ríordáin. We stopped on the road somewhere north of Collon to look
at a tumble-down mud cabin. This was interesting because about half of the building had collapsed, giving a cross-section of the structure and showing the texture
of the mud walls. It was plain that with a few more winters' rains it would melt
into the undergrowth of the roadside and be as if it had never been – indeed tens
of thousands of such constructions must have disappeared from the surface of
the land in the past century or two.

As we looked at it, Ó Ríordáin turned and said: 'Our ancestors crawled out of
places like this on their hands and knees', a statement which was half a comment
on the social history revealed by the ruin and half a reprimand to ourselves for
being so much better off than our ancestors. His remark implied no hostility to
anyone, but, in the minds of many, loyalty to the people of the mud cabins, who so
often in the nineteenth century had their homes broken down by the landlords
and were themselves turned out on the roads, excludes any sympathy for the

people of the big houses in their declining fortunes of later years.

There was a pets' cemetery at Coole, probably something like the one which still remains on a grassy slope at Powerscourt. A few headstones remain, one broken, but they lean against the garden wall and no longer mark the graves of 'Poor Little Prinnie Oct. 1836'; 'Moscow March 4 1881'; 'China May 1895'; 'Gyp 1890', and so on. At the head of each stone is a lightly engraved delicate little spray, and they are obviously all the work of one hand down to the 1880s – a stonecarver whose work spans a period of half-a-century through which he retained the decent standard mason's lettering of the early nineteenth century. A change comes at 1890 – a new hand practising the harsh, rather nasty, sans-serif lettering of late Victorian times. A pets' cemetery with inscribed headstones is a harmless enough sentimental conceit, which would not be out of place in England of the time, but in the west of nineteenth-century Ireland it was somewhat incongruous.

To compare the stones which recorded the deaths of ponies and dogs with the rough uninscribed stones that mark the contemporary famine graves at Quin, only a few miles away, is to be aware of the incongruity. The comparison, or comparisons like it, have been made in too many minds in too many parts of Ireland during the years of hunger and evictions, and have grown into a deep-rooted prejudice. It is a prejudice that no amount or good will or hard work on the part of people like Lady Gregory, or Douglas Hyde or Otway Cuffe has been fully able to overcome, down to our own time.

Yeats, foreseeing of Coole as he so often did of the places he wrote about, the day

> When nettles wave upon a shapeless mound
> And saplings root among the broken stone,

was thinking surely not merely of the decay that comes to all things, but seems to leave more ruins in Ireland than elsewhere. Those of the Anglo-Irish who tried to play their part in the Irish revolution must have been aware of the fact that they were contributing to the destruction of their own curious sub-culture. After fifty years, as old bitternesses and prejudices fade, perhaps we may begin to accept that all the traditions of our country form part of our heritage, and that what was well made, by whomsoever, should not be wantonly destroyed.

[Happily, what is left of Coole is in somewhat better shape now, in 1997, than it was when I wrote the above nearly twenty-seven years ago.]

10

Retreats from the Modern

A plaque on the Aisling Hotel, across the Liffey from Heuston Station in Dublin, records that Wittgenstein spent some time there near the end of his life, working on his final (posthumous) publication, *Philosophical Investigations*. His contact with Dublin would have been tangential; he had come to Ireland, not to engage with the country but to disengage from the world. He was of the third and final Modernist generation. Like Rilke, he displayed the isolation of the artist who finds his intellectual environment unacceptable, and the elusiveness of the arbiter who wishes to retreat from the crassness of his age into his own kind of ivory tower. Rilke's was a real castle tower, at Muzot in Switzerland, as was Yeats's, at Ballylee. Wittgenstein's was perhaps a truer withdrawal, since alienation was a part of his being.

The twentieth century was a time of alienation for Modernist writers and intellectuals, even before the Great War, and for some it was a time of Dantesque (and usually self-imposed) exile. It was then, perhaps more than before or since, that this fraternity exalted to a high degree the shamanistic or priestly function of the artist – a development that had been steady since the middle of the nineteenth century, but just now, reaching its apogee, was beginning to falter as the bonds of bourgeois society appeared to loosen and the power of the centralized state to take on a new character. 'Silence, exile and cunning' was Joyce's formula for the acceptance of this lonely vocation. The deliberate seeking of a Promethean passion by the intellectuals was to be remarkably successful in communicating their message, in spite of their rejection of much of the modern culture that sustained them. They left the deep imprint of their mind on their own and succeeding generations, as much by the figures they cut – artists and thinkers who had become stylites and anchorites – as by the crafted finish of their work. Joyce was perhaps the cleverest at having his cake and eating it, balancing the Objective and the Subjective:

> The artist, like the God of the creation, remains within or behind or beyond or above his handiwork, invisible, refined out of existence, indifferent, paring his fingernails.

This of course is special pleading for 'art', leaving all other questions unanswered;

Previously unpublished.

it is a mystery of religion. It ensured the seer's integrity: he stayed with the world but not of it – not of it even to the extent of making ordinary 'decent' human compromises in daily life: he was the Romantic artist, to be served like the Talmudic scholar, a privileged monster to ensure the salvation of humanity.

There were other detachments. Yeats, far from the bloody barbed wire of the Great War, wrote an epitaph for a friend who was killed in that conflict. Major Gregory met his end in aerial warfare, in which 'chivalrous', and even 'knightly', one-to-one combats were possible for a short while, above and beyond the dirt, squalor, stench and common butchery of the trenches: they appeared to offer a respite of 'gallantry' from the mass murder in the mud.

> I know that I shall meet my fate
> Somewhere among the clouds above:
> Those that I fight I do not hate,
> Those that I guard I do not love; ...

This represented not merely a view of the War, but a turning aside from the abstract public concerns of the twentieth century to traditional loyalties and intimate matters: the modernist rejection of the modern.

Yeats rejected the *Gesellschaft*. He sought a secular – but still mystical – equivalent of the Communion of Saints. Having enjoyed the hospitality of Lady Gregory's country house at Coole, and the conversations there that envisaged a future in which art would reshape the destiny of his ancient nation, he returned to that district and acquired, at Ballylee, a late medieval tower house on the bank of a little stream – a tall stone building with machicolated parapets, which had once had a walled bawn, or courtyard, and could be defended against a neighbour's raid. This became his Walden, at least for a while. The true retreat was within his mind: Ballylee was the sacramental endorsement.

In the past of Ballylee, mirrors mirrored mirrors. A hundred years before, a poor blind poet without noble patrons, barely surviving the wreckage of the ancient Gaelic world, had come to court a local beauty:

> Going to Mass by the Grace of God
> On a rainy day when the wind rose up
> I met the beauty beside Kiltartan
> And straight away I fell in love.
> I spoke to her with mild good manners
> And of her nature she answered me
> By saying, 'Raftery, my mind is easy:
> So come till morning to Ballylee.'

This association pleased Yeats. It spoke to him of the peasantry, of the tradition of poetry, and – through Raftery's predecessors and their aristocratic patrons – of an archaic Gaelic world. The ghost of that old Gaelic poet was such a spirit as we find haunting the imagination of the post-Symbolist poets everywhere. Yeats felt the Irish language and its thousand-year-old literature to be an enrichment of the world in which he chose to live, or to imagine himself living (his own knowledge of the language was poor). But Irish related to a classical antiquity. His tower was a monument of the late Middle Ages, by which time speakers of another language had come to rule. Having roofed its ruin, brooding on – and fretting against – old age, he imagined the people of his own colonial stock.

> And certain men-at-arms there were
> Whose images, in the Great Memory stored,
> Came with loud cry and panting breast
> To break upon a sleeper's rest
> While their great wooden dice beat on the board.

These phantoms of the past were figures from a world of meaning. Yeats saw in all things a living force, a central sexuality. This was the force that held the world together. And, like other writers of the early twentieth century, in those years after 1914 in which Europe tore itself asunder, he heard the crack of doom: 'Things fall apart ...' Trying to grapple with his personal intimations of age and death, he looked out from the windows and battlements of his tower on to a world that had lost meaning.

So too, at about the same time, did his fellow poet, from the castle tower that was his retreat in Switzerland, at Muzot. Rilke was ten years younger than Yeats. Born at Prague in 1875, he too belonged by birth, like Yeats, to a colonial minority (of Austrian Germans among Czechs). His mother, neurotic in her scrupulous and pietistic Catholicism and in her social anxieties, brought him up as a girl, inducing even deeper anxieties in him. He suffered accordingly in the military academies he attended from the age of ten to the age of fifteen. He reacted extravagantly against the bourgeois world to which his birth assigned him and successfully sought comfort in travel and in patronage from the Central European aristocracy. The Great War (which initially he welcomed with naive patriotism) drove him to despair and after it he lived in retreat until his death in 1926. He practised in his poetry, with an intense lyricism, a Nietzschean game of recategorizing all categories, denying the image of the reality of the world in order to remake it. His mystical experience in 1912, under a tree in the castle garden of his friend Princess Marie von Thurn und Taxis at Duino, inspired him to compose the series of poems which he finally wrote down in a fury of activity in 1922 in his tower at Muzot. They are laments for the isolation that consciousness suffers, an isolation which, for him, was at least partly overcome with the aid of the 'Angel' who figures in the poems: an embodiment of some unifying and resolving principle, as it were of a moral and aesthetic field theory.

> But one tower was great, was it not? Oh, Angel, that it was –
> great, even alongside you? Chartres was great – and music

> extended yet beyond, and surpassed us. Indeed, no more than
> a girl in love, alone – oh, alone by night at her window . . .
> was she not as high as your knee? –

He displayed the isolation of the artist who finds his intellectual environment unacceptable, and the elusiveness of the dainty soul who wishes to retreat from the crassness of his age into his own kind of ivory tower. But in his retreat, it should be said, his judgment, like that of Yeats or Wallace Stephens, was wry. Being led by a dislike of the mob into approval of its incarnation, the Romantic 'man on horseback', he admired, for example, Mussolini.

One of Rilke's patrons was the well-to-do Ludwig Wittgenstein, who directed a sum of a hundred thousand crowns to be distributed among worthy artists. Wittgenstein himself was to be at intervals a reclusive exile. He came from the hothouse world of bourgeois Vienna, being the youngest son (in a family of eight) of the millionaire Karl Wittgenstein, who dominated the steel industry in Bohemia and in the Austro-Hungarian empire generally. Karl also was a youngest son – of an assimilated Jew – a Protestant – who had been a successful wool factor.

Karl was devoted to the violin, and his wife, Leopoldine Kalmus, was a pianist. Her eldest child, Hermine, was a painter who admired Klimt; on her account Karl paid for the Vienna Secession Building, which housed the end-of-century élitist breakaway movement in Viennese art. The eldest son, Hans, was musically highly talented, and when Karl insisted that he abandon music and take over the family business, he fled to America and killed himself. The second son Rudi, attracted to the theatre, came under similar paternal pressure: he too killed himself. Karl died in 1913, but – without his direct assistance – his third son, Kurt (a cellist serving in the army) committed suicide in Italy at the end of the Great War. Another son, Paul, became a concert pianist *after* he had lost his right arm. Ravel's *Concerto for the Left Hand* was written for him. Several generations Protestant, the family nonetheless identified with its Jewish heritage, and Margarete, the youngest of three daughters, an admirer of Ibsen and, *ipso facto*, a radical, was in later times to help her close friend Freud to escape from Austria after the Nazis took over in 1938, and was then to insist on being arrested with the other Jews of Vienna, although the Nazis were more than prepared to overlook the Jewish background of the wealthy Wittgensteins.

Karl Wittgenstein firmly believed that the best education could be provided in the home. His wealth enabled him to employ tutors and his household was a salon at which Brahms, Mahler, Walters and Pablo Casals were visitors. Ludwig, the youngest son, was educated at home to the age of fourteen. This didn't equip him for entry to the *Gymnasium*, and he went to the *Realschule* at Linz – where Adolf Hitler had just been a pupil – and then on to Berlin. He was trained to be an engineer, taking courses which involved mathematics and theoretical physics – especially Newtonian mechanics.

Janik and Toulmin in their book *Wittgenstein's Vienna* have provided a lucid exposition of his early formation. They point out that he would have had as a main textbook Heinrich Hertz's *The Principles of Mathematics*. So he would have been brought face to face with those problems of interpretation of the real world that confronted the physicists and thermodynamicists of the turn of the century. He was of course strongly influenced by the hyperactive intellectual activity of his city and of his time. The remarkable Viennese writer Karl Kraus was one major influence. Another was the journalist Fritz Mauthner, who was also a philosopher attempting a theory of knowledge which was wholly nominalist. Mauthner reacted to such abstract terms as '*Volk*' and 'the State' and tried to break them down by analysis to the elements or atoms of language that went to their composition. He believed that thought was indistinguishable from the expression of thought – language. All problems in philosophy were in fact problems of language. The origin of philosophical evil (that is to say, of error) was the tendency shown by many philosophers to reify, to make 'realities' out of complex abstractions – 'matter', 'energy', 'God', 'language', 'culture' and so forth – built up from simple signs for basic processes. Philosophers spoke in metaphors, removed by stages from reality. Mauthner's ideas went back to the British empiricists and to Locke: thought derived from sensory impressions.

This was parallel to the ideas in relation to physics being expounded by Ernst Mach, who exerted an extraordinary influence on his local culture, as Janik and Toulmin have emphasized. Mach's positivism and extreme empiricism, however, came under attack, notably from Planck, who described his biological theory of knowledge as being every bit as metaphysical as the theories he condemned. This criticism was intended to be damaging. The word 'metaphysics' was used pejoratively. The scientists, after a century or two of grappling with the problems of understanding nature, realised that, however much they might disagree about the interpretations appropriate to any current state of research, yet they were steadily building up a body of new knowledge which could be tested and was secure. Theories might be discarded, or superseded without being wholly discarded; but the system worked and could be put into practice. Philosophy, on the other hand, had produced no body of knowledge. Everything was perpetually at issue, and there was no proof of anything. A waste of time. Among thinking scientists in general there was a low regard for metaphysics, or at least a feeling that, so far as *their* examination of reality was concerned, metaphysics might be regarded as being about as useful as theology.

However, a problem remained. Sets of equations might provide a tool by which a working system could be devised that related in *some* way to what actually was. But to what extent did they *describe* reality? Hertz thought that what the equations did was to provide what it has become customary to refer to as a 'model' of reality. (The German word used here is *Bild*, which is more usually translated 'picture', and in English there is a significant distinction between 'picture' and 'model'.) The mathematical arrays, such as Maxwell's equations, for example, provided representations which, for certain purposes, within limits, were adequate to describe certain consequences of reality. And it could be demonstrated that – within the limits – they worked; they had some validity. Hertz recognised the limits. He concluded of Maxwell's equations, for example, that they said nothing at all about the physical nature of the phenomena to which they related. They were logical formulas for dealing with the phenomena.

So the positivist Mach had dismissed the atomic theory as a figment, an attempt to visualize relationships and processes that were in fact beyond observation. But for the generation of physicists coming into maturity as the new century arrived, this was an unnecessarily 'metaphysical' objection. Whether atoms existed, or did not exist, 'in reality', was for most of their purposes irrelevant. If the concept 'atoms' provided a sufficient economy of hypothesis and of effort in the calculations which plainly had *some* relation to reality – that was enough. 'Atoms' proved useful in the manipulation of reality; therefore they were 'real'.

If Planck was impatient with Mach's questioning of the atomic theory, so was Ludwig Boltzmann, the founder of 'statistical mechanics.' Statistical explanation is essentially pragmatic. What works works. Boltzmann described the physical state of a system by placing it in reference to a multidimensional space with coordinates representing all the independent variables. This gives a space of theoretical possibilities; actual events can be specified as probabilities within this framework. In quantum mechanics and other such systems, this worked. And it was the prototype for what Wittgenstein was to call 'logical space'.

Instead of 'meaning', the enquiring mind was being offered practical rules-of-thumb, and, for the Viennese intellectual society of the day, the central questions of philosophy had, for the moment, been reduced to a critique of words: how and what did words *mean?* The young Wittgenstein was attracted to Boltzmann's ideas and wished to study with him. But in 1906 Boltzmann, who had come under severe criticism from Mach and others, committed suicide at Duino. (Perhaps it was his ghost who later took the form of Rilke's Angel.) Wittgenstein went instead to Manchester University in 1908, where he worked on the design of aircraft engines, developed his interest in mathematics, and became acquainted with Bertrand Russell's *Principles of Mathematics* (published in 1903) and, through this, with the work of Gottlob Frege. Ernest Rutherford was at Manchester in those years, studying alpha particles, and it was there, in 1911, that he announced his model of the atom, with its heavy nucleus. In that year, 1911, Wittgenstein went to Jena to see Frege, who advised him to go to Cambridge, to Russell.

In Cambridge Wittenstein entered an environment comparable with but very different from that in which he had grown up in Vienna. The English bourgeoisie had a history quite different from that of the Austrian bourgeoisie; but it too had produced an intellectual élite, one which has sometimes been called an intellectual aristocracy, since its members intermarried so. They stemmed largely from families with an eighteenth-century Quaker, philanthropic or evangelical background and with a common tradition of commitment to personal freedom, families which early in the nineteenth century had entered into close social intercourse, leading to intermarriage. They became professional civil servants, colonial administrators, professors, headmasters, museum curators, editors, publicists. The families included Barclays, Cadburys, Rowntrees, Gaskells, Hoares, Darwins, Wedgwoods, Maitlands, Huxleys, Keyneses, Trevelyans, Tennysons, Macaulays, Arnolds, Wards, Fryes, Stracheys and Stephens. The names are familiar ones in the history of English business, thought, letters and public service in the nineteenth and twentieth centuries, and by the end of the nineteenth century they formed a distinct lineage segment with an ethos of its own. They were endogamous in tendency, but by no means exclusively so; they were open to receive into their number people who met their moral and intellectual standards. Many members of their families became fellows of Trinity or King's College in Cambridge. They had a particular connection with the Cambridge secret society commonly known as 'the Apostles', a group which met for intellectual discussions (often clever silliness) and had a cultivated atmosphere of homosexual camaraderie (even at times when it was not dominated by an active homosexual membership).

From among this élite was formed, in the early twentieth century, the so-called 'Bloomsbury group', which included Lytton Strachey, Clive Bell, Roger Fry, Virginia Woolf, E.M. Forster and – outstanding among these poetasters – Maynard Keynes. Their main cultural achievement was well summed up by Paul Levy in 1979 in his biography of G.E. Moore:

> Bloomsbury, whose well-publicized private lives were and still are emulated in the suburbs of New York as well as those of London, created the *climate* in which middle-class families eat for their Sunday lunch *boeuf en daube*, made to an Elizabeth David or Julia Childe recipe, on a plain pine farmhouse (American 'life style') table bought from Habitat or New York's Conran shop.

Apart from their influence on later suburban manners and customs, the members of the Bloomsbury Group can't be said to have carried the same weight as did their immediate intellectual and genetic forebears. With a few notable exceptions, they are open to the charges of frivolity, self complacency and social callousness. But if they took the rest of the world lightly, they took themselves seriously and they enjoyed through their background an inherited reputation for intellectual seriousness and achievement which they themselves were not put to the trouble of earning.

Wittgenstein met some of them when he came to Cambridge before the War, for the people he sought there, including in the first place Bertrand Russell, were connected with the literary aristocracy. The élite had by then acquired its new philosopher, who had (as many of its members liked to think) given benediction to its ways. In 1903 George Edward Moore published his *Principia Ethica* in Cambridge, and he became, and remained until the War, the guru of a set centred on the Apostles. Moore's concluding thoughts, in the closing chapters of the *Principia*, are to the effect that the good is to be found only in states of mind; and this appealed to a group of people who wished to see themselves both as transmitters of a tradition of moral earnestness based on freedom of thought, and as people released by their intelligence and their appreciation of beauty and truth from the trammels of conventional or social morality. Leonard Woolf, who married Virginia Stephen, compared Moore to Socrates because

> Like Socrates, he attracted a number of friends and followers as different from one another as Plato and Aristophanes were from Alcibiades and Xenophon.

The members of this Grecian circle were Lytton Strachey, Desmond McCarthy, Sir Ralph Wedgwood, Lord Keynes, Sir Edward Marsh and a few others, who are not quite forgotten, because their memory is preserved by the nostalgia of a coterie that hankers for the Indian summer of early-twentieth-century England. Russell wasn't a member: he was a rival rather than a disciple of Moore.

There was more to Moore, however, than providing a cloak for people who wanted to dress up hedonism as altruism – which seemed to be what some of his admirers took from a rather careless reading of the *Principia*. His epistemology was to have an influence on the formation of Wittgenstein the philosopher. Morris Lazerowitz wrote of this influence that:

> Moore's work made many philosophers aware of the linguistic character, or what at first appeared to be the linguistic character, of a particular type of philosophical theory, and Wittgenstein went on to throw a linguistic shadow over the whole of philosophy. The idea which began to take its place among the standard ideas as to *what* philosophy is, to put it somewhat metaphorically, is that language is the stuff philosophy is made of.

The quotation from Bishop Butler which Moore used as the motto of his *Principia Ethica* was to be echoed by Wittgenstein in his work:

> Everything is what it is and not another thing.

Meantime Wittgenstein, skilled as he had been since childhood in the making of machines, and trained in physics – so supplying what had been a gap in the training of philosophical philosophers – made a considerable impression on Russell, who had just then concluded the work he published jointly with Whitehead, *Principia Mathematica*. Wittgenstein spent five terms at Trinity College, Cambridge, in 1912 and 1913 and then went to Norway, where he built himself a hut and lived as a recluse. When the Great War began he joined up and served in the Austrian army on the Russian and Italian fronts. He was decorated more than once for bravery. Numbers of the friends and acquaintances he had made in England displayed another kind of bravery, sustained by their confidence in privilege and by their inherited nonconformist assurance of being in the right, by refusing to take part in the War. This was not necessarily because they were pacifists but partly because they felt a sympathy for German culture that was traditional in their class in England down to the beginning of the twentieth century, and partly because they judged *this* particular war to be unjustified (a much more difficult objection to sustain against the State than one based, for example, on religious rejection of war). Russell, for one, went to jail as a conscientious objector.

It was during the War that Wittgenstein wrote and completed the notes from which he extracted the only book he was to publish in his lifetime, his *Tractatus Logico-Philosophicus*. It was complete when he was imprisoned by the Italians at the end of the War in a camp at Monte Cassino. Through Maynard Keynes he sent his manuscript to Russell, who met him in the Netherlands in 1919 and went through the text with him. It was published in 1921 and Russell wrote the introduction for the English edition. With Russell's Introduction – that is, with Russell's interpretation of the *Tractatus* – Wittgenstein was to disagree fundamentally. But he was also to disagree in due course with himself: indeed, in a sense he did so as he wrote his work; for the *Tractatus* is a unique and extraordinary work in philosophy.

It may be noted in passing that although civilization broke down in 1914 in Europe, its traditions didn't disappear immediately. Both Einstein and Wittgenstein (and they were not alone) found people in England reaching out to them across the insanity of the War. The openness which was then regarded as essential to science and which was a requisite of the liberal tradition that had made the modern Western world, was still founded on bourgeois and aristocratic institutions comparatively independent of the State. Bureaucratic State power had not yet – quite – succeeded in imposing 'national security' on the community of thought as a reason for preventing the free interchange of knowledge; nor had the bureaucracies of industry and commerce invoked the principle of private property (in knowledge) with sufficient success to achieve a similar effect. Scientists and scholars still took pride in their communion of free enquiry, and had not yet been bought – as they since have – by the agents of power.

Wittgenstein very characteristically introduces the *Tractatus* with the words:

> Perhaps this book will be understood only by someone who has himself already had the thoughts that are expressed in it—or at least similar thoughts. ... Its purpose would be achieved if it gave pleasure to one person who read and understood it.

The very short book (it runs to about 75 pages) is two things at once. It is a critique and exposition of symbolic logic, melding the epistemology of Hertzian mechanics, the Viennese subtlety of understanding of language and Frege's and Russell's system of atomization of propositions; and it trumps the lot with the assertion (devastating to academic philosophy) that the emperor has no clothes. It is also a significant and important ethical statement, rejecting the coarseness and vulgarity of thought (blind to the moral universe) that gave rise to the modern world.

No one, of course, except Wittgenstein himself, 'already had the thoughts that are expressed' in the *Tractatus*. It is therefore a difficult work. It was plainly difficult to write and it is not inconceivable that even Wittgenstein never exactly 'had the thoughts that are expressed in it'. The *Tractatus* is highly original (although its genetic code can be read by hindsight): originality is very difficult to achieve, and among the difficulties is that of understanding what one is saying oneself in a newly invented language. Wittgenstein was convinced when he had completed the book that he had at once solved everything and nothing:

> ... the *truth* of the thoughts that are here communicated seems to me unassailable and definitive. I therefore believe myself to have found, on all essential points, the final solution of the problems. And if I am not mistaken in this belief, then the second thing in which the value of this work consists is that it shows how little is achieved when these problems are solved.

Yet, after further retreats, he was to return to work in opposition to the same thoughts.

The work is without chapters or divisions except those implied in its hierarchical numbering system. The system can be illustrated by quoting the propositions under '1':

1   The world is all that is the case.
1.1   The world is the totality of facts, not of things.
1.11   The world is determined by the facts, and by their being *all* the facts.
1.12   For the totality of the facts determines what is the case, and also whatever is not the case.
1.13   The facts in logical space are the world.
1.2   The world divides into facts.
1.21   Each item can be the case or not the case while everything else remains the same.

The subtle difficulty of the system may be observed if we take, for example, proposition 1.21. This appears to counter Laplace, the French mathematician who had imagined a hypothetical demiurge, or demon, who was apprised of the dynamics of the whole cosmic system down to its last detail: supplied with total information at any given moment, the demon could read from it the whole future of the universe, and its past. Laplace was not arguing that such total knowledge of all facts was practically possible, but rather suggesting that a full mechanistic description of the system would include by inference its complete past and future history, since effect followed cause inexorably, and every single event, no matter how great or small, obeyed the laws of motion that had once been set in train. (This *Bild* is essentially what was to give Charles Darwin his central insight into the workings of nature.) When Napoleon asked Laplace what place God had in his system, he famously replied: 'I have no need of that hypothesis.' The system was like Calvin's predestination, but the tables of the Newtonian law replaced divine knowledge. Laplace's demon was to preside over the background of much nineteenth- and twentieth-century thought.

But, if Wittgenstein's proposition 1.21 appears to go against Laplace by stating that the atomic items of the universe are autonomous, the matter is not so simple, for this statement is subordinate to proposition 1.12, which is a Laplacian proposition. The universe in which the item z is the case is not the same as the universe in which the item z is not the case: to however minimal a degree it has a different *Gestalt* and is a different universe.

In spite of his confident statement that he had solved the problems, Wittgenstein immediately realised that he had failed to communicate. Russell's introduction to his book was proof of that. And, secondly, in spite of what he wrote about it, there were weaknesses in his argument. This of course was all but inevitable in a work of exploration of intellectual space such as his. He was trying *from within* the limits of the possible – an exercise familiar to test pilots.

But revision was to come later. In the meantime, the *Tractatus* was Wittgenstein's huge and heroic effort to discern the relationship, if any, between philosophy and living, between what we can usefully say about the reality of which we are a part and the imperative meaning of our existence. It was purification and refinement of Schopenhauer's *World as Will and Representation* – Schopenhauer was one of Wittgenstein's intellectual ancestors. There were other ancestors even less formally philosophical (in the traditional sense) than Schopenhauer. One was Tolstoy, as he expressed himself in his later writings. Another, of great importance, was Kierkegaard, whom Wittgenstein regarded as the most important thinker of the nineteenth century. From them Wittgenstein received guidance for his ethical purpose, which, in his own view, was the main purpose of the *Tractatus*.

Søren Kierkegaard plays a somewhat eccentric rôle in the history of modern thought. Like Mendel's in biology – but over a longer period – his ideas had gathered dust, as it were, waiting to be discovered at the end of the nineteenth century. Kierkegaard was born in Denmark in 1813 and died in 1855. It has been said of him that:

> More clearly than anyone else he understood the shape of modernity, that malaise from which we now suffer.

This assessment by a conservative scholar (John Douglas Mullen) is sympathetic to a man whose reactions to modernity – not to speak of Modernism – were those of a Romantic and a Christian. The combination is important for the understanding of Kierkegaard and of the great significance he assumed when he was brought to the attention of, for example, the Viennese intelligentsia of the 1900s. For within him, and in his writings, the Romantic issued a critique of the Christian; the Christian issued a critique of the Romantic; and the combination of the two expressed a profound rejection of the post-Romantic modern positivist. Kierkegaard was a Christian who renounced his church – because it took its shape from the secular world and failed to be the scandal that he believed Jesus had meant it to be. He was a counter-Hegelian. He *preached* rather than taught in the regular secular way. He analysed at length, and with great insight, the dread, or gnawing anxiety (*Angst*) which he took to be a salient feature of modern life. He wrote about despair.

In his first major work, *Either / Or*, Kierkegaard contrasted the aesthetic and the ethical views of life, maintaining that true morality consists of a relationship between each person and God; that morality therefore is not a social but a personal matter. He embraced Christianity as an 'absurdity to the understanding', a blind leap into the dark: *commitment*.

This was a large part of what Wittgenstein brought to his work: an endeavour to reconcile such a moral will with a latitudinarian understanding. Philosophy's purpose was not to provide us with a series of aphorisms or propositions but to teach us how to live. But it was necessary to begin by understanding.

His *Tractatus* deals first with the nature of language and its relation to the world, and he asserts that 'most of the propositions and questions to be found in philosophical works are not false but nonsensical'. He goes on to develop his view that propositions and thoughts are *pictures* of facts. Then he goes on to make one of his central points:

> 4.121   What expresses *itself* in language, *we* cannot express by means of language. Propositions *show* the logical form of reality.
>
> 4.1212   What *can* be shown, *cannot* be said ...

The basic criticism of the 'philosophers' is that in their logic they deal in tautologies.

The *Tractatus* is a work of necessary destruction, accomplished by the candour of Wittgenstein's approach. His thinking has in common with Albert Einstein's an innocent, almost naive, directness of enquiry. What he offers that is positive rather than negative is largely outside philosophy. Beyond the envelope of our understanding there is a vast reality that we can't reach or grasp.

> 6.432   *How* things are in the world is a matter of complete indifferennce for what is higher. God does not reveal himself *in* the world ...
>
> 6.521   The solution of the problem of life is seen in the vanishing of the problem.
>   (Is that not the reason why those who have found after a long period of doubt that the sense of life became clear to them have been unable to say what constituted that sense?)

The book famously ends with the brief statement:

7   What we cannot speak about we must pass over in silence.

Wittgenstein had performed an intellectual Indian rope trick. Now he discarded the rope. Russell was refuted, Moore reduced. Having completed his demolition – which was thorough, for he brought down his own as well as other philosophers' work – Wittgenstein abandoned philosophy. He taught in Austrian village schools for several years. He designed a modern house for his sister and seems to have contemplated setting up as an architect. He worked as a gardener for a monastery. Then, at the end of the 1920s, he returned to philosophy, and to Cambridge. On visits to Vienna, he became connected with the newly formed 'Vienna Circle' of logical positivists for a while, and in the meantime began the work to be published posthumously as *Philosophische Bemerkungen*. About 1930 he began a substantial revision of his ideas and completed another work, not to be published in his lifetime, *Philosophische Grammatik*. He was to live until 1951, giving lectures most years in the 1930s in Cambridge, succeeding Moore as Professor of Philosophy in 1939. By then he was a British subject, having abandoned his Austrian nationality after the *Anschluss* of 1938. He had also returned for a year to his hut in Norway, where he began work on what was to be published as *Philosophical Investigations*. He served as a medical orderly during the Second World War, resigned his chair in 1947 and then went to Ireland, where he lived for a while in a cottage in the West, afterwards completing his *Philosophical Investigations* in Dublin. After a visit to a friend in America, he died in Cambridge.

Wittgenstein's revision of his own ideas, beginning after he had completed the *Tractatus*, continued to be partly concerned with language. There are already hints in the *Tractatus* itself that the philosophical view, reinforced by the work of Moore and Russell, that language is expository, was causing him qualms. Perhaps the analogy with music – which he adduces – gave him pause. At any rate, the shift in his thinking from the late 1920s onwards brought him further from the view that language consisted for the most part of propositions, to an anthropological and psychological (almost Chomskian) understanding of language and its functions. He opens his final major work, *Philosophical Investigations*, with a quotation from St Augustine on language:

> When they (my elders) named some object, and accordingly moved towards something, I saw this and grasped that the thing was called by the sound they uttered when they meant to point it out. Their intention was shown by their bodily movements, as it were the natural language of all peoples ...

And he goes on to quote:

> 'We name things and then we can talk about them: can refer to them in talk.' – As if there were only one thing called 'talking about a thing.' Whereas in fact we do the most various things with our sentences. Think

of exclamations alone, with their completely different functions ... Are
you still inclined to call these words 'names of objects?'

The poets, in their retreats, also wrestled with words and with these problems.
Yeats wrote:

> O body swayed to music, O brightening glance,
> How can we tell the dancer from the dance?

And Eliot asked:

> Where shall the word be found, where will the word
> Resound? Not here, there is not enough silence
> Not on the sea or on the islands, not
> On the mainland, in the desert or the rainland,
> For those who walk in darkness
> Both in the day time and in the night time
> The right time and the right place are not here
> No place of grace for those who avoid the face
> No time to rejoice for those who walk among noise and deny
> The voice.

And Rilke walked on Wittgenstein's ground:

> Perhaps that's why we're *here*:
> To say house, bridge, well, gate,
> Jug, fruit-tree, window –
> At most: pillar, tower ...
> But to *say* it: that's it;
> To say it, oh, in such a way
> As the things themselves could never
> Have force to think themselve to be.

Philosopher and poets equally found themselves obliged to retreat from the crass
achievement of two centuries' Western thought.
    The Great War in particular did much destruction to the illusion of Progress.
It pointed up the deep and stultifying contradictions in the Western civilization
of the early twentieth century after 'the death of God': the lack of faith in either
the ghost or the machine; the failure both of matter and of the solipsistic self; the
antitheses that could find no syntheses: thinker and thought, speaker and speech,
actor and act. The War, and the moral forces that made the War, also did other
damage. These forces now had their way – the capitalist greed for profit, the
socialist rage for power, the nationalist hatred of the Other – without the restraint
of a universal myth, a common cultural structure. And Wittgenstein for one was

driven to retreat fourteen hundred years to ask ancient questions again:

> Ita verba in variis sententiis locis suis posita, et crebro audita, quarum rerum signa essent, paulatim colligebam, measque jam voluntates, edomito in eis signis ore, per haec enuntiabam.

Augustine's words about words are his new-starting point for an enquiry that had turned in circles since he had begun it early in the century. His great virtue was his refusal to accept the glib Cartesian distinction between the observer and the observed that had usefully carried the thought of the West towards a most profitable understanding of nature but had now reached a limit which must give pause to physicists, philosophers and would-be masters of the universe, and have them call in question the direction in which that formula had taken them.

11

Vanishing Space

It was to 'Realism', in particular the Realism of Courbet, that Manet went to school, but he graduated into something different. His painting, *Le Bain*, subsequently to be known as *Déjeuner sur l'Herbe*, was rejected by the Paris *Salon* of 1863, but was shown in the *Salon des Refusés*, where it gave much offence. It shows two men fully dressed in ordinary street clothes sprawled on the grass of a wooded glade which slopes down to a stream, while one young woman sits beside them, completely naked, and another, in a chemise, climbs somewhat clumsily out of the water. The background is vaguely sylvan, in false perspective like a stage backdrop: a contrived and ironic space. The painting is full of irony, making oblique comments on several matters. In the first place, it refers to the *Concert Champêtre* in the Louvre, then attributed to Giorgione, which depicts a similar, but sixteenth-century, scene. *That*, distanced by time and strangeness of costume, is *art*. Manet's painting of the two commonplace young men in their drab present-day dress, accompanied by the naked young woman who looks calmly and intelligently into the eye of the viewer, or *voyeur*, of the picture, is a joke, a serious joke: art which comments on art. More specifically and forcefully, it is a comment on the use of the nude in *salon* painting of the middle nineteenth century, derived, *via* classicism, from the Renaissance, but now vulgarized. The woman at the centre of the painting is not an odalisque, nor a slave being offered for sale in an oriental (or more accurately, Orientalist) market, nor any other of the hairless, spotless, marmoreal but weightless female bodies being offered to fantasy at this time under the permissive aegis of 'art.' She is a person, not an object.

The disquiet occasioned by the woman depicted not as an object for aesthetic, or lustful, contemplation, but as an intelligence quite capable of contemplating the beholder, is the background tone of the famous passage written close to this time, Walter Pater's description of Leonardo's *La Gioconda* (the 'Mona Lisa') in his work on *The Renaissance.*

> She is older than the rocks among which she sits; like the vampire, she has been dead many times, and learned the secrets of the grave; and has been a diver in deep seas, and keeps their fallen day about her; and trafficked

Previously unpublished

for strange webs with Eastern merchants, and, as Leda, was the mother of Helen of Troy, and, as Saint Anne, the mother of Mary; and all this has been to her but as the sound of lyres and flutes, and lives only in the delicacy with which it has moulded the changing lineaments, and tinged the eyelids and the hands. The fancy of a perpetual life, sweeping together ten thousand experiences, is an old one; and modern philosophy has conceived the idea of humanity as wrought upon, and summing up in itself, all modes of thought and life. Certainly, Lady Lisa might stand as the embodiment of the old fancy, the symbol of the modern idea.

Baudelaire had anticipated him in 1861, when he wrote, in his essay on 'Wagner and Tannhäuser':

> The radiant Venus of antiquity, the foam-born Aphrodite, has not passed unscathed through the dreadful shades of the Middle Ages. Her dwelling is no longer Olympus, nor the shores of a perfumed archipelago. She has retired into the depths of a cavern, magnificent it is true, but illuminated by fires very different from those of benign Apollo.

Suddenly, now, with Manet, anaemic and uneasy fantasy was pruned and governed: something was begun; something was ended.

Manet's work, meantime, was defended by Zola, and by Baudelaire, who wrote of another of his paintings (a portrait of Lola de Valence):

> Entre tant de beautés que partout on peut voir
> Je comprends bien, amis, que le désir balance,
> Mais on voit scintiller en Lola de Valence
> Le charme inattendu d'un bijou rose et noir.

His painting registers an epoch.

Realism, an impulse of the mid-nineteenth century, is the starting point for Modernist movements in visual art, music and literature. Realism was akin in spirit to physical science and had some relationship also to the spirit of the eighteenth-century Enlightenment. It aimed at truth through an attempted objectivity which rejected authority and hierarchy. It embodied a kind of humility, looking to the everyday, the ordinary; eschewing pretentiousness, the grand manner and insubstantial rhetoric. Manet attempted this through his matter-of-fact approach to his subjects and through his handling of his medium. Zola essayed it, in life and work, handling the stuff of ordinary lives, in which lay some immanent meaning. The Symbolists tried to achieve it by taking the transitory and evanescent as manifestations of underlying truth. Oscar Wilde – followed in his different fashion by Bernard Shaw – strove to speak truth through irony, wit and paradox, all of which were designed to penetrate the facades of falsehood erected by the society that was being explicitly or implicitly criticized.

Wagner and Nietzsche, powerful influences on this generation, had to some extent led the way in this search for hidden meaning, which regularly took the form of a provocative defiance of the accepted, a tearing off of masks; and Martin Esslin, in an essay on drama, writes:

> It is no coincidence that the man who did most to naturalize the concept of modernist drama in the English-speaking world, George Bernard Shaw, was an Ibsenite as well as a Wagnerian, and, of course, philosophically decidedly a Nietzschean ...
>
> Behind the vast diversity, the proliferation of forms and -isms, the seemingly diametrical opposition between the different strands of contemporary drama, there still lies that one single impulse, born of the nineteenth century's rejection of the traditional world system that had seemed to contain and explain the ways of the world and to justify the ways of God to Man.

Shaw himself, in his preface to *Man and Superman* in 1903, expressed it piquantly:

> It may seem a long step from Bunyan to Nietzsche; but the difference between their conclusions is merely formal ... Nothing is new in these matters except their novelties: for instance, it is a novelty to call Justification by Faith '*Wille*' and Justification by Works '*Vorstellung*'. The sole use of the novelty is that you and I can buy and read Schopenhauer's treatise on *Will and Representation* when we should not dream of buying a set of sermons on Faith versus Works.

Épater le bourgeois (a part of Shaw's intention, as he confessed in the same preface) had, of course, more than a touch of Romanticism in its background, and Romantic influences were to persist very strongly into the new century; but the interval of Realism marked a true change of direction and intention. The attempt to get beyond sham and pretence and look at things as they really were was a necessary part of the general cultural house-cleaning that Modernism felt to be its task: the removal of old cultural furnishings to make room for cultural forms designed for a wholly new society. Humbug and hypocrisy were to be attacked. There was a real danger – one that was to be catastrophically realised – that rejection of the pretension to virtue would lead to the rejection of virtue itself. Max Beerbohm was to point up this danger, gently, in his little moral tale of *The Happy Hypocrite*.

But the attempt also led, by a natural progression, first to a re-examination of surfaces, then to efforts to discern what meaning, if any, lay beneath the surface. Such efforts were to lead in different directions, some to examine the observer, the 'self', others to analyse the observed, the 'world'. The extraordinary influence that Henrik Ibsen's plays exercised on Europe towards the end of the century derives largely from his capacity to achieve these progressions both through his dramatic technique and through his language. John Fletcher and James McFarlane wrote of others who 'were themselves exceptionally sensitive practitioners of language' that:

> Fascinated by the subtle undertones of Ibsen's dramatic dialogue (mysteriously surviving even in translation) they detect a second unspoken reality behind the surface of things, a *dialogue de second degré* (Maeterlinck); or remark how 'at some chance expression the mind is tortured with some question, and in a flash long reaches of life are opened up in vista' (Joyce); or hearken to characters who 'think about thinking, feel about feeling, and practise autopsychology' (Hoffmannsthal); or see in Ibsen's changing authorship 'an ever more desperate search for visible correlations of the inwardly seen' (Rilke).

The 'second unspoken reality beneath the surface of things', and 'visible correlations of the inwardly seen' were to preoccupy the visual artists too and to lead them to their strange twentieth-century ride to visual oblivion. The Impressionists, liberated in a way by Manet's achievement, had gone on themselves to offer liberation to the bourgeoisie (an offer that was fairly soon accepted). They did this initially by celebrating everyday pleasure. Turning their backs on the portrayal of historical, narrative, or dramatic scenes – but also largely on the 'quiet desperation' of the existence of the nineteenth-century poor – they abandoned the studio with its artificial and contrived settings and were *plein-air* painters, working directly from nature. They painted landscapes, groups of *midinettes* and their men-friends disporting themselves on the Seine or at the seaside, scenes of everyday life. Their technical concern was to convey the visual perception of (usually sunny and pleasant) scenes by rendering the sense of light and colour through their palette and brushwork. They avoided symmetrically or monumentally formal composition and conveyed instead an atmosphere of informality, of the seized, fleeting moment: *Carpe diem.* They presented a shimmering vibrant surface through which forms appeared as if through a heat-haze. It was as though they tried to represent the charged air between the spectator and the scene rather than the scene itself.

At first their work was regarded as incompetent or gratuitously shocking, and they obtained very poor prices initially; but within fifteen or twenty years of the first show they had moved (at least among a discerning small minority of the well-to-do) to the position they have held more or less ever since: the darlings of the *haute-bourgeoisie.* Themselves occupying for a while, through poverty and a taste for low life, the semi-bohemian borderland between the middle and the working classes, they soon contrived to convey to the bourgeois the simple and liberating message: You don't have to live in pretend-castles, be pretend-aristocrats or pretend-saints, or have lofty philosophical-historical thoughts to justify your wealth. Pleasure is easy.

Easy pleasure, however, was not enough to satisfy the sensibility of the age.

Among the Impressionists themselves unease was manifest quite soon. The shimmering surface they created presented its own formal and technical problems. And the group, who had shared a common impulse, developed in different directions. Claude Monet remained most faithful all his life to the principles of Impressionism (which were 'scientific'), seeking always to render through his technique the play of light and colour as perceived by the eye, so absorbed by the endeavour to render *exactly* the visual impression or sensation that what it was an impression of came to be almost irrelevant. When, in the early years of this century, he worked over and over again to render in paint random reflections of sky and foliage in arbitrary areas of the large lily pond in his garden – reflections imposed on the glissant surface of the water and on its shadowy depths – he attempted a critically exact naturalism whose effect was to be that of an almost formless abstraction, like some of Turner's late paintings of atmospheric phenomena. He achieved effects quite similar (although much softer) to those to be produced many years later through a wholly different approach by Jackson Pollock.

Renoir worked together with Monet for a while, but soon went on to depart from Impressionist principles (which stressed a passive spontaneity in the face of nature) by pre-conceiving his paintings, especially in terms of their colour harmonies. From the fairly varied subject-matters of early Impressionist days he began to concentrate on softly fleshy pink-and-white nudes. These studies, both sensual and sentimentalized, found an eager market, extending from Russia to America, at the turn of the century.

Seurat, who died in 1891 at the age of thirty-two, produced a small body of work which, stemming from Impressionism, is its antithesis. He developed some Impressionist techniques, using tiny dots of pigment to build up the colours by the process of 'optical mixing', a close interplay of yellow and blue dots, for example, producing in the eye of the spectator at a little distance from the painting, a sensation of a clearer and brighter green than could be achieved by mixing blue and yellow on the palette. His effects were carefully planned, however, and the masses of colour produced with a multitude of tiny points like the nap on a velvet, simultaneously achieved a rich depth of texture and restored formality to the work. The drawn outline, tending to be blurred in Impressionist work, reasserted itself; further, Seurat's works are classically composed, depicting the pleasures of *modern* life but arranging the scene to convey an Arcadian timelessness and harmony achieved by carefully designing the proportions between the visual units in accordance with the classical modules derived from the Golden Section. He was one of several whose work was labelled Neo-Impressionism. They read, discussed and tried to apply scientific ideas on light and colour; not all in the same way. Dégas, for example – one of the original Impressionists – employed 'optical mixing', but not through *pointillisme*.

A development more important than changes in painterly technique took place in the 1880s and 1890s. Artists began to look beyond the retinal impression of the material universe, to discover the resources from which they could construct a correlative visual world that would offer an interpretation beyond representation. Photography, after all, had carried to its logical, and limited, conclusion the Renaissance development that began with the elucidation of the rules of optical perspective and the use of the *camera obscura* as an aid to drawing. It was possible for owners of the new one-eyed optical machine – the nineteenth-century photographic camera – to go beyond the flat matter-of-factness of its usual products; but only by calling on the graphic rhetoric of painting, a rhetoric already being discarded by painters as bombastic and hollow. Alfred Stieglitz, by the turn of the century, was producing in New York remarkable photographs which expressed the transformed New World of industrialization through what was essentially the sign-system of *salon* painting. The 'medium was the message' here; to some extent the subject matter was also: locomotives, steamships, factories, all telling a story of revolutionary change through a visual vocabulary that had been designed for conservative and aristocratic purposes. It is worthy of note that the 'New York Secession' – the American breakaway to modern art – centred on photography.

The brief moment of hedonism passed with the decade of Impressionism. Questions arose, which were to inform the pervading anxiety that came to mark mature bourgeois culture. The decentralization of European humanity proceeded, as the focal importance of European man steadily diminished—within the solar system, in the universe, in the hierarchy of nature, in the human world, in the eye of divine providence, in sexual command, in the autonomy and authority of the mind. Alienation in the processes of production, anomie in the relationships of society, gathered like a fungus bloom on the withering of life-sustaining myth that followed on the 'death of God'. Many were driven into introspection, despairing or self-complacent. There began what has since become (especially in late-twentieth-century America) a barbarizing obsession with the empty self.

Some, like Léon Bloy, the 'pilgrim of the absolute', strove furiously to deny what had happened to Christendom since the Middle Ages and to sustain in the modern age the fantasy expressed by Hilaire Belloc in the aphorism, 'The Faith is Europe and Europe is the Faith.' Charles Péguy, passionately nationalist and passionately devoted to the old order, held that the world had changed less since the time of Christ than it had 'in the last thirty years' – but felt that this was something that would pass. His illusions and his life were to be snuffed out by the indifferent German machine-guns in the opening engagement of the Great War. Henry Adams witnessed the revolution in New York, and described it in *The Education of Henry Adams*:

> All New York was demanding new men, and all the new forces, condensed into corporations, were demanding a new type of man – a man with ten times the endurance, energy, will and mind of the old type – for whom they were willing to pay millions at sight. As one jolted over the pavements or read last week's newspapers, the new man seemed close at hand, for the old one had plainly reached the end of his strength, and his failure had become catastrophic. Everyone saw it, and every municipal election shrieked chaos. A traveller on the highways of history looked out of the

club window on the turmoil of Fifth Avenue, and felt himself in Rome, under Diocletian, witnessing the anarchy, conscious of the compulsion, eager for the solution, but unable to conceive whence the next impulse was to come or how it was to act. The two-thousand-year failure of Christianity roared upward from Broadway, and no Constantine the Great was in sight.

Robert Musil saw it in the cultural confusion of Vienna and described it in *The Man Without Qualities*:

> Nobody knew exactly what was on the way; nobody was able to say whether it was to be a new art, a New Man, a new morality, or perhaps a re-shuffling of society ... Suddenly the right man was on the spot everywhere; and, what is so important, men of practical enterprise joined forces with men of intellectual enterprise ... The Superman was adored, and the Subman was adored; health and sun were worshipped, and the delicacy of consumptive girls was worshipped; people were enthusiastic about hero-worshippers and enthusiastic adherents of the Man in the Street; one had faith and was skeptical; one was naturalistic and precious, robust and morbid; one dreamed of ancient castles and shady avenues, autumnal gardens, glassy ponds, jewels, hashish, disease and demonism, but also of prairies, vast horizons, forges and rolling-mills, naked wrestlers, the uprising of slaves of toil, man and woman in the primeval Garden, and the destruction of society.

Others looked for some non-European innocence or experience as the way to salvation – in Japan, Africa, the South Seas – following the example of many troubled Western minds since the guns of European ships had first breached the walls of Ceuta in Africa in the year of Agincourt. Tylor's *Anthropology* in 1881 introduced a pseudo-science which was to feed the hankering for myth, and Frazer's *Golden Bough* at the turn of the century (twelve volumes published from 1890 to 1914: an ambitious and world-comprehensive thesis based on wide reading, a creative imagination and a capacity to over-simplify by formula) was to provide grist for the mills of, among others, T.S. Eliot, Oswald Spengler and Carl Jung.

Meantime, the search for alternative worlds continued among the artists. Japan remained a quarry much mined; now more methodically than when the first prints had arrived from the East to open Western eyes to new points of view, to fresh sectorings of optical experience and to felicitous economies in graphic statement. The Pennsylvanian Impressionist Mary Cassatt did important work of study and presentation to make Japanese work better known and understood, as, at a later date, did Okakura Kakuzo in Philadelphia and Lafcadio Hearn through his extensive writings. In France, Paul Gauguin gathered a group around him and took up, in his way, the idea that all art should aim (in Pater's words) at 'the condition of music'. He taught that painting 'acts upon the soul by the detour of the senses; its colour harmonies correspond to the harmonies of sound'. He strove – in theory – to distance the painting from the object: the work of art should bear such a relationship to the scene represented (or rather, interpreted) as memory and dream do to direct experience. Therefore he was against the direct, or *plein-air* approach to nature of the Impressionists. There is something of a contradiction in his teaching; for, in spite of his emphasis on the musical analogy, he also tried to restore narrative and expositional subject-matter to painting, now in the form of the dream-stories of myth. Since there was a complementary contradiction in some musical tendencies of the day – an effort to introduce into music the sounds and even the sights of the world (by a code of equivalent motifs) – perhaps Gauguin was not wholly inconsistent. He fled from what he saw as the ennervating decline of European civilization to the warmth, colour and unspoilt primitiveness (so it appeared) of the West Indies, Tahiti and the Marquesas – a version of the 'noble savage' appropriate to the age of the 'New Imperialism'. Gauguin was his own anthropologist, ransacking exotic cultures for dreams. His communications with his followers were never the blind leading the blind but may sometimes have been a dialogue of the deaf: his precepts, listened to attentively, were not necessarily observed.

His most remarkable disciple was the Dutchman Vincent van Gogh, who was a dark painter where the Impressionists were bright and sunny but who, like them (and contrary to Gauguin's teaching and practice) worked directly from nature. Not, however, through a freely interpreted science of optics. Van Gogh was not interested in the impression light-waves made on the retina of his eye but in the impression reality made on his soul. The intensity of emotion he directed on the world about him – it is clear that he felt a divinity in every atom of creation as acutely as if he were in pain – produced a body of work that led everywhere and nowhere and brought him to madness and death. He is *sui generis*; yet his influence was great on another disturbed spirit, the Norwegian Edvard Munch, and on the German Expressionists, and his personal agonies paradoxically transmuted into a Romantic peepshow of turmoil that would comfort the comfortable, once his strangeness was assimilated, like a storm viewed from a warm safe room.

But the *Zeitgeist* had chosen a different incarnation, in Paul Cézanne. Georges Braque was to write in his notebook that 'Cézanne built, he did not construct'. Cézanne was with, but not quite of, the original Impressionist group. He became something of a solitary, and although his influence on his younger contemporaries was very great, it was exercised through his work – which was only occasionally on view – rather than by personal contact. When he came to Paris from Aix-en-Provence in 1861, and fell in with Pisarro, he began the total and lonely dedication to painting that was to occupy his life. His early work included dark scenes of violence – rape and murder – which were disturbing both in their subject matter and in their restless distorted forms, derived from El Greco, and his dalliance with the Impressionists was brief.

He said that he wanted to make of Impressionism 'something solid and durable, like the art of the museums' and, perhaps more revealingly, that he wanted 'to do Poussin over again from nature'. He was attempting a wholly new start for painting, using the new understanding of light, colour and perspective; drawing on the science of his age and on its enlarged knowledge of the arts of other cultures, to establish a modern canon. He succeeded, and proceeded with great patience and confidence to deconstruct the art of his day. He worked from nature by studying and analysing his 'motifs' intensely – figures, landscapes, still lifes – abstracting the geometry that underlay their structures and re-synthesizing a new geometry to replace it. He said that 'nature must be treated in terms of the cylinder, the sphere, the cone'. His method was to present a picture that was 'representational' in that it showed recognizable objects bearing a visual relationship to the objects from which he had worked; but to arrive at this by first reducing the scene to abstract forms and harmonies. Like Gauguin and van Gogh he showed a firm outline in the finished painting – and he was the most refined of draughtsmen – but the line divided areas or patches of colour on the canvas, and for him the drawing lay in the contrasts of light, shade and hue. To make a comparison with the early Italian Renaissance, he was a Florentine rather than a Venetian – a Botticelli – in his handling of line and colour. Poussin had acquired the skill of creating deep space in a landscape, not by the mechanical projections of optical (monocular) perspective but by modulations of the receding planes which he indicated by a close combination of drawing and juxtaposed colour masses. This spatial imbrication Cézanne learned to do too, as he shows in his repeated studies of Mont St Victoire and other Provencal landscapes. And he did it while at the same time respecting the surface of the canvas: a painting is not a window. This respect, eschewing illusionism and all attempts at trompe l'oeil, is of his time.

And, as the poet Rilke reported of a conversation with Mathilde Vollmoeller in the Cézanne room of the Paris *Salon d'Automne* of 1907:

> 'Here', she said, pointing to one spot, 'this is something he knew, and now he's saying it (a part of an apple); right next to it there's an empty space, because that was something he didn't know yet. He only made what he knew, nothing else.' 'What a good conscience he must have had', I said. 'Oh yes: he was happy, somewhere deep inside ...'

The *Salon d'Automne* at which Rilke made his observations had been founded in 1903 to display the new art. The dominant style at that time was *Art Nouveau*, or *Jugendstil*, a decorative vogue owing much to the Aesthetic Movement in England and to the teaching and practice of William Morris and his followers. Given to sinuous and wiry foliate ornaments, with swelling and attenuating curves, it bore a strange resemblance to the late La Tène art of pre-Roman Western Europe (then not very well known) – an expression, perhaps, of the desire to break with the classical tradition. *Jugendstil* found its main medium in the applied arts, and to some extent in architectural detail – the wrought iron trim at the entrances to the new underground railway stations, for example—and it imparted a certain sickly decorative character to some turn-of-the-century paintings. The strangely neurotic paintings of Edvard Munch have more than a hint of it, as have the very early works of Kandinsky and Braque and a great deal of the work of Klimt and of his fellow Viennese, the kitsch-pornographer Schiele.

But the judgment of Paris, which was to prevail for the early twentieth century, was to be given in favour of a different development, in spite of the *Art Nouveau* atmosphere that turn-of-the-century Paris shared with *Jugendstil* Vienna. A group of painters, including Henri Matisse, André Dérain and Maurice de Vlaminck, who exhibited in the *Salon d'Automne* of 1905 was referred to by critics as 'wild beasts', and as *les Fauves* they have since been known. The group developed, from the theories of the Impressionists and of Gauguin, a new style whose 'wildness' lay in the use of brilliant masses of colour and in daring distortions of form; but fauvism was less a movement or style than a rag-bag of extreme departures from what had been the nineteenth-century norm. This development and others were episodes in a bloodless revolution that was taking place, within the high bourgeois world, at the opening of the century. It was the culmination (beginning about 1860) of the bourgeois revolution itself, which gave birth to the twentieth-century world. Now the revolution was devouring its own children: scientism and Symbolism were both under attack. A new art and a new sensibility were fighting to gain the ascendant, with weapons of startling innovation, scandal, outrage, publicity. The entrpreneurial artists of the new styles employed the shock tactics of the advertizer to startle and intrigue the world. They were acutely aware of a renewed technological revolution. Their success has been abundant, as a glance at the prices their works have been fetching in art auctions will show. They fully imposed their vision on the twentieth century.

The annual *salons* in the various cultural centres were the artists' marketplaces; the struggle for space and conspicuous display on their crowded walls underlay many aesthetic controversies. One of the objects of 'Secession' everywhere was to provide 'exclusive' selections of approved work for the upper end of the market, separate from work that was inferior and often 'proletarian'. The victory of the secessionists was assured by the patronage of enlighened and cultivated businessmen, a new equivalent of the churches and courts of earlier times.

In the middle years of the nineteenth century, the demoralization of the upper classes in Europe, consequent on the French Revolution and on their own loosening grip on economic and political life, was reflected in their accommodation to bourgeois taste – at a time when the bourgeoisie lacked confidence in its own cultural formation, had no style of its own, tried to make do with pastiches of past styles, and looked pathetically to the aristocracy for cultural guidance. Each class corrupted the other in a general vulgarization. But by the closing years of the century, a high bourgeois culture was to emerge, whose values were quite distinct from the aristocratic values of early modern times. This culture now began to attack the debased art that the victory of European reaction in the early nineteenth century had produced. The secessionists of all kinds had the advantage of numerous allies within the royal and imperial bureaucracies, who shared their values at least to some extent, and the fall of the dynasties began. Their attack took strange and barbarous forms.

In his book on *Fin-de-Siècle Vienna* Carl E. Shorske wrote that:

> The modern mind has become indifferent to history, because history, conceived as a continuous nourishing tradition, has become useless to it.

In the nineteenth century, when, presumably, the 'modern mind' in question was formed, history was the dominant mode of thought. Comte, Darwin and Marx, for example, all presented historical processes as models of reality. Why, then did this 'modern mind' reject it?

The answer seems to be connected with the new technological revolution of the end of the century. Henry Ford, the impresario of the production line, is reported to have said that 'history is bunk!' Suddenly, the future seemed to be made available, not by the slow fruition of the past, but by all-purpose, all-solving gimmicks.

Filippo Tommaso Marinetti wrote in *Le Figaro* in 1909 that:

> It is in Italy that we shall launch this manifesto of destructive, incendiary violence which we shall use as the basis for Futurism, for Italy must be freed from its rotten cancerous tumour of professors, archaeologists, cicerones and antique dealers.

The 'Manifesto of Futurism', however, was itself at the mercy of history and was of its time, embodying nineteenth-century ideas. The rebellious son employs the father's language ('*Beauty* exists only in *struggle*), but develops it: 'a work that is not aggressive cannot be a masterpiece'; while at the same time falling back into the language of 'cicerones and antique dealers' ('*masterpiece*').

> We proclaim that the magnificence of the world has been enhanced by a new beauty: the beauty of speed. A racing car hung with enormous pipes like fire-spitting serpents ... a roaring racing car running like a machine gun is more beautiful than the *Winged Victory* of Samothrace. We want to sing of the man who holds the wheel, for its stem passes through the Earth, itself cast into the circuit of its orbit . . .

Manifestos proclaiming art as politics weren't new. The idea goes back at least as far as the utopian socialists of the early nineteenth century. What was new as the twentieth century began was the tone, a compound of arrogance and excitement associated with the sudden rush of new inventions and techniques, most of them in one way or another speeding the pace of life.

As artists, however, the Futurists created, not 'racing cars hung with enormous pipes', but symbols derived from an older technology, that of photography.

But the democracy of technology had not yet impinged on them, and what they failed to notice about the motor cars was that the real artists now were the engineers, not the painters. Photography, however, invented in the 1830s, made good sense in terms of their preoccupations and the possibilities open to them, because faster light-sensitive materials in the later nineteenth century made possible an analysis of motion that was beyond the capacity of the eye. As Hart Crane put it, in discussing the work of Alfred Stieglitz:

> Speed is at the bottom of it all, the hundredth of a second caught so precisely that motion is continued from the picture indefinitely: the moment made eternal.

It was the equivalent of time-lapse photography (a series of photographs of a moving object all exposed on the same plate, such as had been done by Edgerton and Mill in the late nineteenth century) that the painters chose to convey dynamism, as in Giacomo Balla's painting of 1912, *Dynamism of a Dog on a Leash*. This painting has other photographic attributes too: its point of view is that of a camera pointing obliquely downward, and it is framed by cropping: the trotting dog is singled out from its surroundings, and its owner's skirt appears only from below the knee, the rest being chopped away. Such framing, of course, also relates the picture to the Japanese prints that were so influential from the 1860s on (as in the 'camera angles' of Dégas); but for them too, the way had been prepared by early photographs.

While the Balla painting is analytic of movement, Umberto Boccioni's sculpture of 1913, *Unique Forms of Continuity in Space*, attempted synthesis. An inhuman but human-related figure, metallic and streamlined with shapes and attachments suggestive of a racing car, is depicted in full stride. The motion is represented by allowing the figure, especially the fast-moving legs, to occcupy the space through which they would pass in a brief moment of time – the equivalent of a blurred photograph of a moving object. At about the same time an artist less naively *engagé* was playing, both with these photographic suggestions and with the idea of the machine. Marcel Duchamp, in 1912, was producing the series of paintings which he entitled *Nude Descending a Staircase* and the painting entitled *The Bride*. Each *Nude Descending a Staircase* is a 'time-lapse' study of what looks like a metal robot descending from left to right; while *The Bride* depicts a machine with vaguely human attributes.

This was, almost, the end of the revolution in painting, although others were to go on throughout the century painting rectangles of canvas to go on walls. Not Duchamp.

> When Duchamp laid down his brushes and his glass palette after putting the finishing touches on *The Bride* in the autumn of 1912 (write Anne d'Harnoncourt and Walter Hopps) he had reached a crisis in his career. Bored with the very practice of wielding a brush and deeply dissatisfied

with painting as the only means to 'make' something, he not only decided to stop being a painter in the conventional sense but set his mind to work on the whole problem of the artist's engagement with the real world.

The challenge of the camera and the machine had moved to a rapid *reductio ad absurdam*. What was happening was that the artists felt, in some deeply troubling sense, redundant, far in reality from being the avant-garde of the risen people. Car manufacturers and advertizers were supplying the spiritual needs of the new masses of industrial society; art had not replaced religion; industrial artefacts had. The camera, besides being itself a machine and the centre of an expanding technology, was also intimately related to the new technologies of the turn of the century, and as its products multiplied and became a means of wider and wider communication and record, especially through newspapers and magazines, it both fostered new ways of seeing and provided new things to see. As Susan Sonntag put it,

> ... one of the perennial successes of photography has been its strategy of turning living beings into things, things into living beings. The peppers Weston photographed in 1929 and 1930 are voluptuous in a way that his female nudes rarely are. Both the nudes and the peppers are photographed for the play of forms – but the body is characteristically shown bent over upon itself, all the extremities cropped, with the flesh rendered as opaque as normal lighting and focus allow, thus decreasing its sensuality and heightening the abstractness of the body's form; the pepper is viewed close-up but in its entirety, the skin polished or oiled, and the result is a discovery of the erotic suggestiveness of an ostensibly neutral form, a heightening of its seeming palpability

But the artists still devoutly wished themselvs – and in large part thought themselves – to be at the storm centre of the cultural revolution that swept the West with the beginning of the twentieth century. They were attracted – mesmerized, almost—by the subversiveness of new popular art forms suddenly emerging at the time, such as jazz and ragtime. In particular, the interrelating group of writers, painters and musicians in Paris of the 1900s, avid for the new century, for the new world that was being born after the 'death of God', created a kind of anarchic culture of their own – a 'counter-establishment', to use the jargon of a later time. Several of the episodes of the time (such as the theft of Early-Iron-Age Iberian sculptures from the Louvre) are epiphanies of this anarchic transition during which their revolution was accomplished and the counter-establishment became the establishment (as it did after the Great War). Meanwhile, even those like Picasso who were hustling hardest in the commercial market-place, enjoyed, but only in appearance, the irresponsible privilege of solidarity with the dispossessed and could cry with the mob – from time to time – 'Down with everything!'

In 1907 Picasso, partly under the influence of Cézanne's work, partly by turning to certain simplicities of expression in Romanesque art and – increasingly – in the art of non-European cultures, was simplifying, geometricizing, stylizing in his representations: portraits, for example, against flat backgrounds, reduced to definitive planes and to the most basic forms, but given a very powerful presence by his mastery of draughtsmanship. Unable to abandon the studio, the model, the iconic image, he initiated a forlorn but immensely vigorous effort to save painting and keep it profitably in the centre of Western culture.

He worked, through a series of studies, on a painting to depict a scene in a brothel in Barcelona. Originally, tritely enough, it was to show a group of prostitutes, together with a sailor and a medical student. Death was to be represented by a skull: a Hogarthian scene. Death was to be more subtly present in the final version, spatially and ideologically transposed, of *Les Demoiselles d'Avignon*. The painting, as it ended up, resulted largely from a struggle (not wholly successful) to apply the principles of Cézanne's organization of pictorial space in a special context. It is, going far beyond Manet in that respect, a savage assault on the expectations formed by the viewer from a knowledge of preceding European art—partly because Picasso, clumsily but effectively, has made use of the Iberian heads from the Louvre and of African masks to distort and dramatize his portraits of the denizens of a threatening universe, and has applied fauvish colour within a classical composition. But he has also broken wilfully and drastically, with the traditions of painterly perspective and foreshortening and even simultaneity of vision. We are shown a dynamic group, whose position in space is slightly uncertain because we seem to see more aspects or facets of the figures than ordinary optics would permit; yet it *is* a space, within which we seem to move as we look at the picture. And this instability is augmented by an atmosphere of menace: we are looking through the gates of Hell and are enjoined to abandon hope.

This marked a point of departure, and, as was to emerge, a parting of the ways. In retrospect, *Les Demoiselles d'Avignon* can be seen as a spasm of conservatism, Picasso's wild throw of the dice to redeem painting. The poet Apollinaire, along with the art dealer Daniel-Henry Kahnweller, had introduced Georges Braque (a better painter) to Picasso, and Braque saw the final *Demoiselles* in Picasso's studio. He had himself already arrived at a very similar juncture, working as a *Fauve*. It was the year that Cézanne made a considerable impact on the younger painters: the great memorial exhibition of his paintings was put on in October in the *Salon d'Automne*. Studying Cézanne's handling of pictorial space through imbricated planes, and intrigued also by the powerful blocking of faceted volumes, counterpointed with voids, in African sculpture, Braque worked in 1908 at l'Estaque, near Marseille, on landscapes which, when they were refused for the *Salon d'Automne*, were described by Matisse as containing 'little cubes'. When they were shown in Paris in 1909, a reviewer described them as '*bizarreries cubiques*', which gave rise to the term 'Cubism'.

Picasso and Braque began a close collaboration in 1908, producing Cubist work, mainly still lifes, emphasizing form but restrained in colour – which tended to be warm but drab, with harmonies of monotones. The subjects were simple: mandolins, guitars and violins, jugs and pitchers. Cézanne's principle of abstracting basic underlying forms from the object was followed: cubes, spheres, cones; but Picasso and Braque didn't go on to re-synthesize the object. They gave their abstraction (through which the original object could be discerned as through a strangely refracting medium) an autonomy, which reinforced the autonomy of the picture; no longer a peephole in a camera obscura, or a *tranchet* of the visible world, but a complete entity in itself: its own space. Robert Rosenbloom described the effect:

> For a century that questioned the very concept of absolute truth, Cubism created an artistic language of intentional ambiguity. In front of a Cubist work of art, the spectator was to realize that no single interpretation of the fluctuating shapes, textures, spaces and objects could be complete in itself. And, in expressing this awareness of the paradoxical nature of reality and the need for describing it in multiple and even contradictory ways, Cubism offered a visual equivalent of a fundamental aspect of twentieth-century experience.

Cubism created its own visual space-time; for it was possible to see simultaneously the back as well as the front of the filleted and redistributed object. As the two artists pursued their exploration, it tended towards pure abstraction. At the point of their closest collaboration, which was also the point of maximum abstraction, Picasso and Braque were so much of a mind that they painted each other's paintings, as it were, as may be seen in a matched pair of pictures hanging in the Museum of Modern Art in New York. But this was a mere tangent: they were very different painters, and they soon diverged – neither, however, to follow the path of pure abstraction. Cubism meantime had a vogue and gave rise to a period of busy experiment, which, however, retained concrete visual 'subject-matter'. 'Subject-matter' involved the expression of ideas other than purely technical, formal or painterly ones. It engaged the artist, to some extent, with society, even if in a highly ambiguous way. Cubism was seen, both by the community of painters and by those outside that community, as relating in a number of ways to the rapid changes taking place in the world at large. It was soon identified with 'modern art', which, on the eve of the Great War, provoked strong reactions and powerful feelings, often of hostility tinged with fear: it made visible the disintegration of a civilization and seemed to mock its pretensions. This in turn fostered in the artists an unwarranted confidence in their own superior insight and wisdom.

In the Germanies, the artists' endeavour to go behind the surface of things was not directed mainly to formal and chromatic analysis, as in France, but to feelings – to 'expression'. A north German school of painting, which included Paula Modersohn and Emil Nolde, tried to discover in the subtleties of landscape, emotional elements corresponding to human needs and yearnings. Rilke wrote a book about this group: he was a friend of Modersohn's and a sympathizer with the painters' aims. Modersohn gradually stripped away what was 'extraneous', seeking to find a language in colour and form, drawing on the inspiration of landscapes to express what was human. There is in her work a touch of the pantheism of the early Romantics. Then she began to abandon landscape and to move towards reliance simply on the colours and the forms – a development parallel to that of Monet, Gauguin and Cézanne. She visited Paris in 1905 and 1906 and found the key to the revelations she sought, but before she returned for the Cézanne exhibition of 1907 she died, at the age of thirty-one. In spite of her youth and comaparatively small production, she led the way in German painting towards Expressionism.

In Dresden, the group calling itself the *Brücke* pursued a somewhat similar course, while in Munich the moving spirit was Vasily Kandinsky, an immigrant from Russia, who gathered around him the group that included Auguste Macke, Paul Klee and Franz Marc. In 1911, in the group's annual publication *Der Blaue Reiter*, he published *On the Spiritual in Art*. The path he was to follow, leading to pure abstraction, was connected with his rejection of positivism, and indeed of the intellect in itself to grasp truth. He took the Bergsonian view that only *intuition* (the vision of the artist) could perceive reality. Art must be dematerialized in order to express the spirit. In this he was one of a number, on whom Peter Gay, in his *Art and Act*, commented:

> It is simply a fact that in the late nineteenth and early twentieth century many apostles of modernism, though admirers of some aspects of modernity, in general loathed the modern world. And many of them – Vasily Kandinsky and Franz Marc, Victor Hugo and William Butler Yeats – embraced esoteric doctrines and practised spiritualistic rituals that were as hostile to existing Christian sects as they were to contemporary positivism. In the Middle Ages number mysticism had been the superstition of the learned; now, in the time of Mondrian, theosophy became the superstition of the avant-garde.

Kandinsky went on to pursue what he called, in a letter to the composer Schoenberg in 1911:

> the anti-geometric, anti-logical way ... of 'dissonances in *art*', in painting, therefore, just as much as in music. And 'today's' dissonance in painting and music is merely the consonance of 'tomorrow.'

He was by now painting purely abstract compositions in which all vestige of the visual world of forms of things had been abandoned.

He was not quite alone, although he led the way, going ahead along an indicated path where Picasso, Braque and others had veered off. But the Dutch painter, Piet Mondrian, went further. An obsessive, very private, person, he was also a mystic, believing in the power of spirit over matter, and hostile to raw nature, favouring instead the artefact, the work of human hands and the abstracting power of the human mind. In his painting he followed a slow but steady course of simplification, from naturalism through Impressionism to work influenced by Cubism. Stranded by the War in the neutral Netherlands in 1914, he went on to develop the abstract style which he himself was to name 'neo-plasticism'. In its mature form, by the 1920s, this was puritanical in form and austerely restrained in its use of colour: characteristically squares or rectangles of pure primary colours and plain white, separated by narrow bands of black. The paintings immediately suggest the asceticism of an architecture reduced to its most basic elements and expressing a withdrawal from all contamination of its intellectualized structures by the forms of nature. And in 1917 he joined with architects (including J.J.P. Oud) as well as painters and sculptors, in founding the magazine *De Stijl*. They admired the American architect Frank Lloyd Wright who was then enjoying his first vogue (to be followed after a long interval by a second). Vincent Scully, Jr., wrote of them that

> ... it was clearly through *De Stijl* that the International Style of the twenties found its characteristic shapes. The process, whatever it also owes to both Cubism and Futurism, can be traced almost step by step from the illustrations of Wright's work in Wasmuth ...

Meantime, in neutral Switzerland, a group of artists was engaged in a flight from their time (to borrow the title, *Die Flucht aus der Zeit*, which one of their number, Hugo Ball, gave to his published diary). They were young men and women for whom the war being waged all around their refuge was madness. Perhaps more than any others of their time they have stamped their mark on the Western culture of the late twentieth century.

They professed to reject, in extreme and zany ways, the bourgeois culture which they found responsible for the war madness. It was Ball who gave the group its focus, and one of its members, Hans Richter, wrote of him:

> It is impossible to understand Dada without understanding the state of mental tension in which it grew up, and without following the mental and physical footsteps of this remarkable sceptic ... On 1 February 1916, Ball founded the Cabaret Voltaire. He had come to an arrangement with Herr Ephraim, the owner of the Melerei, a bar in Niederdorf, a slightly disreputable quarter of the highly reputable town of Zürich. He promised Herr Ephraim that he would increase his sales of beer, sausages and rolls by means of a literary cabaret.

The Cabaret Voltaire, where these anarchic spirits spent their rowdy nights, was at No. 1 Spiegelgasse (Mirror Street). In No. 12 lived Lenin, exiled from Russia, who regularly met with his fellow revolutionaries, Radek, Axelrod and Zinoviev, at quieter locations in Zürich. The narrow alley was indeed a mirror – which reflected the world from an unusual, but significant, angle. The group at the Cabaret included the Germans Hugo Ball, Emmy Hennings, Hans Richter and Richard Huelsenbeck, the Alsatian Hans Arp, and the Romanians Marcel Janco and Tristan Tzara. There were poetry recitals: readings of the work of French, German, Russian and Swiss poets, including Kandinsky and Max Jacob. Different kinds of music were played. Delaunay's and other pictures were exhibited. The group composed and published.

The term 'Dada' was coined in Zürich to describe the movement, which had something of the atmosphere of Jarry's circle in Paris at the beginning of the century, much of the provocative attitude of the Futurists, much of the deadpan practical joking of Duchamp's art. The Cabaret performers enjoyed presenting jazz (which they termed '*Negermusik*'), sensing its subversive quality. They practised nonsense verse that went beyond Lewis Carroll and Edward Lear:

> This is how flat the world is
> The bladder of the swine
> Vermilion and cinnabar
> Cru cru cru
> The great art of the spirit
> Theosophia pneumatica
> poeme brutiste performed the first time by
> Richard Huelsenbeck dada
> or if you want to, the other way around
> birribumbirribum the ox runs down the circulum
> Voila here are the engineers with their assignment
> Light mines to throw in a still crude stat
> 7,6 cm Chaceur
> and the Soda calc, not to forget the 98/100%
> Here is the beagle damo birridamo holla do funga qualla di mango
> damal da dai umbala damo
> brrs pffl and the beginning
> Abrr Kpppl encore commencer and again
> the beginning ...

With the end of the War Dada spread to other centres and engaged quite a number of artists who were attempting to make sense – or reasonable nonsense – of what had just happened in Europe. Dada produced a number of manifestos, and one of them, Tzara's of 1918, had its effect in Paris in 1920, when Tzara arrived there and set up, with André Breton, Francis Picabia, Louis Aragon and others, the *Litterature* group. In Cologne in 1919, Johannes Bargeld, Max Ernst and Arp caused political upheaval with a Dadaist performance. In Berlin, Huelsenbeck arrived from Switzerland in 1917, to find a hungry population facing defeat in war, far removed from the complacency of neutral Zürich. He helped found a

Club Dada, whose membership included Hannah Hoch, Johannes Baader and George Grosz. The Berlin Dadaists became involved in the brief communist occupation of Berlin (although the communists soon disowned them); they opposed the Weimar Republic, and to the property-owners they were Bolsheviks.

In fact at this stage they were virtually nihilists, against everything, each Dadaist group condemning other Dadaists; condemning also those (such as Apollinaire) who had led the way to their position; mortally opposed to other ways of showing revulsion from the existing social world (Expressionism, for example). Their manifestos expressed the nihilistic hatred that was already taking shape in numerous European political movements after the War:

> TO THE PUBLIC
> Before going down among you to pull out your decaying teeth, your running ears,
> your tongues full of sores,
> Before opening your cholera-infested belly and taking out for use as fertilizer your too fatted liver, your ignoble spleen and your diabetic kidneys,
> Before tearing out your ugly sexual organ, incontinent and slimy ...
> Before all that,
> We shall take a big antiseptic bath
> And we warn you
> We are murderers.

Dadaism in this semipolitical form, running to unrestrained extremes of expression and behaviour, extremes that gave voice to the extraordinary tensions generated by the War and by the social systems that produced the War, lasted just a few years. It gave rise, however, to the art movement known as Surrealism (taking Apollinaire's term), which was initiated, or announced, by Breton in 1922. Surrealism took over, to manipulate for its own purposes, the teachings of Freud. Breton thought that 'a certain psychic automatism which corresponds quite well to the state of dream' might be produced by hypnotic sleep, and the group who originated Surrealism—including Breton, Louis Aragon and Max Ernst—experimented with individual and group hypnosis. The First Surrealist Manifesto (1924) defined, as in a dictionary, what they were about:

> SURREALISM, noun. Pure psychic automatism by which it is intended to express, either verbally or in writing, the true function of thought. Thought dictated in the absence of all control by reason, and outside all aesthetic or moral preoccupations.

These nihilistic reactions against the world that had produced Verdun, the Somme and Passchendaele, were to have an enduring effect in the coming years. Surrealism, strangely enough, was to prove to be the form of modern art that best communicated – after a due interval of familiarization – with the general public, and it backs much of present-day public culture, from television and magazine advertisements to pop videos. 'Pure psychic automatism by which it is intended to express, either verbally or in writing, the true function of thought. Thought dictated in the absence of all control exerted by reason, and outside all aesthetic or moral preoccupations.' This could serve as an exposition of the underlying philosophy of the mass movement of Nazism and as an account of much that was to happen in Europe in the 1930s and 1940s. As Hitler wrote in *Mein Kampf*:

> In the field of propaganda particularly one must never be guided by aestheticists or *blasé* persons: not by the first, because otherwise propaganda's form and expression would after a short time, instead of being suitable for the masses, only have attraction for literary tea parties; but against the second one ought to guard oneself carefully for the reason that their shortage of fresh sentiments of their own is always looking for new stimulants ...
>
> All advertizing, whether it lies in the field of business or of politics, will carry success by continuity and regular uniformity of application.

The reaction against the nineteenth century took other forms, most notably, in German Europe, through 'Expressionism', which derived, at a remove, from Romanticism. Oskar Kokoschka's work in particular illustrates the history of the early twentieth century in Central Europe. He entered the Vienna School of Applied Art in 1904 and was engaged for a while by *Jugendstil*, under the influence of Klimt. From the beginning he brought to his painting an intensity of vision that is reminiscent of Van Gogh. An increasingly nervous sketchiness characterized both his drawing and his colour as his very personal style developed. 'Expression' was all. As Werner Haftmann put it:

> This freedom to pour swarms of images on canvas, to capture trance-like states in an objective, figurative scenario, to achieve self-representation in painting – this was Kokoschka's contribution to German Expressionism.

A contribution too, it might be noted, to every talentless and undisciplined student's self-deception, and to the consequent outpouring of worthless art-school artefacts and even worse verse.

A view of Kokoschka's work as a whole, through a long life (such as was available through the very extensive exhibition put on some years ago in the Tate Gallery), reveals an anguished person, unhappy partly for personal, partly for public, reasons. The Great War caused him something of a breakdown, and in Dresden at its end he was known as 'mad Kokoschka'. He had a dressmaker of that city fashion for him a life-size doll to which he could make love; his love, however, was unrequited and left him as unhappy as before. He remained a figurative or representative painter, but in a frenzied sketchy manner, with scribbled brushwork and intense colours drawing an emotional meaning from landscape or portrait partly by means of a furious impasto which gives us, not so much a view of Prague or the sense of 'the philosopher: Thomas Garrick Masaryk' as an insight into the turbulent emotions of the painter. He spent his life in flight from those aspects of the twentieth century that, for three generations, were to blight life in Central Europe.

But Expressionism was merely one direction in the centrifugal escape from the past that Western painting registered from about 1860 to about 1930. By the time Hitler came to power in Germany, the energy of that explosion had been spent. The painters, Braque, Picasso, Dali, Mondrian, Kokoschka, and many others, went on marking time, each in his own way, until they died off one by one. New generations of artists found that 'publicize or perish' was the recipe for making a living, and, in New York in particular, during and after the Second World War, an entrepreneurial group of impresario-critics managed an art business whose most valued and reliable markets were the great multi-national corporations emerging as arbiters of the world's taste in those years, and the media of popular culture, from cinema and glossy magazines to television and rock videos. The painting, that framed rectangle of canvas hanging on the wall, which had been the symbol of the cultivated mind in the West for half a millennium, faded away like the Cheshire cat around its grin. A walk along the American galleries of the Museum of Modern Art in New York reveals the progress: white brush strokes on canvas; 'Abstract painting, red' (Reinhardt, 1952: darker squares of red on lighter); 'Ornament III' (Newman: a maroon canves with an uneven central vertical red stripe); 'American Flag' (Johns, 1954). Finally there are huge canvases, each painted evenly all over in one colour and framed to provide opaque coloured stops to the spaces of multi-storey atriums in great Post-Modern corporate buildings. And, by the 1990s, painting had all but disappeared from the repertoire of the artists. The painters had vanished into their elusive space, and it had vanished with them.

12

The Great War

In the last third of the nineteenth century, a drumbeat of violence sounded in the consciousness of the West, with a throb at first subdued but coming gradually to a crescendo. The rulers of the world, one by one, in their hearts and in their thoughts, had abandoned the principle of order in favour of the principle of struggle. Darwin, Marx, Wagner, Nietzsche, Freud and a hundred other prophets, great and small, offered variants of the same message. The world was not governed by reason, but by Will, energy, force. God's blessing was manifest in power.

Bismarck's wars in Europe and the American Civil War across the Atlantic settled certain matters. Germany had become the chief power in Europe. The American Union was to continue and slavery was abolished. But a great deal remained unresolved. Whole peoples nourished thoughts of revenge. And whole classes. The Paris Commune, set up after the Prussian defeat of the French, itself committed many atrocities, but when Paris was re-taken in May 1891 by the founders of the Third Republic, led by Adolphe Thiers, they took vengeance on the Communards in a way that was to divide the French bitterly for a century. They slaughtered something of the order of 25,000 people in the city, and in London *The Times* commented on 1 June:

> The crimes of the Insurgents have surpassed the most gloomy forebodings of what would be accomplished under the Red Flag ... But its seems as if we were to forget the work of these maddened savages in the spectacle of the vengeance wreaked upon them. The wholesale executions inflicted by the Versailles soldiery, the glee, the ribaldry of the 'Party of Order', sicken the soul.

And if the principle of 'struggle' was to divide class from class, it also seemed to many that it was the principle dividing 'race' from 'race.' God, with infinite wisdom and skill, as the Revd Josiah Strong of Cincinnati wrote in 1885, was training the Anglo-Saxon race for an hour sure to come. 'Teutonic race' or 'Caucasian race', or half-a-dozen variants on these, might be substituted according to the situation and background of the prophet.

The plenitude of material goods pouring out of the ever more numerous fac-

Previously unpublished

tories was joined, as the century drew to a close, by an abundance of exotic articles and commodities flooding in from new colonies. A series of great industrial and colonial exhibitions, in Europe and America, spanned the years from 1851 to 1914, displaying to the humble workers of the West the products of their labour and the spoils of conquest. In the 1870s and 1880s the new department stores began to change the patterns of commerce, again, among other things, introducing the exotic products of 'the colonies' to wider and wider markets. In the last decade of the nineteenth century a new popular press, throughout the West, began to replace the improving texts by which a section of the working population had tried to educate itself. New sensational stories, some purporting to be news of the day, ranged from fanciful adventures to scandal and pornography. The 'yellow press' never neglected to preach the lesson taught by an English ditty of the time of the Congress of Berlin in 1878:

> We don't want to fight, but by Jingo if we do,
> We've got the ships, we've got the men, we've got the money too!

Conflict, implicit or explicit, became a feature both of the internal and of the external affairs of all the nations. The form and nature of the conflict varied. The United States of America continued to be 'united states' (after a fashion) at the end of a grim and premonitory war that had begun four years earlier in a land that was turbulent but still largely adjusted to the conditions of peace. The war went on to engage the passions, the energies, the economies, the industrial and domestic resources of whole populations. It saw an almost casual overruling of the provisions of the Constitution that was ostensibly the sacred text at issue, and it witnessed the stubborn pounding of bullets and cannon-balls into flesh and bone in battle after battle: a democratic war. And, shortly after its end, the actor John Wilkes Booth, in Ford's Theatre in Washington, shot dead the melancholy and victorious President and cried, '*Sic semper tyrannus!*'

'*Sic semper tyrannus!*' was to resound, in one version or another, for the next fifty years. The social order was fragile.

There were movements for radical social change in the last quarter of the century, and they may be divided into three broad categories: meliorists or gradualists who believed that the lot of the workers could be improved by trade-union action within the existing political structures and that power could ultimately be obtained, or at least shared, without violent revolution; Marxists and others who believed that the proletariat, in the most industrialized countries, could be led through political awareness towards revolution – the seizure of power from the bourgeois State; and the radical revolutionaries who held that violent action, here and now, could destroy the existing State; and that then the workers would rise and take power.

Within the last category the most conspicous group was the Anarchists. They were by no means a unified group, since they eschewed organization: they wished to do away with all governments, hierarchies and power structures. They were most effective, not in the countries advanced in industrialization, but on the fringes of the industrialized world; and a minority among them tended to make a virtue of this necessity and to argue that acts of spectacular and exemplary violence in the more backward nations would spark off revolts leading to the collapse of the State, the end of government and the freedom of all. In the sixties, Michael Bakunin, and later his successors, believed that the correctly directed act of terror, striking like a lightning bolt, could bring down the structures of oppression. It should be noted that existing governments shared with the anarchists this faith in the virtues of violence; they differed widely from the Anarchists, however, in their command of the means of violence. Bakunin himself dashed from one European revolutionary occasion to another, until the experience of the terror unleashed by the bourgeoisie on the defeated Paris Communards in 1871 seems to have taught even him the advantage enjoyed by the State in any competition in frightfulness.

But a handful of conspiratorial and violent anarchists, nihilists and other extreme opponents of the existing régimes contrived to give a colour of menace to the whole age, and to force even the most powerful and autocratic rulers to live with the knowledge that they were in daily and hourly danger of personal destruction. In 1878 a young woman called Vera Zasulich attempted to kill the St Petersburg police chief by shooting him, point blank. In 1880, by being delayed on his way to dine, the Tsar was saved from an immensely destructive explosion in the Winter Palace in St Petersburg. In 1881 a group of conspirators failed to kill him with a land-mine, but – due to the determined resolve of another young woman, Sophia Perovskaya – a back-up plan was put into effect, and Alexander II and some bystanders were killed by two bombs.

Tiny numbers were involved in these conspiracies, but they gave the dominant classes the sense of a dangerous underworld whose denizens were ever a threat to the social order. This abyss was to be explored by Dostoevsky: Peter Verkhovensky, in *The Possessed*, shows us the face of the extreme in nihilism. Turgenev and, in a different way, Tolstoy, also examined the political manifestations of 'the spirit that denies'. The anarchist with the bomb became one of the archetypes or mythic figures of the age.

With some remissions, assassinations continued, like a progressive disease of the ruling classes. Dynamite went off in London, bombs in Barcelona and Paris. The president of France, Sadi Carnot, was stabbed to death by an Italian anarchist in Lyon in 1894. In 1897 another anarchist killed Antonio Canovas, prime minister of Spain. Yet another Italian in 1898 killed the Empress Elizabeth of Austria in Geneva. An Italian-American from New Jersey shot and killed King Umberto of Italy in Monza in 1900, and a Polish-American anarchist, inspired by this act, shot President McKinley dead in 1901.

A bomb was thrown at King Alfonso of Spain on his wedding day in 1906, and in 1912 a second Spanish premier, José Canalejas, was assassinated by an anarchist. Others besides anarchists became involved. In Russia a group led by Alexander Ulyanov was unsuccessful in an attempt on the life of the Tsar Alexander III: the conspirators were hanged. Ulyanov's brother, a student embarking on a career, found that as the kin of a would-be regicide he had lost all hope of regular advancement. He took the *nom-de-guerre* 'Lenin' and devoted his life, as a Marxist, to revolution. The series of assassinations continued in Russia, including two ministers of the interior, Sipyagin in 1903 and Plehve in 1904, and in 1911 the prime minister, Stolypin. In June 1914 a Serbian nationalist group assassinated the Archduke Ferdinand, heir apparent of the Austro-Hungarian empire, who was visiting Sarajevo.

Meanwhile the public show of the State was chiefly military. Soldiers with shining swords and bayonets, brilliant uniforms and waving plumes, paraded along the boulevards of the cities. Flags had become sacred objects that, on solemn festivals, were shown in masses of colour, covering the facades of whole streets, rippling in the breeze to generate in the crowds the excitement of belonging, of being the devoted and dedicated members of the Nation, all together against the alien world beyond the sacred frontiers.

After 1871 the West was internally at peace for a while, and the achievements of modern Western civilization were constantly lauded; but it maintained a culture of War. It was, both in Europe and in America at this time, a world of the very rich, conspicuous in their opulence, luxury and wastefulness, and of the very poor, wretched in their hundreds of thousands in slums and sweatshops. There was no love between the rich and the poor, but fear and hatred. But there was also between them the middle class, of functionaries and clerks, shopkeepers and physicians, fearful of the disruptive and destructive possibilities inherent in that hatred. For the members of that class, the preservation of the State was essential, and the warlike cult of the State was their special care.

Which way would the masses turn? No one, at the beginning of the twentieth century, could be quite sure. Would they rally to the Nation? Or would they turn on the ruling classes?

Wars external to the West continued. Among the powers the most consistently belligerent had been Great Britain, which had fought the French (and others) intermittently throughout the eighteenth century; had engaged in the long war against Napoleon that ended in 1815; had gone on to an almost continuous series of colonial wars, against Gurkhas, Mahrattas, Ashanti, Bengalis, Afghans, Zulu, Sudanese and a host of others throughout the nineteenth century; had twice bombarded its way into China in support of drug merchants bringing in opium and had then taken part in the international invasion of China at the turn of the century; had fought the Russians in the Crimea in the middle of the century and the Boers in South Africa at its end, and early in the new century had massacred Tibetans defending their mountains. All this with a comparatively small regular army and without conscription. British grand strategy, such as it was, depended on the powerful navy, which for a long time could descend, literally from the blue, in any part of the earth, to uphold British world-wide commercial and imperial interests. By the end of the century, however, Britain was being passed out by other nations in terms of capacity to produce the materials

needed for modern large-scale warfare and world power. The British successfully courted the greatest emerging power, the United States of America. Secretary of State Hay, in the issuance of the 'Open Door' notes on China at the turn
of the century, registered the new diplomatic fact, that America was stepping in
to maintain British liberal economic interests, jointly with its own, throughout
the world. The object was to open the whole world to the trade and investment of
the richest nations.

But the driving forces of capitalism were by no means the only, or the chief,
ones at play. Competition – 'struggle' – took other forms. The countries comparatively new to industrialization had not yielded State power to liberal
bourgeois ideas to the same extent as had Britain, France and the United States.
The dynastic rulers went along with the rôle of competitive entrepreneur that
had been offered to them, but largely from a desire for power rather than money.
And each state tried to protect its frontiers by expanding its power beyond them.
The rulers of Austria, trying to stamp out brush-fires of Slav nationalisms, endeavoured to extend their control south-eastward through the Balkans. But the
rulers of Russia, attempting in turn to contain the extravagances of Pan-Slavism,
had offered their protection to the Balkan Slavs.

The murder of Archduke Ferdinand in Serbia proved to be the occasion for
that adjustment of the balance of power in Europe that many had desired. Austria
made impossible demands on Serbia, but, when the Serbs all but acquiesced,
refused to accept the surrender. Meantime, the German empire had offered support to Austria; Russia supported Serbia.

The moment long expected had come. Mobilization now became the concern
of the governments. The deadly timetables of call-up and deployment, based on
the scheduling of trains and the synchronizing of postal, military, railway and
supply systems in operations lasting days and weeks, meant that mobilization,
once begun, could neither be readily undone nor, worse, undertaken anew for a
long time. But, should war really be imminent, the countries quickest to mobilize would have great and possibly decisive advantage. Every army wanted to
mobilize first. Every army that mobilized was an urgent threat forcing another
army to mobilize. The tyranny of timetables helped to impel the European powers, within weeks, into a general war.

All were prepared for war: it had been in the air for years. It was expected, like
a thunderstorm, to clear the air. The European conflicts of forty or fifty years
earlier had been short and decisive. Few took heed of the long-drawn-out American struggle of 1861–5, which had settled down into stubborn trench warfare
and the strategy of attrition.

The events of July and August 1914 shed a lurid light on the temper of Europe. A peace movement had been making a show for a decade and a half, attempting to stave off the conflict everyone expected, by calling on people not to
take part in it. All over the West, socialists of all shades had been telling the
workers not to go out to kill their fellow workers of other nationalities on behalf
of 'capitalist' competition. Nor was war of any obvious advantage to the capital-

ists (although it would offer its pickings); yet, through their newspapers and through government propaganda, they supported the nationalists who extolled 'my country, right or wrong'. And, when war was declared, pacifists, socialists, feminists, capitalists, conservatives, liberals and radicals, with near unanimity came to the same conclusion: the cause was sacred – of this state or that, to whichever the victory-seeker chanced to belong.

There was relief from tension: *alea jacta est*. A cross-section of articulate opinion in 1914 shows that the culture of war was already formed: what happened was a welcome retreat from the unreality of peace to the reality of human existence: the survival of the fittest – killing and being killed.

> Now God be thanked who has matched us with His Hour,
> And caught our youth, and wakened us from sleeping.

So wrote Rupert Brooke in England in 1914. He was echoed in Germany, in France, in Austria, in Russia. Crowds cheered in the streets of the capitals as the soldiers, regular and conscript, marched to the railway stations where the trains waited to take them like cattle to slaughter. And slaughter there quickly was.

The war began with the quarrel between Austria-Hungary and Serbia. Russia supported Serbia. Germany supported Austria. France came in with Russia. Great Britain vacillated for a while but declared war when Germany invaded Belgium. In due course, Turkey, Italy, China, Japan and the United States of America, as well as smaller powers, were to be involved.

The German plan was to hold the French along the southern part of Germany's western front while launching a ferocious attack on the northern part of the frontier, through Belgium (whose neutrality was to be ignored). The northern armies would swing south behind the shattered left of the French line, capture Paris and defeat the French decisively, before the Russians – whose mobilization was slow – had fully mustered their forces. Then the main German armies would entrain for the east, to defeat the Russians.

There was behind this strategy – and behind many of the plans made to counter it – a moral, political and social blindness induced by fantasies of outright victory. The end was absolute: almost all means were justified. The media of mass communication now available darkened understanding, as rationality, moderation and truth were sacrificed to the end of absolute victory. Kipling summed it up:

> Once more we hear the word
> That sickened earth of old:–
> 'No law except the Sword
> Unsheathed and uncontrolled.'

An atmosphere of hatred was created among the populations such as had darkened the American air at the onset of the great American Civil War. It was not just that the soldiers had to nerve themselves for battle. Whole populations had to see the opposed populations as other than human. Lies and exaggerations were employed to create throughout civilized nations the mentality of lynch mobs. *Raison d'état* and *Realpolitik* were carried far beyond Machiavellian cold calculation to demand fervour and fanaticism as in the service of a religion.

The soldier going to kill was persuaded that his own death, should it occur, would be martyrdom, bearing witness to the rightness of his cause; his blood, should it be spilled, would be the seed of his motherland's future. Charles Hamilton Sorley was one among many who saw the moment as a mystery of religion:

> Earth that blossomed and was glad
> 'Neath the cross that Christ had,
> Shall rejoice and blossom too
> When the bullet reaches you.
> Wherefore, men marching
> On the road to death, sing!

A furious impatience to accomplish the victory and bring the war quickly to a decisive end governed the actions of the armies. The autumn of 1914 saw immense bloodshed and a callous contempt for the usages of civility. Permanent Belgian neutrality, for example, had been solemnly guaranteed in 1839 by the ministers of England, France, Russia, Austria and Prussia in one of the several nineteenth-century endeavours to secure a rational and peaceful international order within Europe. In 1914, the German chancellor, Bethmann-Hollweg, insisted that England must bear the blame for the fearful consequences that would follow should the British insist on German withdrawal from Belgium – 'all for just a word – "neutrality" – just for a scrap of paper'. Neither the chancellor nor the distressed British ambassador to whom he spoke noticed at the time the terrible implications of that phrase, 'just for a scrap of paper'.

The Belgians defended their neutrality and the Germans – who had not expected this – responded with barbaric behaviour to crush the effrontery of weakness resisting might. In a war of movement they almost reached Paris, but were then driven back towards the frontiers again. Meantime the Russians lost a whole army to the Germans in a six-day battle near Tannenberg, and destroyed an Austrian army in a sixteen-day campaign that culminated in the battle of Lemberg. By the end of 1914 immense numbers of men had been killed and maimed on the battlefields, immense numbers of prisoners taken, immense quantities of matériel consumed or destroyed, immense damage done to towns and farms. And the war was just beginning.

On Germany's western front the armies bogged down in stalemate, but in the east the Russians, Germans and Austrians advanced and retreated, while in the south, the Italians, now in the war on the Allied side, attacked in 1915. In that year two attempts were made to circumvent the European stalemate and win the war by other means. The Germans begn unrestricted warfare at sea, among other things sinking the liner *Lusitania* off the Irish coast. The Allies aimed a blow at

Germany's allies, the Turks, and attempted landings at the Dardanelles which were bloodily defeated.

In 1916 and 1917 the generals on both sides tried to overwhelm the enemy on the European fronts by mounting tremendous bombardments and then sending huge masses of men against entrenched machine guns and cannon. In destroyed landscapes, desolate wildernesses of splintered trees, barbed wire, shellholes and polluted mud, men week after week scrambled out of the trenches in which they lived to try to kill men in the opposite trenches. They died by the thousand, by the hundred thousand, by the million. They accomplished nothing. The governments refused to negotiate a peace. It was to be victory or nothing.

The French army mutinied along the line in 1917 but the mutinies were put down by summary executions. The British had, from the beginning, been shooting those of their own soldiers who cracked under the strain. The Russian mass armies, having endured extraordinary sufferings and privations, began to drift homeward in 1917 after the overthrow of the Tsar. When the Bolsheviks seized power late in that year, Russia eventually made a separate peace and dropped out of the war. At sea there was slaughter in the war of submarines against merchant ships. The heavy warships of Germany and Britain fought one another to a standstill, with great loss, off Jutland in 1916. In 1917 the United States entered the war against Germany, but before trained American troops became fully effective on the Western Front, the German armies in 1918 mounted a last great effort, broke through the elongated killing grounds of the trenches in northern France and Flanders, and drove on Paris again. This offensive collapsed in defeat and they were driven back once more as the Americans began arriving in decisive numbers. An armistice came into effect at eleven o'clock on the morning of the eleventh of November 1918, and the guns fell silent after more than four years.

It would be very difficult to exaggerate the importance of the Great War for the way European nations were to develop in the twentieth century. Its effects on the United States of America, distant and isolated from the breakdown of civilization, were comparatively slight. On the other hand, the Americans had had a foretaste of modern war two generations earlier and had experienced the profound changes that ensued in their society. The Great War, unlike 'World War Two', and in spite of the involvement of China, Japan, Australia, New Zealand, South Africa, Canada, the United States and other non-European nations, was essentially and centrally a European conflict – resembling therefore a civil war in many respects. The bourgeois-liberal states (as they then were), France and Britain, fought the aristocratic-bourgeois states, Germany and Austria-Hungary, which were aided by primitively autocratic Turkey. Japan supported the Allies merely as a hyaena circling the battlefield, and China's subservient impotence is irrelevant to these matters. Russia, the industrializing autocracy without an effective middle class, is the oddity: the Western powers' disliked but needed ally, with an endless supply of cannon-fodder.

It is this oddity, however, that defines in some ways what happened in that fearful decade between 1910 and 1920. The Western European order, such as it was, fell apart, not to be adequately restored. 'Progress' came to a sudden stop. The armistice of 1918, although it was to be followed in 1919 by peace settlements that ratified victory over Germany, was to last uneasily only for twenty years. The Russian, German, Austrian and Turkish empires collapsed and were replaced by new systems, largely makeshift. The Russian collapse, early in 1917, was followed by a revolution that brought communists to power and took Russia early out of the war, and effectively for many years out of the European polity. Revolts and disorders marked the end of the war throughout Central and Eastern Europe, and the Austrian and Turkish empires were broken up into unstable and multi-ethnic successor states, on a crude and imprecise principle of 'self-determination'.

Germany lost territory but remained a large intact state, an unstable liberal republic whose ruined, half-starving and embittered people believed themselves betrayed. France, in spite of its recovery of the lost provinces of Alsace and Lorraine, remained depressed and demoralized from its enormous losses in young men and from the vast damage that had been done to the country. The United Kingdom broke up with the creation of an independent Irish Free State. Britain lost a whole generation of its governing class and suffered also a huge loss in fortune and in its capacity to be a great power – although the illusion of power persisted. Germany, although defeated and humiliated, paradoxically achieved one of its war aims. The collapse of the old European order left it with the potential to be without doubt the most powerful state on the Continent.

The summer of 1914, before the guns spoke, had been a balmy one, and after the war it became a symbolic synecdoche for Western Europeans. 'The golden summer of 1914' stood for the golden age before everything changed – for the late nineteenth century when, by and large, there was peace within most of Europe, frontiers were open, industry was expanding, health and literacy were improving, and rudimentary social service arrangements were beginning here and there to ease the lot of the poor. The view, of course, was idealized. It gave expression to a great and widespread sense of loss; and what had been lost was a kind of innocence, a sense of security, superiority and confidence which Europeans had enjoyed. Previously, war had happened (mostly) elsewhere, and had been approved of on the whole, almost as sport was approved of, as a healthy form of necessary competition, in which 'valour', 'gallantry' and 'nobility' could be displayed by young men.

By 1916, if not before, all that had changed forever and become a mockery – first of all to the men in the trenches, whether, like Ivan Goll, they expressed themselves in German, or, like Wilfred Owen, in English:

> Before sticking your bayonet into his groin, did not one of you see
> the Christ-like look of his opponent, did not one of you notice
> that the man over there had a kingly heart full of love?
> Did not one of you believe in his own and mankind's conscience?
> You brothers, fellow-men! Oh, you heroes!

I am the enemy you killed, my friend.
I knew you in this dark: for so you frowned
Yesterday through me as you jabbed and killed.
I parried, but my hands were loath and cold.
Let us sleep now ...

Voices of the literate and the articulate. The anonymous voice of the trenches, sardonic and without more illusion, had its own comment:

The bells of hell go ting-a-ling-a-ling
For you but not for me;
And the little devils how they sing-a-ling-a-ling
For you but not for me.
O Death where is thy sting-a-ling-a-ling,
O Grave, thy victor-ee?
The bells of hell go ting-a-ling-a-ling
For you but not for me.

13

A Terrible Beauty is Born

Fifty-nine years ago Patrick Pearse surrendered his sword (it is interesting that he was wearing one) to General Lowe. It was half-past two on a Saturday afternoon, one hundred and twenty-two and a half hours since the Volunteers had entered the GPO in Dublin.

What happened in those five days is clear enough. It is possible to reconstruct with fair accuracy, and almost minute by minute, the events that followed the seizure of buildings in different parts of Dublin and the reading of the Proclamation of the Republic.

The events were bloody: it is still with some sense of shock that one re-reads the accounts of the violence that exploded suddenly in the sunny streets in a week of what was later colloquially known in Dublin as 'rebellion weather'. The British, initially surprised, reacted somewhat slowly and fumblingly, but as they brought the weight of their numbers and their guns to bear, their military success was inevitable. Their failures were political, and the chief one was being surprised, so that the insurgents could hold Dublin for a week. As Mr Harold Wilson reminded us some years ago, a week is a long time in politics. In Irish politics there can hardly have been a longer week, in this sense, than that of Easter 1916.

If there is little dispute about the main facts, there is much dispute about how the achievement of that week is to be interpreted. From the moment it happened, it was seen to have been highly significant in *some* way. Farce, in the first place (for that is what the Irish Volunteers, with their marches in the streets that parodied the parades of a real army, seemed to many people) gave way to tragedy. They fought bravely; this was generally acknowledged. What is perhaps more important in the impression they made is that they fought ferociously. From the first moments of the uprising, none, although hardly any had ever heard a shot fired in anger, seems to have had any hesitation in killing those formally designated the enemy – that is, anyone wearing the king's uniform on Irish soil – so long as that enemy was opposed to them. To prisoners they behaved chivalrously. More civilians than Volunteers or soldiers were killed, but the number of soldiers killed was quite impressive. The Easter Rising may have been romantic, may have been gallant, but it was very bloody. It was shocking; the shock brought

This appeared in the 'Roots' column in the *Irish Times* on 29 April 1975.

about political changes so profound that not only do they still affect us but it can be said with confidence now that 1916 had a permanent effect on subsequent Irish history.

One of the first interpretations of what had happened was that a German plot against England had been foiled, partly by misadventure.

While the insurgents had no more interest in German war aims than they had in British war aims, the fact that their action took place in the middle of the Great War made them *de facto* allies of the Germans, and of course, they had indeed had dealings with Germany to secure arms for their cause. However, they were, essentially, among the small minority of Europeans of the time who rejected the murderous conflict of the great early-twentieth-century empires as something which did not concern them, or did not concern them enough to persuade them to go out and offer themselves as targets to strangers, whom in turn they would try to kill. They killed strangers all right, but they were strangers on their own streets.

Most interpretations of that week, however, see it as one which changed, perhaps permanently, the direction of Irish politics. 'A terrible beauty is born.' Yeats put it in highly romantic terms, but almost everyone else has made basically the same interpretation. Scales fell from eyes, almost immediately after the surrender, and even before the executions began. More and more Irish people saw their relationship to the British empire quite differently after Easter Week, and from half-acquiescing in the dominion over palm and pine – with the corollary obligation to go out and try to maim or kill Germans, Austrians or Turks – they came for a while to think of Ireland as an independent entity again, and to accept the motto which a tiny minority had displayed on Liberty Hall: 'We serve neither King nor Kaiser but Ireland.'

The swerve into a new direction was so abrupt and so sharp that, again from the very beginning, some people speculated on what might have happened in Ireland if this swerve had not occurred. What 'if England had kept faith?', as Yeats mused, referring to Asquith's failure, in the face of armed Orange revolt, to enforce the will of parliament as expressed in the third Home Rule Bill (so like Wilson's recent failure in the face of the UWC strike of a year ago). As well as the note of admiration for those who acted, forcefully, bravely and tellingly, there is in the Yeats 'Easter 1916' poem a note of regret for the failure on the other side to display the integrity shown by Pearse, Connolly and their comrades.

From time to time since then, and most notably in recent years, people have sounded that note of what-might-have-been, or if-only. This, however, is fairly pointless. The possibilities of what might have happened if what did happen did not happen are limitless and incalculable. If the Easter uprising had not happened in 1916 it might have happened in 1940 – for who is to say that in the unknown situation after a non-rising, England would have 'kept faith?'

But it happened when it did, and on 29 April 1916, it ended with Dublin in ruins, many of its citizens dead, and with Pearse's surrender. It must have been a gloomy and depressing moment for the Volunteers and the Citizen Army. They could see the destruction all around, they could see the dead or wounded bodies, of their comrades as well as of others, they had been greeted with indifference or hostility by the ordinary people of Dublin to a large extent, and they had been beaten. Wellington commented on the result of Waterloo that 'there was nothing worse than a battle won except a battle lost', and, for the insurgents, Easter Week had been a battle lost. They had not fought on a foreign field for a cause which was indifferent to them but among their own streets for the cause, as they saw it, of the people of those streets – who had not thanked them for the death and destruction their action brought.

Yet the change was already happening, because what had been done was so drastic that it must, and did, change fundamentally all appraisals of the relationship between Britain and Ireland. The self-contempt, which is apparent in so many Irish expressions of political and social ideas from the middle of the nineteenth century onwards, was suddenly checked. It was checked, not because of the profound political ideas of the insurgents: their ideas were little known and were for the most part not especially profound. It was checked because the insurgents had carefully conformed to the ideas and ideals of the dominant British society. They had been brave; they had been chivalrous; they had eschewed the slavish cynicism which was their allotted attitude and had shown the sincerity which enabled them to kill designated enemies without hesitation – a highly regarded virtue at the time of the First World War. They had reinterpreted history, in terms which their contemporaries could understand.

Pearse handed General Lowe his sword. General Lowe was, it would seem, somewhat puzzled by this for a moment, but he was also trapped by it, or rather by the whole paraphernalia of military nonsense which makes it possible to recruit armies of men to fight strangers for obscure reasons, and to which, of course, by his profession, General Lowe must subscribe. Instead of rejecting the out-of-date and useless piece of ironmongery, he accepted it and handed it to one of his officers. Pearse, a pathetic, almost ridiculous, figure, as the surviving photograph shows, imposed his own view of the situation on the victors and made real in that moment of defeat the Irish republic. The insurgents of 1916 fought according to their opponents' rules and, if they did not win, they demonstrated that they knew how to play the game. This was a kind of victory in itself, and was important in bringing about the great change, which happened and cannot be undone.

14

A Matter of History

Certain events have a special quality: they assume very quickly the character of myth. These tend to be events which, for one reason or another, bring large numbers of people to the sudden realization: 'I have seen history being made!' The Battle of Britain is a good example, the Kennedy assassination perhaps another. For us, the Easter Rising has been such an event, its mythic quality caught and expressed by Yeats: 'A terrible beauty is born.'

The periods which produce such a heightened sense of the making of history have often been troubled ones; yet many of those who live through them look back on them as to a golden age –

> Bliss was it in that dawn to be alive;
> And to be young was very heaven!

Many of those who were active in the events of the period from 1916 to 1922 in Ireland have spoken in particular of the feeling of *unity* – among all classes and sorts of people – which sustained them in the struggle against the British that followed the Rising. There was a sense that the rest of life had been something of an anti-climax, after the sadness of *disunion* culminating in the Civil War. There is much evidence of a similar widespread nostalgia in England, among those who fully accepted Churchill's phrase about their finest hour. The war against Germany was the last moment of glory, followed by England's rapid decline. Later generations, however, soon become impatient with such nostalgia.

Here in Ireland, the last time a really sizeable number of 1916 veterans pinned on their medals and marched to the banners and bands of a nation celebrating its glorious and bloody birth was in 1966, the fiftieth anniversary. But even by then there were discordant notes struck. A column of the IRA – at that time neither Official nor Provisional, but in the full flush, after the inglorious failure of the Border campaign of 1956–62, of their attempt at unarmed political agitation – was involved in a fracas with the Gardaí as it marched along O'Connell Street in Dublin towards Glasnevin cemetery; Nelson's Pillar was blown up just before the State celebrations which were to centre on the nearby GPO; Mr Lemass had paid his famous visit to Stormont, and had suggested that the Sean Bhean Bhocht,

---

This was a Thomas Davis Lecture, broadcast on RTE Radio on Easter Monday, 1976.

the Poor Old Woman of nationalist myth and balladry, might well now be forgotten.

A few years later, in 1969, I wrote:

> The new entente of Fianna Fáil and the Ulster Unionist Party withstood its first strain when, in 1966, the fiftieth anniversary of the Easter Rising came to be celebrated. Captain O'Neill, in spite of protests from the Unionist right, permitted well-mannered commemorations in Northern Ireland. The Dublin government, with pomp, ceremony and an air of finality, buried the republican dead.

That 'air of finality' was not universally noted, and, since then, the 1966 celebrations have come to be regarded, in some quarters, as a serious contribution to the present Northern trouble. This view in turn affects the perspective in which the Easter Rising itself is viewed: myth begets myth.

'Old moulds are broken in the North', wrote the poet John Montague a few years ago, words which were quoted by Mr Lynch, then taoiseach, in an important speech. They are broken in the south too. The southern State struggles with sudden and overwhelming economic problems, resulting from a combination of the world recession, the link of the currency to a rapidly depreciating Sterling, and the strains of new membership of the European Communities. It has, to sustain it, a good infrastructure, built up in the years of independence, and the habit, now formed over sixty years, of self-reliance. It is physically and visibly changing at an alarming pace, and the spectacle of gathering chaos north of the Border has diminished greatly the old rhetoric of the nationalist revolution. We are in a situation, not revolutionary, but of rapid and bewildering change. The flare-up of resentment against England which occurred after the Bloody Sunday massacre of January 1972 has long since died away in bewildered shame at the bombings, and with it much of the preoccupation with 'old unhappy far-off things, and battles long ago'. Violence is feared, and the Easter Rising, or at least its celebration, is seen as almost an embarrassment.

Yet, as the episode recedes in time, the bewitching and bewildering glamour of myth fades, and it becomes easier to treat the happening as what it was and is: a matter of history. The occasion of the fiftieth anniversary stimulated not only a good deal of triumphalist celebration, but also much re-examination of the evidence by historians and others.

One of the others was the late Father Shaw, whose highly critical analysis of Pearse's philosophy, although written for the occasion, was interestingly and perhaps unfortunately witheld at the time by the editor of *Studies* because it seemed out of tune with the general note being struck in 1966. Fr Shaw's paper, when in due course it was published, opened what has been essentially not an historical but a political debate on the meaning of 1916: this has been the character of the 'revisionism' of the past few years.

Fr Shaw to some extent tackled a straw man: the tradition that Anglo-Irish relations had been, as it were, a long-drawn-out contest between Beauty – that is, Ireland – and the Beast – Great Britain. He singled out, however, for destructive analysis, the rhetoric of Pearse, taking exception in particular to the many passages in which Pearse equated Irish nationalism with Christianity, the salvation of Ireland from British tyranny with the salvation of Man. Here Fr Shaw declared his interest honestly enough; he wrote not only as a dedicated Christian but as a Catholic priest, shocked at the blasphemy he found in many of Pearse's words. In another respect he did not fully declare his interest – his own political views, formed by a family background of well-to-do midland merchants who supported Redmond's party, supported the British recruiting campaign in the First War, and bitterly disliked the tradition which Pearse represented, no matter *what* words were used to express it. The Shaw criticism, however salutary it may have been in contesting the messianic and mystical nationalism of the fifties and sixties, was unhistoric.

Pearse's language and imagery did not in fact represent the republican nationalist tradition, but were borrowed from the language and imagery of the imperial tradition of the day. It appealed to other republicans, because one of their tactics was to turn the ideological weapons of the imperialists back on themselves. Pearse could speak the language of their enemy: this was one of the reasons he was chosen, not so long before 1916, by those who planned revolution, to be a spokesman and leader. The same qualities which appealed to them and suggested him as a suitable figurehead are the qualities which have made him, *par excellence*, the representative and symbol of the Rising: his rhetoric of resurrection after blood sacrifice became for a long time the received version of what the Rising was. But this was, to a large extent, the rhetoric and imagery of the Great War, of which, in one aspect, the Easter Rising was a minor but significant episode.

> It is these soldiers of ours to whose keeping the cause of Ireland has passed today. It was never in worthier, holier keeping than that of these boys, offering up their supreme sacrifice of life with a smile on their lips because it was given for Ireland. May God bless them! And may Ireland, cherishing them in her bosom, know how to prove her love and pride and send their brothers leaping to keep full their battle-torn ranks and to keep high and glad their heroic hearts!

Those words were written not by Pearse but by John Redmond: they refer to the Irish fighting in the ranks of the British army and were written in 1916 in the effort to persuade more to join them. Pearse, to a certain extent, shared Redmond's view of the War, and had himself written, a few months earlier, one of the passages to which Fr Shaw and other more recent writers have taken the greatest exception. He wrote:

The last sixteen months have been the most glorious in the history of

Europe. Heroism has come back to the earth. On whichever side the men who rule the peoples have marshalled them, whether with England to uphold her tyranny of the seas, or with Germany to break that tyranny, the people themselves have gone into battle because to each the old voice that speaks of the soil of a nation has spoken anew. . It is good for the world that such things should be done. The old heart of the earth needs to be warmed with the red wine of the battlefields. Such august homage was never before offered to God as this, the homage of millions of lives gladly given for love of country.

However, it was not only fifty or sixty years later that people took exception to these words. James Connolly promptly described them as 'blithering idiocy' in the pages of his paper, and it is highly unlikely that many of those who fought in Easter Week would have shared Pearse's views on this particular matter. It is perhaps more to the point that the praise and glorification of death became part of a tradition of nationalism *after* 1916, when the Rising became mythologized as the rebirth of the nation. No doubt, simplistic interpretations of that sophisticated and highly complex poem of Yeats helped to bring about this rather sick version of the republican tradition:

> I write it out in a verse—
> MacDonagh and MacBride
> And Connolly and Pearse
> Now and in time to be,
> Wherever green is worn,
> Are changed, changed utterly:
> A terrible beauty is born.

Or, more to the point, perhaps, the refrain of that other, shorter, poem:

> There's nothing but our own red blood
> Can make a right Rose Tree.

Yet it was Yeats who first asked the question that Dr Conor Cruise O'Brien and others have more recently asked:

> Was it needless death after all?
> For England may keep faith
> For all that is said and done.

But these are not historians' questions. To suggest, explicitly or implicitly, that in one way or another our history took a wrong turning, from the pursuit of political ends by parliamentary means to the pursuit of them by violent means is to make the mistake of trying to direct history to suit our present views or needs. This cannot be done. The past is what happened, not the infinite possibilities of what might have happened; and it is not history's concern to follow the will-o'-the-wisps of might-have-beens. Further, as Dr F.S.L. Lyons wrote, some years back when the rebirth myth was being celebrated, 'There is no surer way of going wrong about the past than to interpret it in terms of the present.'

Meantime, the detailed studies published by Fr F.X. Martin on the history of the Irish Volunteers, the studies by Dr León Ó Broin of the British administrative side of things, and the essays, papers and volumes produced in recent years by almost all the historians working on twentieth-century Irish history, have added considerable depth to our knowledge of what happened here sixty years ago. The Rising still stands out, in spite of or because of all this work, as an extraordinary episode, if only because it made such military nonsense. For a small and poorly armed force, facing a large regular army at wartime strength, and *in* wartime, to seize the centre of a city and fight a purely defensive positional battle instead of taking to the hills for guerrilla warfare, made no military sense. Perhaps this is why it took such a simplified form in myth and has been seen as a bloody ritual, designed to awaken sleeping giants. What happened afterwards has been seen as the intention of the men who took the Post Office: their execution, the awakening, the 'resurrection' which followed. This is not quite the way historians show it. As always, the clarity, of events and of purpose, is imposed by the pattern of later events, and the editing out, in recollection and narrative, of all that proved to be irrelevant to later developments. But the historical research reveals the muddle, confusion, uncertainty, agonies of indecision, abysses of ignorance of what was going on, which almost always prove to be the reality of major events.

Pearse again, with his private visions, poorly related to the Ireland of his day, has greatly helped the myth by *seeming* to foresee all that was to come to pass. But his was the kind of somnambulistic certainty which characterizes 'hearts with one purpose alone, winter and summer', whether the purpose be good or bad – like the sleep-walker's surety of judgment which Hitler later claimed, with some justification. It is a precarious certainty, and appears to have been much troubled at times during the Rising. The Dublin looters and the slum-dwellers who spat upon and reviled the defeated insurgents did not conform to his fanciful image of the risen people. And again, Pearse, living in a dream, was not – even if he may have seemed it in later years – either the Rising or its architect. The pattern of its making is now much clearer than it was, the great importance, for example, emphasized by Fr Martin, of Seán Mac Diarmada and his work of organization and direction. Pearse was chosen by the planners and organizers because what they were planning and organizing was in itself a somewhat visionary enterprise and they needed someone who could explain it in high-sounding words. In his oration at the grave of O'Donovan Rossa, and elsewhere, Pearse had shown that he had this capacity.

The other side of the Rising has also been much investigated in recent years. It is worth asking why, in the first place, the British opposition to repeal of the

Union and to any form of Home Rule had been so long and so sustained. Lord Salisbury, in the eighties, explained it in terms of the fixed sentiment of a nation, which, he said, could not be brought to reverse itself except by military force. The long years since the introduction of the first Home Rule Bill had underlined the meaning of his words, and more and more it seemed to Irishmen who desired some form of independence or autonomy that it would continue to be deferred or resisted, no matter how many bills came before parliament. The third Home Rule Bill, although on the statute book since 1914, in the form of an Act of Parliament whose operation was suspended, had already been lost in substance as a result of the armed defiance of the Ulster unionists, supported by the British Tories, and the out-manoeuvring of Redmond in the back-stage negotiations over the exclusion of Ulster counties. This issue was not settled, but merely deferred, by the outbreak of the Great War, and it is pointless to speculate how the issue might have been joined had the 1916 Rising not occurred.

But the Rising is to be interpreted not merely in terms of IRB conspiracies or the organization of the Irish Volunteers. It is also to be interpreted, as it as been, in terms of British miscalculations, misunderstandings and misjudgments. It was, as I mentioned earlier, an episode in the Great War. This – not the foundation of the present Irish State – is its historical context. It was in part a seizing of an opportunity which appeared to be provided by the War, in part a protest at the recruiting campaigns which were bringing large numbers of Irishmen to fight in a cause considered by the Volunteer and Citizen Army leaders not to be Ireland's, in part a blow struck at what was seen to be behind the War, the imperial system. All this appears from the analyses of letters, speeches, directives, propagandist and other articles and other documents, which have been made in recent years. In the heightened atmosphere created by the War, with its constant flow of news of battle, of propaganda and of urgings to join the fight, it is plain that among those who rejected the British connection there was a pressing desire for *action*. This emerges clearly from the accounts of the reactions to the countermanding order issued by Eoin MacNeill to call off the Easter Sunday manoeuvres which – as he discovered only at the last moment – were in fact to become an insurrection. This countermanding order, which deferred the Rising for a day and very greatly reduced the numbers taking part, is the classic instance of the confusion in which the event took place. MacNeill was one of the many who saw the Volunteers as essentially a defensive force and who discerned, correctly enough, that in military terms the Rising was madness. For them, it was a moral problem. Some, like the O'Rahilly or, at a humbler level, Liam Ó Briain, having done their best to stop it taking place, also found that their conscience required that, once it *did* take place, they should be there nd part of it. This very confusion, however, as, among other matters, León Ó Broin has elucidated, further confused the British, who thought they had prevented rebellion and were taken unawares when it happened belatedly and went off at half-cock.

It is a central part of the myth – not necessarily untrue, but highly stylized into a kind of saga – that the great British miscalculation was the execution of the leaders. This is perhaps so: certainly the executions had rapid and demonstrable effects on public opinion. Bernard Shaw pointed out promptly to the British and indeed the other Allied powers that by preaching what he called the 'Sinn Féin' doctrine of the rights of small nations to self-determination – part of the wartime propaganda – they were teaching dangerous ideas: and he went on to ask how many who preached this doctrine would have been prepared to defend it heroically in the blazing ruins of Sackville Street. The answer to this rhetorical question, of course, was that many of them would – at least so far as the heroism went. The Easter Rising may have been an insurrection of poets and intellectuals – another part of the myth. If so, several of them were very minor poets; and there were other Irish poets and intellectuals who fought as heroically, for a cause which they also understood to be Ireland's, in France or the Dardanelles. We come back to the War, and to the larger history which informs the whole of that year of 1916 for Ireland. The echoes of the firing squads of May had hardly died away when, on the first day of July, the murderous machine-guns of the Somme were reaping Irishmen like ripe corn.

Here, in this parallel and in this contrast, is probably to be found the chief *historical* significance of the Easter Rising. The separate and opposed traditions of nationalism and unionism already stood in hostile confrontation. The Rising separated two traditions in Irish nationalism, traditions which had been moving apart since the death of Parnell. Parnell had held his party to a course which never took them too far from the radical nationalism of the countryside, from fenianism, and from the ultimate aspiration to a *republic*. A republic was not just a state separated from Britain; it was a state opposed to the whole hierarchical, deferential type of society which in Britain was symbolized in the crown and the empire. Redmond and his party, by 1914 (in contrast to some of their earlier positions), had come to accept the crown and the empire and the kind of society they symbolized. Redmond, in all honesty and sincerity, committed Ireland to the War, in so far as was in his power, as an instance of good faith in Britain's promises for Ireland's future as a partner in empire. The Rising asserted a counter-view, and asserted it in the only way – as Shaw pointed out – in which fundamental political views may in the end be asserted, that is in arms. The separation of traditions which was thus violently brought about had, of course, complex consequences, and the myth of the Rising arises from a reading back into it of some of these consequences. It is seen as the rebirth of the nation and as the birth of the modern Irish State. Both might be questioned by historians, but both these mythic interpretations have for a long time suited the purposes and needs of politicians and their followers. Now, it seems that politicians require a different myth, while their followers seem to be afraid, at the moment, of the bloody truth about the origin of states and the resolution of political differences.

Dr O'Brien, in a deeply thought lecture published in the *New York Review* under the title 'An Unhealthy Intersection', and reprinted in August 1975 in the *Irish Times*, has some observations on history and myth. Having referred to the preoccupations of many politicians with the question of how they will go down in history (and this was certainly a preoccupation of Pearse and of a number of his companions), he goes on to say:

> This is essentially a literary question, since history is a branch of litera-
> ture – which people often forget – and many of them answered it in a
> literary way, through the composition of memoirs; memoirs for which
> many of them were preparing by preserving material during their political
> lives.

And later he says:

> Politicians are like other people in being the products not only of actual
> history, which is generally unknowable and unknown, but also of 'history'
> as it is generally taught in their time and place, which in most times and
> places will be an inspirational myth, designed to unify the nation and in-
> spire it with a sense of pride in its past.

Here, in the context of a lecture concerned with politicians and literature, is the kernel of some of the views, not only on 1916, but on many other aspects of our history and the way it has been taught, which have been given expression in recent years. It must be said that there is a great deal of truth in it; that in the Easter Rising there was a great deal of presentation of words and gestures for 'going down in history', and that the mythic version of the story of the Rising has been used to further the purpose described. Indeed one may go further and find, as many have recently, that some of the inspiration for recent violence is to be found in this kind of myth, this kind of attitudinizing for the history books of the future. The refrain of the song which has become the anthem of the Provisional IRA goes as follows:

> Where are the lads who stood with me
> When history was made?
> O grá mo chroí, I long to see
> The boys of the old brigade.

But again, in fact, we move away from the matter of history here. History is no more unknowable and unknown than a great many other areas of human experi-ence, in spite of myth. Dr O'Brien's solipsism denies the possibility of discerning objective historical truth, and no doubt we can never arrive at *absolute* objective truth about anything. His own writings in recent years have shown a tendency to handle history in a distinctly literary way, in terms of individual psychologies enacting a drama upon a stage. This makes possible the interpretation he offers, but it is not the only way of studying the past.

There is at least the objective fact that the Easter Rising happened. We know in considerable detail now from the work of historians *how* it happened, and quite a bit about *why* it happened. The consequences are many and varied, and still working themselves out. But they certainly affected, for good or ill, the way our twenty-six-county State was formed, and the way partition took its shape. The Rising has inspired myth, but is itself a matter of history: it happened, and it forces us to take note of it. It has helped to form us.

15

The Battle of the Somme

It is possible that more Irishmen died in battle on 1 July 1916, than on any other single day since the beginning of time. This melancholy calculation does not in itself demonstrate that the battle of the Somme is of great historical importance for Ireland, but it does demand that it be taken into the reckoning. Not all the Irish who took part in the opening of the Somme offensive were in Irish regiments, and it is impossible to ascertain the precise total of those who fell on that first day, but at least 2,500 died of wounds received on the first day of July – probably considerably more. The British army as a whole suffered nearly 60,000 casualties on the opening day of the offensive, of whom about a third were dead.

Among the battles of the Great War, the Somme is significant because it registers, for the British part in the war, an important change. Fighting had been going on for the best part of two years. The war had opened in 1914 as one of movement, with the German thrust through Belgium and deep into France, almost to the gates of Paris. When the Germans were forced to fall back, stalemate developed on the western front, but throughout 1915 it still seemed that a strategy of indirect approach or the opening up of freedom of movement through a breakthrough might bring the war to a conclusion. Irish casualties had already been quite heavy in a British attempt at an outflanking move in 1915 – the unsuccessful invasion of Turkey at Gallipoli – and the reaction in Ireland gave rise to a wider questioning of the purpose of the war.

By the end of 1915, defensive weapons and techniques had prevailed over offensive, and the warring powers were deadlocked. Two alternatives were open to the western allies. One was to make peace; and up to the summer of 1916 the Germans were offering compromise terms – they expected, of course, to profit from their initial successes of 1914. The German peace moves had no chance of acceptance. They were not revealed by the handful of people in Britain who knew of them, and the second alternative was vigorously pursued. This was to crush the central powers by simultaneous French, Russian, British and Italian offensives, on different fronts. However, this did not work. The Germans began a major offensive first, against the French, at Verdun, and a fearful and bloody battle of attrition began. The Russian and Italian offensives were not successful. By the summer of 1916 the French were near collapse, and were putting pressure on the British to move forward the date of a joint offensive on the Somme, one to which

Previously published in the *Irish Times*, 24 August 1979.

now they could not contribute as many of their own troops as had originally been intended.

Alone among the allies, Britain had not had the Continental system of conscription, and had no mass army available for call-up when war began in August 1914. There was instead a well-trained professional army, which furnished the British Expeditionary Force in France and Belgium. The new war minister of 1914, Kitchener, unlike most of his colleagues, believed that the war would last several years, and immediately set about recruiting a completely New Army, of volunteers, to provide an equivalent of the mass conscript armies of the Continent. The initial enthusiasm for the war, assisted by an extraordinary campaign of lying propaganda – a model of its sinister kind – which was mounted with great success as soon as the war began, brought tens of thousands thronging into the recruiting stations.

A feature of the New Army (or 'Kitchener's Army') was what came to be known as the 'pals' battalions', formed when large groups of people who already knew each other, in streets, factories or offices, joined up in units and continued into military service the comradeship of neighbourhood or work-place.

Ireland had several private armies, as well as the forces of the Crown, when the Great War broke out. The earliest of these to be formed was the Ulster Volunteer Force, recruited to resist in arms, if need be, the imposition of Home Rule, armed with German weapons and prepared as a last resort in the summer of 1914 to fight the British army. Kitchener appealed to the Ulster unionist leader Carson, for the use of the UVF in the European war. Carson was at first reluctant. The UVF had no quarrel with Germany – and indeed owed something to German help – but, as the war was going very badly for the BEF in the autumn of 1914, he offered the UVF on condition that Home Rule would not be applied while the Ulstermen were in service against the Germans. As a concession for this help, the UVF was kept together as a unit, the 36th (Ulster) Division, which formed part of the New Army.

The other major private army in Ireland was the organization of nationalist Volunteers formed at the end of 1913 as a response to the founding of the UVF. After the outbreak of the European war, John Redmond, leader of the Home Rule cause, and one of the ruling executive of the Volunteers, in a famous speech at Woodenbridge, County Wicklow, pledged his party's support for the British war effort. Ireland would show, by her wholehearted contribution to the war, that under Home Rule she would be a friend and ally of Britain, worthy of self-government.

The Volunteers split, the vast majority, known thereafter as the National Volunteers, supporting Redmond's position, a small minority, retaining the name Irish Volunteers, rejecting any alliance with Britain. The Irish Volunteers supplied the main part of the force that rose in insurrection against British rule at Easter, 1916. Redmond's Volunteers, unlike the UVF and in spite of his request, were not permitted to form a distinct unit of the New Army, and those of them who joined were recruited into the Regular Army or dispersed among English and Scottish regiments.

In his book, *The First Day on the Somme*, which is largely based on a number of individual case-histories, Martin Middlebrook traces the experiences of one of them. Paddy Kennedy's father and two uncles had been soldiers in the regular British army. He was born in Dover barracks. When the Irish Volunteers were formed in 1913, he joined the Manchester company. His first military engagement, a bloodless one, was when British troops attempted to intercept a unit of Volunteers – of whom Paddy Kennedy was one – escorting German-supplied rifles from Howth to Dublin (blood was shed later that day when a Dublin crowd taunted the British soldiers). On the outbreak of war Kennedy joined the Clerks' and Warehousemens' battalion of the New Army in Manchester and on 1 July 1916 was a soldier in the 30th Division which, with very heavy casualties, stormed Montaubon in one of the chief British successes of the day. Later in the battle, towards the end of 1916, when a war-weary battalion of the 30th Division was being punished, he had the miserable task of serving on a firing squad to execute a fellow-soldier for cowardice. He survived not only the Somme, but the war, winning the Military Medal and three mentions in dispatches.

The New Army had been trained and made ready, and now, at the beginning of July 1916, it was committed and formed the main part of the force assembled for the offensive. It was stiffened with regulars (many officers distrusted the amateur, or war-time, soldiers recruited under the Kitchener scheme, but the regular British army had already been greatly reduced in strength in the actions of the previous 23 months). Although forces from various parts of the Empire were already involved in the war, these did not take part in the new offensive, with the exception of the 1st Newfoundland Regiment, and a small unit, the Bermuda Volunteer Rifle Corps. Otherwise the operation was carried out by United Kingdom forces.

Seventeen divisions took part of which one (the Ulster division) was wholly Irish. The 8th division, of regulars, included a battalion of Royal Irish Rifles; the 34th division, of the New Army, included four battalions of Tyneside Irish; the 4th division, of regulars, included battalions of the Royal Irish Fusiliers and the Royal Dublin Fusiliers; the 29th division, of regulars, included battalions of the Royal Dublin Fusiliers and the Royal Inniskilling Fusiliers; the 32nd division, of the New Army, included a battalion of the Royal Inniskilling Fusiliers; the 7th division, of regulars, included a battalion of the Royal Irish Fusiliers; but there were very large numbers of Irish serving also in Lancashire, Scottish and London battalions. It was something of an irony that Irish forces which had been organizing to confront one another—and drawing, on both sides, on German sources of supply – two years earlier, were now assembled side by side on the Somme.

The tactics to be employed in the offensive were simple and unsuccessful. A prolonged heavy artillery bombardment was to cut the German wire and destroy the German dugouts. Then the British force was to advance, walking across the line destroyed by the guns, and to begin rolling back the Germans. A breakthrough, to be exploited by cavalry, was not planned for.

From the beginning, this plan proved to be a failure. The ferocious bombardment was not sufficient to cut the wire, except here and there in patches; nor did it destroy the dugouts. The advancing soldiers had to carry heavy equipment (including bales of barbed wire), mostly uphill, across a wide space of fairly open country. As the bombardment lifted, the Germans re-emerged in their trenches, and their machine guns and heavy guns played on the advancing British. Some units never reached the German lines. Others, including the Ulstermen, did so, but were without support on their flanks and could not hold what they had gained. Although the operation failed within the first hour or two, this (because of communications and other difficulties) was not immediately apparent to those in command, and further waves of men were sent in during the course of the day, to reinforce failure.

The appalling casualties had effects which were not immediately obvious. Verdun and the Somme marked the commitment of both sides to a kind of warfare which seemed to pass all reason in its total commitment to narrow and limited objectives. Human lives, human dignity, human aspirations, came to be treated as trivial in comparison with the vanities of already out-dated nationalisms.

The New Army was innocent: it was made up of classes and a generation of people misled into their thousands of lonely, untimely and agonising deaths by *Boys' Own Paper* or *Chums* delusions about adventure, loyalty, glory and patriotism. The old sweats, who supplied the levies of the old regular army, and the officer class, which supplied a proportion of its sons in every generation as a sacrifice in honour of its own right to privilege and rule, were replaced by a mass of people, from the upper working class, to the lower middle class, and the upper middle class, who demanded that war should have meaning and purpose other than the pursuance of diplomacy by other means; that every war should be a crusade of good against evil. This, certainly, is how the Great War was presented to the masses in every country involved. But the disillusionment with war which was to characterize the decades after 1920 set in with the new kind of warfare whose horrors first became widely obvious in 1916.

On the first day of the Somme, officers were killed at a far higher rate than other ranks; the character of the British army changed as a result. The cosiness of 'pals' battalions was destroyed: casualties were so heavy, replacements so numerous, that the notion of small communities joining up as comrades and going together to war could no longer be sustained.

Even enormously heavy casualties in war do not necessarily have a demographic effect. Arithmetically, they can be made up very rapidly – all the more so since they are usually almost all male. But, as they tend to be highly selective in other ways too, they can have very considerable qualitative, if not quantitative, effects on the society which suffers them.

The loss of England's 'lost generation' did not noticeably affect the members or growth of the gross English population. It changed, rather, the character of English society.

It is arguable that the Somme and its aftermath changed Irish society too. A handful of those who took part returned to Ireland and supported, some in arms, the republican cause in 1919–21. Most remained loyal to the comradeship of courage and endurance of the trenches; but they ceased to be relevant to the course of Irish political history. The courage of the Ulstermen demonstrated that the threat of the UVF in 1913 and 1914 had been no bluff, but the courage of their Catholic compatriots did nothing to bridge the gulf between nationalist and unionist. The Irish Volunteers who, though initially a small minority, were to dominate the Irish scene, were very definitely on the other side – and the gulf widened.

The failure on the Somme was deep rooted. Russia collapsed in the First World War. England and France did not, but they did not win: they were losers who ended up on the winning side. American intervention in 1917 deprived Germany of victory, and 20 years later, when the war was resumed, German strength was fully apparent, and the English and French war-efforts were little more than side-shows in the ferocious conflict between Germany and Russia. The point at which the tide in European affairs could be seen to have turned was 1916. Nowhere was the turn of the tide more dramatic than in Ireland, where the events of April, May and July highlighted the remarkable contradiction that is this island's tragedy.

16

The Ambiguity of the Republic

We have entered a new period of Irish history, a time of troubles because it is a time of accelerated change. The myths with which – whether we accepted them or not – we have lived for many decades have suddenly ceased to have the appearance of life and are assuming the faded look of old photographs. That the GAA should finally have abandoned its famous Ban is surely an event to be noted, and it is far from being the only such omen in the aftermath of the crisis years 1969 and 1970. It is not only in the North that 'old moulds are broken'.

One of the broken moulds may well be that which shaped the Irish political tradition from the middle of the nineteenth century on. That tradition took its form from nationalism, and was expressed in a cycle of hope, failure, apathy and renewed hope, or, to put it another way, of illusion, disillusion, cynicism and renewed illusion. This was a dialectic suited to a history of the dispossessed. But the touch of affluence, even an affluence as bogus as ours of the 1960s, has broken the chain. There is now a widespread mood of uncertainty, fear and dismay, The recent breakdown in our politics has produced not so much the old familiar reaction to failure, the feeling that 'the one crowd is as bad as the other', but rather a desperate wish that all the queen's horses and all the queen's men might try to put Humpty Dumpty together again. It is a vain wish, but this perhaps is a good time to consider what Humpty Dumpty was.

The twenty-six county state which has, characteristically, passed under a number of dubious aliases in the past half-century (in our present constitution the state is given legal definition but no name) came into being in a cloud of ambiguity and unreality. To find out what its original ethos was (as distinct from the beliefs and aspirations of the various groups which helped to bring it into existence) one must look, I believe, to the Treaty debate rather than to the 1916 Proclamation or the Democratic Programme of the First Dáil. The debate concerned itself with formulae and symbols of sovereignty. It dealt with the handing over of power from one group to another: it all but ignored the existence at that time of a full-fledged, functioning, armed and hostile separate state in the north-east corner of Ireland. Although the tricolour of the 'republic', with its make-believe union of Orange and Green, flew over the law-courts, civil service offices and prisons, what really triumphed was the Harp without the Crown. The revo-

Previously published in *Atlantis*, November 1971.

lution was of the kind foreseen by Connolly. '"After Ireland is free", says the patriot who won't touch socialism, "we will protect all classes, and if you won't pay your rent you will be evicted same as now. But the evicting party, under command of the sheriff, will wear green uniforms and the Harp without the Crown, and the warrant turning you out on the roadside will be stamped with the arms of the Irish Republic. Now isn't that worth fighting for?"' Although the constitution of 1922 was, as Dr Dudley Edwards points out, more liberal in character than that of 1937, it nonetheless enshrined not so much the Rights of Man as the rights of property.

Ambiguity has characterized Irish political aspirations for a long time, perhaps a century and a half. This is perhaps because the nation with which Irish nationalism became identified as it developed in the late eighteenth and early nineteenth century was *not* the whole people of Ireland, in spite of the efforts of Thomas Davis and such to give it that meaning. In practice, in the working out of history, Irish nationalism has shown itself to be a movement not so much against English rule in Ireland as against the rule of England's colony in Ireland, the colony established largely by the Cromwellian and Williamite settlements of the seventeenth century. In the last analysis it appears as essentially a struggle of Catholics to replace Protestants in the government of Ireland, disguised, since the main Catholic weapon was mass support, as a struggle for the Rights of Man in Ireland.

At the very beginning of the nineteenth century nationalism had already developed powerful myths, whose potency was at its height when the present two states in the island came into being in 1920 and 1922. On the southern side was the myth of the Irish nation, a nation which, in spite of the obsession of the myth-makers with history, is regarded as being in some way distinct from its own history. In terms of this myth there was and is an Irish nation, one and indivisible, whose territory is rightfully the whole of Ireland—a historic nation which has been engaged in a centuries-long struggle against foreign rule. To give full meaning to the myth it has been necessary to sit in judgment on practically all episodes of our political and cultural history for the past 800 years (or even longer), rejecting some as being contrary to the ethic of the myth, and approving others. That a consciousness of the nation in this mythic sense did not exist until probably the beginning of the nineteenth century is treated as irrelevant.

Something resembling this aspirant 'nation' came into being after the end of the Middle Ages largely as a result of the economic, social and religious revolution in England and Europe which everywhere brought about a threat to old-established interests. This threat in Ireland forced together Old English and Old Irish (and indeed, although they are often overlooked, Old Scots) in an alliance – under the banner of Catholicism – to safeguard their several heritages of power and property. Support for the conservative side in Stuart times and in Stuart wars created the Catholic nation, and since the Old Irish aristocracy was involved, the dying Catholic civilization tended to become bound up with them. The loss of the native aristocracy left an eighteenth-century Catholic nation which had little political shape or form beyond what it had received from the fragments of the Gaelic aristocratic culture of the past. Much of its popular literature was Jacobite, although the emigrés themselves, the 'Wild Geese' of the myth, as soon as or sooner than their Scottish counterparts, swung round, even in their exile, to the Hanoverians. As Colonel Daniel O'Connell wrote from Paris in 1778, on receiving the news of that year's measure of relief for Catholics:

> A Revolution so unexpected and so long wished for must needs procure, in the course of some years, an accession to the power and prosperity of the Kingdom of Ireland, and unite in one common Sentiment of loyalty the hearts of that long-opposs'd and long unfortunate Nation. One step more still remains to be made – I mean the Liberty of spilling their blood in defence of their King and Country.

One of the earliest exponents of the new ideology of the nation, the 18th- century historian Sylvester O'Halloran, in his *Introduction to the Study of the History and Antiquities of Ireland* (1772), expressed views which might almost be seen as an anticipation of those of the 'republic' when he wrote:

> For, although unhappily for this ancient kingdom *unnatural* distinctions have but too long been kept up by artful and designing enemies, to the almost entire ruin of the whole; yet are we in fact, but *one* people, and as unmixt a race as any in Europe. There is not at this day a Milesian, or descendant of Strongbow, whose bloods are not so intimately blended, that it would be impossible to determine which should preponderate ...

But in the same context, he writes, of the Stuarts and their Hanoverian successors:

> The Irish, who before this period, were perpetually in arms struggling for their liberties, the moment they beheld a prince of the royal line of Milesius wear the British crown, immediately declared themselves peaceable subjects; and what the force of four hundred years could not accomplish, the simple accession of one prince compleated. By the compacts between him and the Irish, all distinctions were forever to cease; and the laws of England, or rather those of Ireland, were to be implicitly obeyed over all the kingdom, as may be seen in the acts of James I and Charles I. Since that day, all ranks of Irish own the power of the kings of England, as Monarchs of Ireland the Irish of British origin from natural affection, and those of the old stock, from the pleasing consideration that they are still governed by a prince of their own blood. Such is the light in which they behold his present Majesty; and warmer or faithfuller subjects his extensive dominions cannot produce.

Such guidance or leadership as that Catholic nation received was, for long, conservative, coming from such sources as the church, the old native aristocracy and the Gaelic poets. It was only at the very end of the eighteenth century, when revolutionary political and social ideas began to be preached in Ireland, that rival candidates for leadership – social revolutionaries – emerged. But the Catholic nation's self-consciousness was not very sharp until the nineteenth century: it was largely the operation of a colonial system with its foolishly ruthless exclusiveness that gave the mass of the people a full consciousness of corporate identity. Tom Moore, and after him Davis and the Young Irelanders, expressed the new ideology, but in the meantime O'Connell, a man who never came to share in full the new romantic nationalism, was aiming at something very different, at civil rights in fact. As a dogmatic nationalist (Arthur Griffith) was later to say of him:

> With the fall of Napoleon and the consequent accession of strength to England, the idea of Ireland as an independent state was dismissed by the majority, and the doctrines of English philosophic Radicalism replaced with them the dreams of national independence. The public life of Ireland became more or less avowedly provincialised. Bentham was read as a prophet and Burdett proclaimed as a leader. Reform substituted Nationality as the watch-word of patriotism, and Irishmen were fain to believe that in material improvements, the amelioration of the conditions under which they lived, and in their assimilation in rights and privileges to the people of England, lay the way of salvation. In a languid agitation for Catholic Emancipation and a semi-academic movement in support of Reform measures, the rich blood of the Nation dissolved into serum.

O'Connell symbolises the ambiguity in the Irish political tradition at an early state. His ikon appeared in the cottage kitchens along with those of Robert Emmet and other romantic leaders, including Parnell, but O'Connell was grudgingly honoured – the tribute paid to him by the Irish people after his heyday had gone by was from the head; that paid to Emmet was from the heart. The head rules, but O'Connell's fault was that he did not sufficiently deal in what might be called the higher Blarney (although he had plenty of a more humble variety of blarney). The ideal political hero in Ireland is someone like Parnell, offering the appearance of romantic Fenian extremism in a context of safe secure parliamentary moderation. Parnell was good at this: *fortiter in modo, suaviter in re.* Éamon de Valéra was better. And if we were, as in *1066 and All That*, to Ask the Irish Question (one version of which is: 'What on earth do the Irish want?'), a possible answer is that the Irish want this kind of ambiguity. The ideal hero is indeed Christy Mahon, the Playboy of the Western World.

The 'idea of Ireland as an independent state' to which Griffith referred has been exposed to the proof of real life in the past half-century, but in a way which itself is ambiguous. What we have had is an 'independent state' *in* Ireland – and an alibi, since there has also been in Ireland throughout the period another state which is not independent (although arguably more free). This curious situation has enabled us until very recently to go on having our cake and eating it, an activity which appears to suit our political temperament very well. The cake which we both have and eat is known in the southern part of divided Ireland as 'the republic', and the recent goings-on within the Fianna Fáil party (the Party of Reality as they liked to think of themselves until reality faced them) bear witness to the ritual or sacramental character of the Irish Republic which has been the central mystery of the Catholic myth for most of this century.

Now that the realisation of change is upon us, so is a flood of words, explaining or explaining away. Ambiguity is, if anything, overstressed. We have, for example, a two-level biography of the master himself, the President, which is a study in ambiguity. Its very authorship is veiled in a cloud: one is tempted to suggest that it was composed by Thomas P. O'Neill (Tomás Ó Néill) – perhaps that should read Tomás Ó Néill (Thomas P. O'Neill) – and translated into English by the earl of Longford and into Irish by an tAthair Pádraig Ó Fiannachta. But one knows that at least two of these have a command of both languages. Perhaps they all conceal another (ambiguous) identity, for the blurb of *Eamon de Valera* (Dublin & London, 1970), tells us that 'The President ... agreed that he would cooperate in two ways in the writing of an authoritative biography.' The ambiguity is compounded by the fact that contrary to Mr de Valéra's long-standing custom in public speechmaking, the *'focal tosaigh dos na Gaeilgeoirí'* is a great deal longer than the real message to the public. Indeed only two of the three volumes of *de Valéra* (Baile Átha Cliath, 1969, 1970), have so far appeared. Its principal difference from *Eamon de Valera* is that it is much fuller in detail and that it prints many extracts from source documents which are not quoted as fully or at all in the English-language version. The quotations, although we may take it that virtually all the originals were written in English, have been translated into Irish – an extremely important point when one is dealing with the words of Mr de Valéra, whose command of Irish has always been inadequate to his purpose but whose command of English, for diplomatic or political ends at least, has been very subtle indeed. When one is dealing with a legalistic, hair-splitting, logic-chopping mind, of a man who could refer to a dictionary in order to define his country's international status, shades of meaning are of great importance. Unnecessary translation (how many readers of *de Valéra* will be unable to read English?) diminishes the value of these volumes.

The work/works on the President's life and career are and will remain useful. Mr Ó Néill / O'Neill is a competent historian who guarantees by his co-authorship that the rules of the game, for what they are worth, are adhered to, Fr Ó Fiannachta writes a lively Irish and has a commitment to something, and the presence of Lord Longford's name on the billing is in itself an undertaking that the whole business is worthy of a U certificate and will not bring a blush to the cheeks of anyone under sixteen. The two volumes constitute in other words an ingenious improvement on the common type of work in which an eminent politician, placed by his eminence in a favourable position of access to at least a part of the historical documentation of his own times, makes a suitable selection from that documentation and publishes memoirs in which he demonstrates to his own satisfaction how right, wise and clever he was in all his actions, but especially on the occasions when it might seem to an unsympathetic world that he was wrong, unwise and stupid. The ingenuity here consists in the use of intermediaries. We are faced with masks behind masks. What emerges from the study is Mr de Valera's Mr de Valera: the achievement of his life (this may be inferred from shifts and subtleties of emphasis) was the 1938 agreement with Neville Chamberlain. We can infer too that what ruined his chances of solving all Irish problems through the special relationship with Chamberlain was the IRA campaign on the eve of the Second World War. The history of Humpty Dumpty as revealed to us here, in spite of Mr O'Neill's strict adherence to the rules of the Cambridge game, is the history as retailed in Alice's Wonderland.

The editor of the *Irish Press*, Mr Tim Pat Coogan, has had a second look at the same period, having completed a general survey in *Ireland since the Rising*. His study of *The IRA* (London, 1970), made the running, in terms of publication dates, a little ahead of Mr J. Boyer Bell's study of the same organisation, *The Secret Army* (London, 1970). There is, inevitably, a good deal of overlapping between the two works, but from a close comparison it soon emerges that Mr Bell's, apart from being better written, is a great deal more balanced, comprehensive and accurate. This is not to say that it would be fair to describe Mr Coogan's book as inaccurate – although there are slips here and there. But it is undoubtedly a partial work, unsympathetic to its subject (that is, not merely unsympathetic to the IRA but unsympathetic to the *subject* of the IRA). It seems that Mr Coogan did not receive in full the cooperation which was essential for writing a study of an underground and, of its nature, poorly documented organisation. His own view emerges fairly clearly: the Lynch view (and Mr Lynch, if not Mr Coogan, it should be remembered is as expert in ambiguity as Mr de Valera) that if we call our state a republic it is a republic and there's an end of it: the aspirations of Tone, Mitchel and Pearse have been fulfilled. One's understanding of the IRA is not therefore enlarged by *The IRA*, although gobbets of information may have been added.

Mr Bowyer Bell, an American who spent some time in Ireland about his affairs – and ours – on the other hand has produced an outsider's book which has assembled the evidence in a workmanlike manner; more than this, he has posed one or two pertinent questions. Why does the IRA go on and on and on, in spite of failure after failure after failure? This is a question worth asking. As Mr Bell points out, in most parts of the world underground militant revolutionary organisations either succeed or fail. They do not simply persist. He does not really attempt to answer the question; although he acknowledges, as must anyone who looks into this matter, that the ambiguities of official policy make almost inevitable the perpetuation of such cargo cults as are embodied in the various IRAs. The history of the Irish government in 1969–70 will make an extended footnote to the fifty-year history of the IRA. What does emerge clearly from both works, although more so from Mr Bell's, is the great importance, for the twenty-six counties, of the existence of the six-county state, insofar as this underground movement is concerned. It may indeed become clear – Mr Bell glimpses this but not Mr Coogan – that the IRA persisted because they were needed. That, at any rate, it would seem certain, is why they are there now.

Other books have taken a wider view of our recent ups and downs. Mr D.R. O'Connor Lysaght, who produced a very penetrating pamphlet in late 1969 on the Northern crisis, has essayed the broad sweep of a study of *The Republic of Ireland*, which he subtitles 'An Hypothesis in Eight Chapters and Two Intermissions'. This is a serious attempt at a Marxist assessment of our recent history, which falls short of its purpose largely it would seem because Mr Lysaght has been somewhat overwhelmed by the materials produced by his own research: the wood is lost in the abundance of trees. However, he has done two things very well: he has detailed and documented the history of the state since its foundation with due regard to social and economic matters and without the deference to the establishment canon which is customary in studies of this period, and he has sketched the lines on which an analysis of our politics and society might be attempted.

History of a more conventional kind is represented by a series of Thomas Davis lectures published under the title *Ireland in the War Years and After* (Dublin, 1969). This is complementary to the central part of the de Valéra biographies and deals with a period which these stress as being of prime significance. The lectures cover the period down to 1951, when Mr de Valéra gave way to Sean Lemass as taoiseach, and they deal with Northern Ireland and, among other things, with the two episodes of coalition government which demonstrated more clearly than their years of rule, Fianna Fáil's mastery of the tricks of the Irish political game.

Finally, *Conor Cruise O'Brien Introduces Ireland* (London, 1969). This is a collection of essays to which I have contributed myself – but only on 'Antiquities', which fall well outside the main themes of the book. This has the fading brightness of the very best kind of tourist literature:

> An Irishman invited to 'Introduce' Ireland is faced with an odd kind of challenge. The lady is of venerable age and already of wide, though mixed, reputation. To the 'introducer' she 'means' as they say 'a lot' though what exactly she does mean he cannot quite be sure ...

And so on. As Dr O'Brien goes on to say, later in this passage,

> In these conditions, writer and reader are unwittingly drawn into a kind of collusion in the invention of a special country; the Ireland of literature.

True, but the Ireland of literature is only one kind of invention. The Ireland of politics is the invention of more dangerous collusions. What collusion is now going on, to produce the invented Ireland which will serve our purposes and supply our alibis in the new European system remains to be seen. It seems likely, whatever else, that it will still have an IRA and still have those attached to it who maintain the ambiguity of the Republic.

17

The Ebb of Irish

It might seem, to the person who has never handled it, that census material, once it becomes available to us, should provide accurate, tidy and instantly usable data. Unfortunately it is not so. A census depends for its accuracy on a chain of many links, which, like all chains, is only as strong as the weakest of them. It depends in particular on two ends of the chain: enumerators who are capable, conscientious, considerate and courteous, and a population disposed to cooperate and place its confidence in the good will, integrity and discretion of the authorities.

Census accuracy, like the level of literacy, probably reached its peak in these parts of the world about half a century ago. Since officials are more venal, governments less scrupulous, and corporations—avid for information of credit-worthiness and other matters—more pressing in the weight of their demands than they used to be, people nowadays are reluctant to entrust full information on their affairs to a functionary or to an official form. It is possible, for example, that the mere head-count of population for Greater London may be out as much as a quarter of a million in recent censuses because of the existence of a huge floating population which shrewdly reckons that the less the Government knows about its circumstances, or even existence, the better.

So it was in early nineteenth-century Ireland. Both people and procedures were unreliable. The questions asked about language were incomplete, obscure, or so marginal (sometimes footnoted on the enumerators' forms) as to be omitted frequently.

The present-day investigator of such material must employ all kinds of careful checks, extrapolations and corrections. But the censuses, beginning in 1821, certainly provide more complete and useful information than the guesses and estimates which preceded them. At least they attempt to be comprehensive, and they established rudimentarily uniform procedures for the inquiry from Antrim to Cork.

The taoiseach, Dr FitzGerald has published a paper in the *Proceedings of the Royal Irish Academy* that deserves much wider notice. Its title ('Estimates for Baronies of minimum level of Irish-speaking among successive decennial cohorts: 1771–81 to 1861–71') is not one to have an immediate appeal for the general reader, and it contains somewhat forbidding columns of tables. But a very considerable amount of work has gone into extracting these particular facts from

---

This was published in the *Irish Times* on 10 June 1985.

166

the census figures of many years, and in the process Dr FitzGerald has succeeded in adding substantially to our knowledge and understanding of the way in which the Irish language finally retreated before the advance of English.

Working backwards from the fairly full and reliable 1881 census, Dr FitzGerald's paper has examined the Irish-speaking population in ten-year age-groups in baronies. The barony is now a wholly obsolete division of land, but it is among the very oldest of our land units. Baronies have the advantage, for any kind of historical or antiquarian investigation, that they represent more 'natural' divisions or regions than the larger and more recent counties, and that they frequently correspond roughly to ancient population groups.

The accuracy of Dr FitzGerald's results diminishes as we go back from 1881, and diminishes more sharply as we move into the late eighteenth century. Yet, even then, the margin of error remains small enough so that we can be confident that we are receiving a true, if somewhat fuzzy, picture. It is the first really detailed *statistical* picture of the decline of the language in the period in question. Earlier examinations of the subject, by Corkery, Seán de Fréine, Maureen Wall and others have given us powerful impressions of the process and of the pain and guilt involved. Cultures die no more easily than persons.

What the paper does is to measure the minimum level of Irish-speaking 'amongst successive new generations of young people in different parts of Ireland between 1771 and 1871'. Ten maps tell the story very graphically. If we look at the map for the age-cohort born in the decade 1771–81 to see what minimum percentage of them was Irish-speaking, we find a fairly dramatic contrast. Connacht and Munster were (for this group of people) quite solidly Irish-speaking, most baronies showing more than 80 per cent.

But along the frontier of this great region with the English-speaking east there is a buffer-zone. The baronies running down from Donegal Bay along the west shore of the Shannon, and then running east to the Barrow north of the lower Suir, show a lower percentage of Irish – mostly between 60 and 80 per cent. North Tipperary shows a sharp falling away from the pattern of the rest of Munster, but the percentages of the Munster-Connacht borderlands are carried into Donegal in the north and Kilkenny in the south-east.

We might say that Leinster and Ulster were English-speaking, Connacht and Munster Irish-speaking, but that Connacht and Munster, for this purpose, included west Donegal and most of Kilkenny.

But the pattern is further complicated. A wedge of Irish-speakers (among those born in 1771–81) runs inland from the shores of Dundalk Bay, through Louth, north Meath and parts of Monaghan and south Armagh. And there are stubborn residual areas (20–40 per cent Irish speaking) in much of north Leinster and patchily throughout most of Ulster. There are only two really solidly English-speaking areas: a huge tract almost from the Shannon south-eastwards to the Wexford-Wicklow coasts, and another large tract around Belfast, including north Down, south Antrim and north Armagh.

That simply sets the picture at the beginning of the survey. It depicts the linguistic habit of people born around the time of the American War of Independence and the Industrial Revolution. The pattern of those born some 90 years later (1861–71) shows a drastic withdrawal to something more closely resembling (although still more extensive than) the Gaeltacht areas of recent times. North Clare is still Irish-speaking (in this cohort) as are north Donegal, Connemara and West Mayo, West Cork and the Kerry peninsulas and the Waterford coast. Over a large part of Munster some Irish survives, but an English-speaking wedge has been driven across Tipperary and east Limerick to the lower Shannon area. Irish has all but died in the Glens of Antrim, but a stubborn patch still survives in mid-Ulster.

However, the main conclusions are not to be found in the contrast between Map 1 and Map 10, but rather in the tables and maps that show the process of withdrawal stage by stage. It is like the ebbing of a tide. We know that there were events that might have been expected, in theory, to issue the order, as it were, 'End Irish now', simultaneously in all parts of the country.

At any given moment, for example, the National School system had the same aims in Kildare and Kerry. But culture – the way people behave – doesn't issue such a simultaneous response. It stubbornly resists change.

As Dr FitzGerald puts it:

> First, there is consistency in the intensity of Irish-speaking amongst each cohort in *neighbouring areas*, with graduated 'buffer zones' of lower intensity of Irish-speaking intervening between areas where there was a high level of Irish-speaking and areas where the language seems to have been disappearing or to have disappeared so far as a particular cohort is concerned. Secondly, it is consistent *over time*.

This is not as simple or as obvious a matter as it might appear at first glance. there are various local discrepancies, discontinuities, or oddities, which are listed by Dr FitzGerald in his summary of conclusions, but what he has shown us (clearly, for the first time) is on the whole a consistent process.

Facts can of course be confusing – quite upsetting to many a theory – but they are the essential fibre for our historical digestion. The importance of the change from Irish to English, in its effects on almost every aspect of Irish life, is difficult to exaggerate. This change is a fundamental process of the past three centuries.

It plays its part in each of the major traumas (and there have been a number in that period) that affected Irish society. The Gaelic world died from the top down. Its political superstructure was destroyed in the sixteenth century. Its social and cultural superstructure was destroyed in the seventeenth century. Its social fabric was destroyed in the eighteenth century. Remnants, and only remnants, survived into our own time.

The language itself is only part, although the central part, of that world. The language revival of this century has been partly successful. A great many people speak, read or understand some Irish who, without the revival, wouldn't. But this has very little to do with the old Gaelic world. Revivalism, virtually by definition, is a feature of English-speaking Ireland, whose values, however sympathetic to the past, are quite different from those of Gaelic Ireland.

What we see in Dr FitzGerald's tables and maps is the last stage of the destruction. This does not require the passing of judgment. It happened. People were reluctant to give up their language, but they gave it up because it was necessary for the survival of their children. Irish, having lost the social and political order that belonged to it and sustained it, had become the language of poverty and destitution. The language that had produced a great literature gradually became the language of the illiterate.

This does not emerge from the evidence marshalled in the taoiseach's paper. We know it from a somewhat more anecdotal kind of history and from some previous studies of a different kind. What we now know, in much greater detail than before, is how and where the last retreats occurred. It may seem a matter of small account exactly how, in what parishes and baronies, the language died, decade by decade. It might be argued that it is the overall picture that counts. But history, ultimately, can be understood only in its actual workings in the confusion of past reality – which means parish by parish. And it is the fine detail that modifies and corrects our view of the whole. It is detailed work on various aspects of life, for example, that has been modifying our understanding of the great famine of the forties. It seems more and more that the fundamental changes which we associated (not wholly inaccurately) with the famine, actually were beginning to take place somewhat earlier.

The growth of population, for example, seems to have stopped, if not gone into reverese, before 1845, in many parts of the country. And drastic social change, it is becoming plainer, had already begun. The famine undoubtedly accelerated many kinds of sovial process, and undoubtedly also exerted its own powerful and important influence on the hopes, outlook, self-confidence and emotion of a great part of the people. But profound change was already taking place.

The famine was most severe precisely in those areas of the west which were predominantly Irish-speaking. A parish with 3,000 people, 90 per cent Irish-speaking in 1841, although it had only 1,500 people in 1851, might still have been 90 per cent Irish-speaking. But demoralized. Such halving of local populations occurred virtually *only* in the remote western areas.

The tables and maps in Dr FitzGerald's study suggest other questions. Was there particularly acute social stress in the fringe areas – of, say, 30 per cent Irish – between the overwhelmingly Irish-speaking regions and those that were overwhelmingly English-speaking? Can we relate outbreaks of violence or other such symptoms to the fringes? If we match percentages with dates, it seems that this is a possibility worth pursuing. Contemporary Ireland, as we all know – and most of us admit it – is riddled with ambiguities, evasiveness, and self-doubt in its social and political and religious life.

It is arguable that this stems from the cultural destruction, partly self-inflicted, that a whole society underwent in the past three centuries. Not nearly enough investigation has been done of this most profound of changes. Dr FitzGerald has successfully applied a magnifying glass to one aspect of it.

18

Bloody Sunday

The province which came to be known as 'Northern Ireland' was based indirectly on a political reality: that most Irish Protestants had come to be strongly opposed to Dublin Home Rule, and that there was a concentration of Protestants in north-east Ireland, forming in places local majorities. The province was directly founded, however, on something politically simpler – a gerrymander. The boundary established by the Lloyd George government, and ratified through the Government of Ireland Act, 1920, was that agreed by members of the Ulster Unionist Council, who sacrificed those they represented in Donegal, Cavan and Monaghan in order to achieve a territory whose area and population would be as large as possible, while at the same time maintaining a secure and comfortable majority for their political views. There was no question of a plebiscite, county by county or barony by barony or parish by parish, by which communities could opt in or out of the new arrangements. It was a decision in the style of Tammany Hall, leading to smaller gerrymanders, like that by which for fifty years a minority ruled the city of Derry. It created both a new home rule province and a major and enduring problem.

Like most issues involving any real transfer of power, the survival of the new province (for a time) was decided by force. The republicans who had been fighting a guerrilla war against the British tried to make it impossible for the new administration of the six counties to function. That administration fought back and – helped by the outbreak of civil war among the nationalists – won. But there were atrocities and there was much bloodshed, 232 people being killed in the six counties in 1922 alone.

The manner of Northern Ireland's creation had consequences. The nationalists, crushed by force, were also alienated. The unionists, triumphant but fearful, like an African tribe in precarious majority in a post-colonial State, not only practised but glorified one-party rule. In the travesty of bourgeois democracy which ensured, votes were all-important for the survival of the provincial system, which like Tibet under the indolence of the later Manchus, was allowed its local autonomy of corruption so long as it maintained a secure frontier for the declining empire. The votes, in turn, were maintained by the constant reiteration of the important political distinction between Catholics and Protestants and by the manipulation, on confessional lines, of the social system.

Published in the series 'Wars and Rumours' in the *Irish Times*, 1979.

Through the Depression years (and Northern Ireland had a minor depression in the '20s and a catastrophic depression in the '30s and has been, compared to the rest of the United Kingdom, depressed since the First World War) this system worked well – years in which the flow of money was from Ulster to England, rather than vice versa. Ironically, it was the reversal of the flow, when the British Government belatedly set about the creation of a 'Welfare State', that contributed largely to the dissolution of the system.

An elaborate apparatus of discrimination could deprive Catholics of houses and jobs and for a long time succeeded in countering their higher birth-rate, but British social welfare cut right across the system. Catholics, even if inadequately housed and unemployed, were given the means of survival in Northern Ireland; more important, they were given the possibility of higher education and thereby the means of articulating their grievances. These were not third-world grievances: they were the dissatisfactions of the alienated in the developed and affluent western world. Northern Ireland was far from being what some of its opponents represented it to be in the post war period – a fascist State ruled by a Protestant *Herrenvolk*. It was highly vulnerable to political action.

Political action, on the issue of civil rights, however, only commenced after the stresses set up by the contradictions in Northern Ireland's political, social and economic system had already revealed sinister forces and led to bloodshed. The 'Troubles' stemmed initially, with elegant logic, from the ecumenical movement. They began (like the 'Troubles' of the earlier part of the century) with a 'Protestant backlash' – in this case the 'Malvern Arms murders', the revival of the UVF, the declaration of war on a then quiescent IRA in Belfast, the reaction to John XXIII. 'I am sorry I ever heard of that man Paisley or decided to follow him', said one of the men charged with the Malvern Arms murders in 1966 (when four Catholics were shot as they left a pub in the early hours of the morning of 27 June).

The bloodshed, however, was on a very small scale until the civil rights movement provoked Stormont into actions which were confusing and therefore embarrassing: British enough in a colonial context: un-British in a United Kingdom context. To which context did Northern Ireland belong? The answer was, and remains, unclear.

For three years, from late 1968 until late 1971, the civil rights movement won sympathy from liberal and left opinion in Britain. It provoked Stormont violence and gathered wider and wider popular (but, by the end, almost exclusively Catholic) support, embarrassed the British administration, which was forced to reassert its claimed authority over Stormont and Northern Ireland, and became a major problem for the permanent British establishment which had no intention (whatever passing politicians might lean to) of relinquishing the province.

The formation of the Provisional IRA, the beginning of their bombing campaign, the attacks on the British army which had been brought in to reinforce Stormont rule, the confused effects of internment: none of these sufficiently mitigated the problem. Very large numbers of people were marching in the streets, proclaiming to the world that they were deprived of their civil rights.

In his manual *Low Intensity Operations* Brigadier Kitson, a counter-insurgency expert who advised the British Army at the beginning of its operations in Ulster, wrote of movements like that demanding civil rights in Northern Ireland:

> There are two main difficulties which confront the organisers of a non-violent campaign when it comes to controlling their followers, both of which are capable of being exploited by the Government. The first of these is that a large number of people have to be involved compared, for example, to the numbers required to conduct a programme of sabotage or terrorism, and the second is that the participants themselves are not disciplined members of a clandestine organisations, but crowds of citizens or groups of students who may resent tight, political organisation as part of their beliefs ...
>
> With the major weaknesses of non-violent action in mind, it is possible to consider a general framework of operations suitable for combating it. For the purposes of this study no account will be taken of the simplest method of all, which is to suppress the movement by the ruthless application of naked force, because although non-violent campaigns are particularly vulnerable to this sort of action, it is most unlikely that the British government, or indeed any Western government, would be politically able to operate on these lines even if it wanted to do so.

Reluctantly accepting this limitation, the writer goes on to say that:

> In practical terms the most promising line of approach lies in separating the mass of those engaged in the campaign from the leadership by the judicious promise of concessions, at the same time imposing a period of calm by the use of government forces backed up by statements to the effect that most of the concessions can only be implemented once the life of the country returns to normal.

However, although it is this second, 'practical' line of approach which has on the whole been followed in Northern Ireland (where the British government, like the American in Vietnam for a long period, appears to have derived political decisions from military advice), the simplest method, the application of 'naked force', was attempted with remarkable success at the beginning of 1972. On Sunday, 30 January, soldiers opened fire on a large civil rights demonstration which, like all such assemblies (especially in Derry) at that time, included a large unruly stone-throwing element. This was not another Amritsar massacre, a flash of imperial rage against the scandal of insubordinate natives. It was much more restrained and calculated: aimed fire, singling out youths and young men, of whom thirteen were killed there and then; a nicely measured 'whiff of grapeshot.'

The effective non-violent civil rights movement came to a sudden end, such movements indeed being, as Brigadier Kitson had written, 'particularly vulnerable to this sort of action.' The adverse political effects were dissipated rapidly by the burning of the British embassy in Dublin on the following Wednesday, by the loss of nerve of the Northern civil rights movement when it came to organising a great non-violent demonstration at Newry on the Saturday following 'Bloody Sunday' in which masses of people from the Republic were initially intended to join, by the Official IRA's inept atrocity in reprisal at Aldershot, and by the Provisional IRA's own massacres of citizens later, in Belfast ('Bloody Friday'), Claudy, and elsewhere. The rapid setting-up of a tribunal of inquiry into the Derry shooting also went a long way to undoing adverse political effects (in spite of the fact that the British judicial system is singularly unsuited to the discovery of the truth about any such event).

It is true that the political struggle in Northern Ireland degenerated into a very unpleasant conditions of sporadic violence. But at the time it was not forseen that this would continue for long. To quote again from Brigadier Kitson's work (published in 1971), he wrote on his opening page that:

> It can be argued that the recent past has been exceptional, that Northern Ireland and Vietnam will both be settled within five years, and that with the withdrawal of all but a small remnant of the British Army into Europe, the requirement to fight insurgents or to take part in peace-keeping operations will cease. Since this view is held by some influential people both inside and outside the army, it is necessary to make out a case for being ready to take part in these operations.

The expressions of outrage in the Republic were countered by a show of another kind of force, economic sanctions, unofficial but effective, in reprisal for the burning of the embassy. Once British displeasure began to affect the pockets of the south, the retreat from involvement with the nationalists of the North began, which has been more or less continuous ever since.

Anglo-Irish relations were more directly and immediately affected. The assertion of imperial authority in the shots of 30 January was logically and swiftly followed by the resumption by the Imperial Government of direct rule over Northern Ireland. Ulster Home Rule ended in 1972 after the experiment of half a century. The attempt to cobble up a new settlement to serve as an equivalent for the 1921 Treaty, however, did not produce a quick result, and the Sunningdale device, of a kind of *panchayat* democracy, failed.

The Wilson Government, having surrendered to its own army in the province during the Protestant paramilitary putsch of 1974, reverted to pro-consular rule, and settled down to the slow business of wearing down the IRA while maintaining as 'normal' a state of affairs in Northern Ireland as possible. On the whole, in the short term at least, this policy has been successful. A population which, in the interests of the minor comforts deriving from untrammelled use of motor-cars, is prepared to kill about three hundred people a year and maim a great deal more, soon finds that it can tolerate as normal – or nearly so – a smaller loss from civil strife and political discontents. The declared aim of 'an acceptable level of violence' has been achieved: the embarrassment is minimal.

But the end of Stormont in circumstances of violence has nonetheless undone the makeshift settlement of 1920–1, re-opening, it seemed, old political questions, but perhaps in fact opening new ones. It was change – not, as might seem at first glance, the lack of it – that lay at the root of the violent upheaval that began in Ulster in the 1960s; economic, social and demographic change. Such changes have been occurring throughout Ireland, transformed in a quarter of a century. The politics of nineteenth-century nationalism, or anti-nationalism, do not fit the reality of the later twentieth century, and there is much evidence to show that, in an island which has returned to its 1800 population of five million people, fewer and fewer of the inhabitants can understand, let alone support, such politics. Where two parts of Ireland for half a century had been drifting apart in separate preoccupations, they have begun to come together in common perplexity.

19

Peace in Our Time

Peace movements are interesting manifestations of the working of the twentieth-century system of communications. As long as there have been wars there have been private or local expressions of distaste for the killing, maiming, rape, rapine and destruction which wars entail. But, until recent times, by and large, the people who suffered from wars had no means of bringing their dissatisfaction to bear effectively upon those who conducted the wars. Means of rapid communication and dissemination of information and ideas were built up in the western world in the nineteenth and twentieth centuries, but before 1914 these, when used for discussion of the meaning of war, were largely in its favour.

For a long time wars in Europe had tended to be short and decisive, lending support to those who favoured a neo-Darwinian interpretation of the world: may the best man win; and the man who wins is the best man. Tolstoys were rare. Victory was virtuous. War was cleansing, and was the supreme test of the values of the west, the proof that Gatling guns were not making the powerful nations soft, but that these nations could still produce an élite of young men of dedication and courage.

After 1918 things were different. 'Gallantry' was not ultimately what people saw in the trenches, with their lice-ridden filth, their seeping clouds of chlorine gas, and their appalling slaughter from high explosives. People who had access to the new means of mass communication now often exalted peace just as much as, a decade or so earlier, they and their predecessors had exalted war. One's patriotic duty was no longer to defend the national honour bloodily against all comers, but to save the nation, if possible, from the appalling damage which, it was now clear, could be caused by modern warfare. In 1939 there were still many people about in Europe who derived their ideas on these matters from the period before 1914, but, by and large, the Second World War was fought by people who no longer believed in the glory and value of war. However, while the war itself was on, there was no significant peace movement, on either side.

Peace movements seem to occur not as the cause but as the effect of whatever it is that brings wars to an end – a change, probably, in the will of both sides for victory. In 1968, I remember the changing atmosphere in the United States, where I then was, when President Johnson was forced, chiefly by opposition to his Vietnam policy, to declare that he would not stand for a further term of office in the

Previously published in the 'Roots' column in the *Irish Times*, 21 January 1975.

election of that year, and to begin the Paris peace talks. There was at that time, as there had been for long, a vociferous peace movement in the United States, with frequent protests and demonstrations, and the election primaries had shown that opposition to the Vietnam war was being effective at the polls.

But what is a peace movement? Was it the young people marching in the streets because they objected to being sent into danger of death or mutilation on the other side of the world? Or is it more significant that, before peace began to express itself significantly through the voting machines, *Time*, *Newsweek*, and the *Wall Street Journal* had already turned against the American commitment in Vietnam? Did the direct American involvement in Vietnam, in other words, end because the events on the battlefield itself decided that the whole business had become too costly for those whose interests had involved the United States in the first place?

To put the matter another way, it seems possible that 'peace movements', especially when they have the explicit or tacit support of the kind of establishments that make wars, are not basically altruistic (although they will always have altruistic people in them, sometimes leading them) but selfish. And they usually reflect a balance achieved on whatever battlefield is in question. Peace is preferable to war: no one, or hardly anyone nowadays questions that. But those who fight a war rate certain objectives below peace. A peace movement takes sides, even if in a curiously roundabout way, saying: what you are aiming at is not worth the cost.

The confused and confusing Irish struggle, like the confused and confusing Vietnamese struggle, has a long history behind it. People have come to it with very fixed ideas about what they want in Ireland. Very often they have come to it in the context of the cultural time-lag which has marked so much of Ireland's history. War, for a great many of the young people of Europe today, the equivalent of those who went, willingly enough, into the mass slaughter of the First World War, is a bad joke. They no longer find glamour or honour in the business of risking one's life and limbs to kill or maim other people at the behest of distant politicians, inspired by a piece of coloured cloth flapping on a flagstaff. The spirit of Henty and of the *Boys' Own Paper* is still, however, maintained by the volunteers of the Provisional IRA, whose trade journals show that they still cultivate the sentimental romanticism of Thomas Francis Meagher – 'Meagher of the Sword'.

> There are times when arms will alone suffice, and when political ameliorations call for a drop of blood, and many thousand drops of blood. Opinion, I admit, will operate against opinion. But, as the honourable member for Kilkenny observed, force must be used against force. The soldier is proof against argument, but he is not proof against a bullet. The man that will listen to reason, let him be reasoned with; but it is the weaponed arm of the patriot that can alone avail against battalioned despotism. then, my

> lord, I do not disclaim the use of arms as immoral, nor do I believe it is the truth to say that the God of heaven withholds his sanction from the use of arms. From that night in which, in the valley of Bethulia, He nerved the arm of the Jewish girl to smite the drunken tyrant in his tent, down to the hour in which He blessed the insurgent chivalry of the Belgian priests, His almighty hand hath ever been stretched forth from His throne of light, to consecrate the flag of freedom – to bless the patriot sword. Be it for the defence, or be it for the assertion of a nation's liberty, I look upon the sword as a sacred weapon.

This kind of fustian is probably essential, at least as a rationalisation in the background, for those whose trade is the bloody one of killing. It is embodied in the regimental traditions of the British army, as well as in the motivation of IRA volunteers. But it does not follow that those who animate 'peace movements' are wholly opposed to this kind of romanticism. On the contrary. The cry, 'Let us have peace!' often appears to be a romantic or sentimental counterpart to the cry 'Let us have war!'

We are hearing both now in Ireland, as they have both repeatedly been heard in the past two centuries. Perhaps, English-speaking and Anglicized as we are, we suffer from having a derivative culture, of whose values we are not wholly sure. Perhaps we echo too much the rhetoric rather than the reason and values of the culture which is our model. Perhaps, after so many failures to solve the 'Irish question' it is time to realise that both warmongers and peacemongers are expressing the question wrongly.

There are some striking similarities, of an almost technical nature, as, for example, in the role of British civil servants between the peace negotiations of 1921 and those of the past couple of weeks. In 1921, too, there was a surge of desire for a cessation of hostilities, a surge which took place among not quite the same people as had given mass support to the desire for revolutionary change. Nineteen twenty-one led to no permanent peace in Ireland, no satisfactory settlement. Again today, we have peace being demanded by a surge of opinion, but a surge among people who, by and large, did not demand an end to injustice at a time when war could have been not ended but averted. War and peace are transient issues, conditioned by the main issue, which is the permanent ordering of our society.

20

The People's Choice

Most people in present-day Ireland, if pressed on their political philosophy, would claim to support the democratic notion of the popular will as the source of political authority. Yet many of these same people have long been obsessed with legitimism, a political attitude more appropriate to believers in the divine right of kings, or in the processes of divination by which the reincarnation who is the true new Dalai Lama may be discovered.

It is an attitude useful to those who wish to avoid present-day realities which run counter to their political aspirations or fantasies. It has led, for example, to the extraordinary reverence paid down the years on the unionist side of the great divide to the 'constitution of Ulster', which they persuaded themselves was in some mystical way more than a mere British act of parliament. Yet the totalitarian dictatorship of Mr Whitelaw for more than a year past in Northern Ireland was as consonant with the true constitutional position of that area as was the negligent tolerance extended for many years previously by Westminster to the peculiarities of Unionist rule.

No doubt the great majority of Unionist supporters believed as sincerely in democratic systems as did most people in the western world. But they narrowed down the meaning of such systems to the simple arithmetic of majorities and minorities in political votes within their own arbitrarily defined area of six counties, leaving aside as inconvenient a great many other elements in the basic theory of democracy, including the personal liberties (which were denied in the permanent Special Powers Act) and the notion of the general will, which required the *consent* of large minorities. And even their often-expressed faith in the principle of majority rule has been gravely shaken when that principle is again applied (as it almost was in 1912) to the United Kingdom as a whole. Legitimist principles appear as soon as Ulster unionists are threatened, in an adverse sense, with the United Kingdom to which they claim so vehemently to belong. Then, it seems, the majority has not the right to do *wrong*.

But Ulster unionists have at least, in the last resort, some grounds for falling back on legitimism. They can appeal beyond the popular will, because, while being genuine democrats up to a point, they are not quite republicans. They can always fall back on the crown, or even on the great sacred cow of Ulster, the Bible, in a final appeal to fundamentalist superstition. What is more curious and

Previously published in the 'Roots' column in the *Irish Times*.

interesting is that many who not only call themselves republicans but arrogate to themselves that title are as ready to appeal beyond the popular will to their own fundamentalist legitimism.

It seems to me that we have here an Irish political tradition not nearly sufficiently examined. Those on the whole who have investigated Irish history since 1920 have concerned themselves with the patent affairs of a functioning and, after a shaky start, stable 26-county state, which soon received the general assent of its population and which presents enough complexity and interest in its development to be studied like any normal small state. Yet all the time there has been within it, as within the much more dubiously situated north-eastern pseudo-province, an intransigently dissident small minority, organized and persistent, whose allegiance was legitimist. For much of the period of the 26-county state's existence there has been, somewhere, a group of people in a back room who were convinced that they were the 'true government of the Republic'. For all I know there may still be such a group. Certainly, the non-recognition of the existing State, south as well as north, by some groups implies the recognition of some legitimate State. What?

It is an important question, since we are dealing with groups who have shown quite remarkable persistence over a period of more than half a century, in spite of being not only repeatedly defeated, but reduced at times to vanishing point. This indeed is the central theme of Bowyer Bell's history of the IRA: this remarkable survival. And these groups have not only survived; they have re-emerged to make a considerable impact on the politics of Ireland in the 1970s, when constitutional crisis has come in the North and threatens the South. To what then do these groups give their allegiance? The nineteenth-century Fenians gave theirs to 'the Irish republic virtually established', when Ireland was under British rule; but this was essentially an expression of aspiration and determination. It depended on the sense that the majority of the people of Ireland shared the aspiration, and that therefore, in terms of democratic theory, the Fenians were giving their allegiance to what the general will desired.

There are flaws, some of them very obvious, in this; but the Fenians, nonetheless, could claim to be republicans in the full sense of the word. It was their tradition, in large part, which animated the political struggle that took place in Ireland in the early part of this century, when basic republican principles were observed to the extent that appeal was made to the will of the people. It has been a recent fashion to present the 1916 Rising as a departure from this principle, but this is an over-simplification which ignores the fact that those who organized the Rising were very much bearing in mind two important circumstances: that democratic parliamentary procedures had been successfully thwarted by a combination of armed unionists and conspiratorial (and, on the military side, mutinous) Tories, and that large numbers of Irishmen had been misled into killing Germans, with whom they had no quarrel, in an imperialist war in which they had no part.

In a sense this intuition on the part of the 1916 leaders was justified not only by the result of the conscription crisis of 1918 and the subsequent election, but by the total discrediting of the Redmondite party as a result of their resort to imperialist violence.

The republicans of that period, then, appealed to the people, and were justified. Separation from England had long been the aspiration of a majority of the ordinary people of Ireland; separatism therefore was republican. But republicanism is a system of beliefs and principles which is not connected with Anglo-Irish relations. Irish separatism is an aspiration which is not necessarily republican. The million-strong minority in the island who did not desire separation – at that time, at any rate – were not sufficiently regarded by separatists who had democratic principles, partly perhaps because they had expressed their dissidence by a highly undemocratic resort to arms and to an alliance with British reaction.

But, throughout the Anglo-Irish struggle of 1919–21, there were those who realised that the 1918 election was an election, no more. It had provided an opportunity to the people to express their views on a single black-and-white issue presented to them. They had been offered a considered and debated constitution; they were basically deciding whether they wanted to be ruled at home by Irishmen or, as for the previous century, from London by Englishmen. Their answer was significant, first because in five-sixths of the island it was overwhelmingly in favour of Irish rule; second because in the other sixth it was overwhelmingly in favour of English rule.

It is *that* vote to which, essentially, our present-day 'republican' legitimists appeal. A snap decision, in a time of crisis, on what was in effect a single issue has become, for them, the fundamental basis of an Irish state. The living Irish people, who plainly *do* recognize our courts and government in the 26 counties, are not regarded as a source of authority by supporters of the divine right of 1918. Thus, in support of their fundamentalist political bigotry, they have intervened, with disastrous results, in the constitutional crisis in our island.

Our crisis, however, is not singular, and not due to the legitimists. They represent in it merely the intransigence we have inherited from our past – both unionist and separatist. We have also inherited the idea that the people who live on this island should decide how it may be governed, an idea expressed equally in the Ulster Covenant and in the 1918 vote. This is the idea 'republicans' might profitably develop.

The Voice of Bigotry

In Belfast last week I bought the issue dated 15–28 September of a journal I read frequently, if not regularly, the *Protestant Telegraph*. This issue is not unusual in providing a very good illustration of one of the deep and seemingly ineradicable roots of the present troubles in Ireland, religious bigotry.

There have indeed been several references to the article on page 2, signed 'Dr Ian R.K. Paisley', in which that politician employs the old technique by which the popular press used to say 'This filth must be stamped out' – while giving its readers an eyeful of the filth in question. Here, however, Dr Paisley's topic is not the comparatively harmless one of sex or nudity, but religious hatred. His article is a little sermon in which he tells Protestants not to burn down Catholic churches or kill Catholics but he leads up to this injunction by making his readers' flesh creep at the murderous wickedness and intolerance of the Roman Church.

> Let there be no doubt about it, if Rome got full sway in Ireland the Protestants would face a campaign of genocide ... Protestant churches would be closed or burned as in Spain and Colombia and Protestants slaughtered and imprisoned. This has always been Rome's tactics and only a dupe to her Jesuitical propaganda could think otherwise.

And the injunction itself is given in a somewhat left-handed way, prefaced by an excuse for those who do not purpose to obey it:

> In the confusion of the Ulster tragedy some misinformed and misguided Protestants should not stoop to Rome's practices indulging in the killing of Roman Catholics and in attacking Roman Catholic churches.

The whole passage is put in such a way as to leave the reader, who is ostensibly being dissuaded from murder and arson, with the impression that these in the circumstances would be no more than an understandable and forgivable sin.

This happens to have attracted notice, but similar pieces have regularly appeared in the same paper. Last January, for example, Dr Paisley had an article in almost identical terms on the front page, but with a rather weaker precept against

Previously published in the 'Roots' column in the *Irish Times* in September 1973.

182

murder and a more lurid fantasy of the horrors that would ensue should the Church of Rome come to dominate Ireland. There are thirty-seven items in the current issue, including a letter to the editor but excluding advertisements. Of these, sixteen are directly anti-Catholic in content. Others are directed against the Republic, against Mr Heath, against Mr Wilson, or against other real or imagined enemies. Apart from a syndicated Bible-commentary column (by Dr Bob Jones of South Carolina) there is only one piece of positive rather than negative intent – an announcement of the choice of an Ulster Democratic Unionist candidate for the North Antrim seat, vacant in the Assembly. Some of the items constitute incitements to hatred, notably that on the front page which insinuates that the murder of ten-year-old Brian MacDermott was sectarian in character.

Religious bigotry is not peculiar to Ireland (although quite a few people nowadays write and speak as if it were) any more than it is peculiar to either side of the main religious divide. It is found wherever people hold strong religious convictions, and it is not even confined to Christians – although the long history of Christianity is such that the term 'Christian' would seem more appropriate than the more commonly applied 'un-Christian' in referring to hatred, murder, torture and revenge. What is being enacted in the North in this respect is the effect of a cultural time-lag. It is a continuation of the long and ferocious quarrel of the churches which has continued since the Reformation. Similar hatreds and resentments fester almost everywhere, awaiting only suitable circumstances, such as Northern Ireland has unhappily provided, to manifest themselves as eruptions of public evil.

The ecumenical movement, which seeks to end the quarrel of the churches, has become the target of the intransigent and has in them increased the bitterness, if this were possible. Dr Paisley himself first came to prominence in the early 1960s as a noisy and demonstrative opponent of ecumenism, which played the same part for him, in his rise in politics, as the 'Jewish conspiracy' did for Hitler. Ranting against Rome has of course been from the beginning a pastime of Protestant preachers of the more enthusiastic sort, and it certainly has a long tradition in Ireland. Jemmy Hope, for example, in his memoirs gives an interesting account of this kind of sermon in the Antrim of his youth, two hundred years ago. It is in the context of a community, deeply divided on a number of other issues as well, that exhortations which are, in theory, concerned merely with matters of theology and belief, become inflammatory. This has been the situation in Ireland for centuries, and continues to be the situation in the North. The 'siege mentality' so often spoken of as that of the Ulster Protestant, has become in journals like the *Protestant Telegraph* a form of paranoia. This of course has had justification in the past few years, when the Protestant community and its institutions have been under attack, by bomb and gun, as never before.

But the reason for the 'siege mentality' has existed much longer than that, even if it is not necessary to trace it back to the Catholic uprising of 1641. It has not, however, been the Protestant faith which has been under siege, since the emergence of Catholic nationalism early in the last century, but the Protestant

Constitution. That Constitution is still clung to by people like Dr Paisley, even though it has long been no more than a shadow of a shadow. Protestant constitutions, Catholic constitutions and Hindu constitutions cannot survive in advanced societies of the modern world, which must be pluralistic to function. England has already abandoned Northern Ireland in this much more fundamental way than any withdrawal of troops or civil servants. The *Protestant Telegraph* expresses and exploits the enraged bewilderment of people who find themselves, like an all-but-extinct species, stranded in a strange world.

In trying to assess complex historical events, one is always tempted to emphasise unduly the causes which seem spectacular. Perhaps in this way, the 'siege mentality' has been over-emphasised in the recent efforts to understand the source of the Northern trouble, and the intransigence of both sides exaggerated. Reading the *Protestant Telegraph* is a good corrective to the face value of Dr Paisley, who, as a Westminster MP and a Northern Assemblyman, is an important politician. But the religious group to which he belongs is very small in terms of numbers, and its paper is not, in that respect, representative of Northern Protestantism. The one million and the half-million people in the North who are conventionally represented as opposed armed camps are not homogeneous groups. They are individuals, not by any means all bigots. Some have no religion at all. A few even have no politics.

22

Eggs and Omelettes

Last week I referred to the change in attitudes which had brought greatly in-creased danger of destruction to our field monuments, as these are no longer protected by superstitious fears or by a sympathy for the past they represent. This is only one such danger arising from the change-over from a 'traditional' to an 'advanced' society which has been taking place in Ireland in the present cen-tury. Nor is it only field monuments which are threatened: we are passing through that dangerous stage of development when an anxiety to modernize, to join, as it were, the modern world, encourages an ignorant haste to disown our old identity in the hope that thereby we will the more quickly acquire a new one.

Our progress into the brave new world has been halted, for the moment at least, by the world-wide recession. This brings not only hardship and difficulty, but also some opportunity to pause and reconsider whether we are wise in all our rejections and in all our acceptances. We might, for example, be a little more moderate in our enthusiasm for the European Community, which has disadvan-tages for us as well as advantages and has been sold to us with many spurious as well as with valid arguments. We might be less quick to abandon our 'special relationship' with the peoples of North America and to rush to adopt in its place the shallow anti-Americanism common to Right and Left in Britain, and there derived essentially from an envy which is inappropriate here. We might take note of the evidence that our society in these recent years, which have seen the general level of prosperity raised, has been developing in the direction of greater in-equalities and, among our urban communities at least, of greater stress and hard-ship for the poor.

Conservationism has become fashionable in the Western world at large, in reaction against changes which were both rapid and destructive. We have picked it up like other fashions, but so far it has been ineffective. Some conservationists, themselves comfortably situated, have been heedless of the need of other people for jobs – which often can be provided only at some expense to the existing envi-ronment. Other conservationists can readily be made to seem heedless of such needs, even when they are not. Just the other evening, for example, the minister

---

Previously published in the 'Roots' column in the *Irish Times* on 1 April 1975. The references to the oil off-loading business in Bantry Bay were written, of course, before the great Whiddy Island disaster.

for local government, Mr Tully, in a television interview, when he was being questioned about the most recent oil spillage in Bantry Bay, suggested that some people in sheltered positions, like television interviewers, would oppose any kind of 'dirty industry' although such industries might provide a living for large numbers of other people. This, of course, is to sidestep the issue that the Gulf Oil enterprise, while it is undoubtedly dirty, is not, so far as Ireland is concerned, an industry at all, in any serious sense, but rather a casual exploitation of Irish resources on behalf of activities which essentially take place outside Ireland and with little relevance to this country. Its value to Ireland is to be assessed not simply by counting the relatively small number of jobs it provides, but rather by weighing this against the damage caused by repeated leakages of oil to the natural beauty and amenity of the south-west coast, to the natural life there, to the fishing industry and to the tourist industry.

The tourist industry has been important in the development of the sixties and early seventies. More than other industries it illustrates the dilemmas of such development; for a large part of its stock-in-trade embodies the tension between past and present. The industry cannot sell the sun, or warm seas; it must sell, simply, 'Ireland'. It is, *par excellence*, the industry of self-exploitation. For one thing, it has been found in more than one survey and inquiry that one of the chief attractions this country holds for tourists is archaeology. For another, it is the 'traditional' aspects of present-day Ireland that the Tourist Board, in its advertizing abroad, emphasizes: the quiet, relatively traffic-free roads, the slow pace of life. The friendliness and hospitality of Irish people are also emphasized.

It is plain that there must be in this not merely an element of self-exploitation, but also a large element of destruction of the very assets which are being exploited. The more tourists are enticed into the country, the less quiet it will be, the less traffic-free the roads, the less slow the pace of life – and the less likely the people are to remain friendly and hospitable. The more it becomes a business or an industry, the more corrupting tourism becomes, as we all know from experience here and abroad. As visitors multiply, they soon cease to be looked on as guests and become 'marks' or 'punters', while an elaborate system of commissions, tips, and other forms of 'squeeze' takes as much money from them as possible. As for the landscapes and archaeology; these too suffer from the exploitation, with the construction of beach developments, motorways, marinas, carparks and other conveniences, while exhaust fumes and a variety of forms of chemical pollution are, as it were, cultivated in close proximity to ancient carvings. We are still far short of the stage of self-exploitation through tourism which has been reached in some other places (such as Cornwall, to take one relatively near to home) where the visitors so greatly outnumber the natives in the season, that services like water and sewage begin to break down under the strain.

This industry, like others, has met with a severe set-back in the current recession, exacerbated no doubt by the Northern troubles. It is reported that the Tourist Board is indeed at present doing some reconsidering, about such matters as planning for desired numbers and types of tourists, and the decentralization which some years ago produced the regional tourist boards. If this is so, it is an important development, for the industry, like some others, had become short-sighted, it would seem, in aiming at short-term results with insufficient heed for long-term consequences.

Tourism provides a paradigm for the processes of development which may sacrifice too much in enthusiasm to achieve a limited gain. This is a particular danger for a small state like ours, all the more so when capable and energetic people are involved. Smallness makes for flexibility: it is possible to carry through drastic policy changes relatively rapidly. This has been demonstrated throughout the economy in the past few years, especially since we joined the European Communities. Such flexibility in turn confers obvious benefits on a small society in a world subject to the kinds of sudden change we have seen in both economic and political affairs in the past couple of years. But it has its dangers, for it makes it all too easy to abandon or jettison – with little hope of recovery – parts of our heritage which we may impatiently regard as having no further value, until we discover, too late, that we were mistaken.

The passion for demolition is not altogether to be decried. It is a sign of energy, which may almost as readily be directed to construction as to destruction, and is preferable perhaps to mere apathy. It can be tolerated to a high degree by large, forceful and rich cultures. But what we destroy, in our efforts to clear the way for a new prosperity, is something which we have neither inherited in abundance nor can readily replace. We can enjoy neither an American instinctive confidence in the future nor a European instinctive confidnce in the past. The professional and administrative class which makes the decisions for us is rootless and insecure, enjoying little confidence of any kind. Its values are uncertain. Its destructiveness has yet to be matched by a convincing constructiveness. A revolution is being made in Irish society by people without an ideology or a clear objective. We have, in unpleasant circumstances, been given a brief lull in this process. We might use it to consider that while it is not possible to make an omelette without breaking eggs, it is quite possible to break eggs without making an omelette.

23

The Future of the Irish Past

Last year's series of lectures organised by the Printing Industry Cooperative Society dealt with affairs in Ireland since the Treaty, in other words with the very recent past. It seems to me that the very choice of the general title for that series – 'Ireland since the Treaty' – expresses the view of the organizers that we in this country have reached a point of transition, that passions and conflicts of opinion which exercised Irish public life for many years have died down, and that there is something of a lull in our affairs which gives us an opportunity to pause and reflect, to examine our position anew and see where we have come from and where we are going. This view is borne out by the title of the new series which begins tonight – 'Ireland in the Coming Years' – and by the guiding lines which have been laid down for the lecturers.

'What issues are now emerging? How much rethinking of our national position is necessary? To what extent are our policies and public attitudes based on tenets which are no longer believed in private?' These are the questions asked on the cover of your programme, the questions which the lecturers are required to examine.

Now, last year you heard learned papers from people who have spent many years studying our institutions, our recent history and the social and economic questions which affect our public policies, and, reading the programme, I have no doubt but that this year you will hear more such valuable papers. But my talk tonight is not of that kind. I am not an expert on any subject which is relevant to the political and economic controversies of the day – my own field of research is concerned with periods which are safely remote in time. However, since what I have been asked to talk about is our Cultural Heritage, in the widest sense of the word 'cultural', our way of life if you prefer, no special expertise seemed to be required since I shall be discussing something which we all know. The facts are

This was given as a lecture to the Printing Industry Cooperative Society in the Shelbourne Hotel, Dublin, on Friday, 7 November 1958. It was the opening lecture in a series on 'Ireland in the Coming Years', following on a series given in 1957–8 on 'Ireland since the Treaty.' I was involved in the planning and organization of both series, which were designed to examine – in a period which seemed at the time, and still seems in retrospect, to mark a low in Irish morale – the substance and the potential of the Republic that had finally been proclaimed barely ten years earlier. The lecture is printed here as it was delivered then.

available to all of us, and my function tonight is not to supply information but to express opinions.

It is significant that the organizers of this new series chose to begin with a talk on this subject, because, or so it seems to me, the real roots of some of the troubles which afflict our country today are not economic, as is so often said, but cultural. Large-scale emigration expresses a loss of confidence in Ireland, a feeling, I believe, not only that the country has failed to provide a livelihood but that it has failed to provide a life for many of its people.

Some feeling of disappointment was probably inevitable. For generations a large part of the Irish people had been led to look forward to national independence as to a Promised Land. Alien rule could conveniently be blamed for all our ills; native rule would do away with them all. Nobody, I am sure, ever made this claim in so many words; but when all energies are concentrated in a difficult struggle, people tend not to look beyond the immediate end. When that is achieved, disappointment ensues. Things are never as simple as often they have to be made to seem.

The political movement which led ultimately to the establishment of the Irish Free State has been, at least since the days of the Young Irelanders, also a cultural movement, or closely associated with cultural movements. The United Irishmen of the late eighteenth century took the culture of Ireland in their time more or less for granted, as, to a greater extent, did the Volunteers. Their concern was with political and economic questions. But since the time of Davis, Irish nationalists have been opposed not only to English rule in Ireland but to the culture which existed in most of the country under English rule. They struggled to replace English rule by Irish self-government, and Anglo-Irish culture by – what? At this point the picture becomes rather murky, and that murkiness persists and bedevils our affairs to this day. It became a commonplace of Irish nationalist thought that Ireland was an ancient nation whose glories had been eclipsed by seven centuries of foreign domination. It is a proposition which begs a number of historical questions, but there it was, and is. It might seem far-fetched to suggest that anyone seriously envisaged a full restoration of the twelfth-century nation which had been invaded by the Anglo-Normans, but in the early part of this century books were published commending the Brehon laws to the nationalist movement; one for example by L. Ginnell, another with the significant title, *Liberty, Order and Law under Native Irish Rule*. Only ten years ago a small political party which was contesting elections for Dáil Éireann displayed in its head office a large coloured drawing – the plan of a proposed new capital of Ireland on the Hill of Tara. The head office of the party, however, was not on Tara but in Dublin. For this is the duality which affects all such unreal thinking. The public, or remote, ideal might be a modern Gaelic city on Tara (there was, incidentally, no such thing in ancient Ireland); the private, or immediate, ideal was to achieve some measure of success within the despised culture that had the overwhelming practical advantage of being in existence.

I have deliberately chosen extreme examples to illustrate a confusion or conflict of ideas which I believe has deeply affected the Irish Nationalist tradition and therefore the ideological formation of our present Republic. Those of our people – and they were many – who supported nationalism in its various forms and degrees in the past century-and-a-half felt that Ireland should not merely be self-governing but *different*, specifically different from England, and that this difference should be rooted in our past. 'Not free merely, but Gaelic as well' is how Pearse put it, and it is clear from his writings that he was not thinking of language only. 'Irish Irelander' was the popular term for someone who thought on those lines. The Irish nationalists wanted Ireland to be distinctively *Irish*. This was the aim of the Gaelic League – to revive not only the Irish language but Irish culture. The importance of the part played by the Gaelic League and the GAA in the struggle of 1919–22 is well known; but it was a political part. The significant point is that these cultural organizations provided a perfect recruiting ground for revolutionary politics. It was the same people, more or less, who desired political and cultural change. In the outcome, however, they put the one into practice, the other only into resolutions and policies. It is easier to overthrow governments than habits. Apart from that, no clear picture was ever provided of the Irish culture which it was intended to revive. That culture included the Irish language – so much was agreed on – but it was two centuries since the Irish language had been the main language of Ireland. The Gaelic past was to be restored, but the truth is that there were very few people who knew very much about the Gaelic past, and the whole idea has many of the aspects of a pipe-dream. Besides, there were other ideas involved. Many of the early activities of the Gaelic League, and indeed of Sinn Féin, show the influence of the nineteenth-century reaction against the Industrial Revolution, the ideas of William Morris and his fellows.

The ideas and ideals of 'Irish Ireland' have faded somewhat with time, but their effect is still strongly felt. Our concern here is with the present and the future. It is still the policy of all our main political parties to revive the Irish language. Less is heard now of policies for reviving other elements of Irish culture, real or fictitious, but there are still dozens of organizations, groups and individuals protesting vigoursly at the growing influence of English and American culture in Ireland.

The fact is, of course, that this is an English-speaking country which was governed and administered for centuries by the English and which has been anglicized in customs, manners and even thought by the habits and experiences of those centuries. By comparison with Asian, African or American countries Ireland is clearly culturally a part of Europe. But by comparison with other European countries Ireland is just as clearly, I think, a part of the British Isles. I need only mention language, laws, public institutions, styles of building – but there are hundreds of minor ways in which the British element in our culture may be discerned: to mention a few at random: food; our early-closing of public houses; our custom of playing the national anthem after cinema and theatre performances. This is not to suggest that there are no differences in culture between

Ireland and Great Britain, or indeed between one part of Ireland and another, north and south, east and west, country and town; but I think that an unprejudiced observer of European culture who was dealing in generalizations would group Ireland and England just as closely together as he would Germany and Austria. It is an inevitable result of the course of our history that this should have come about. But what is the trend today, after more than thirty-five years of self-government? Is Irish culture moving away from or still closer to British culture? This is quite a difficult question to answer, certainly by a generalization. Undoubtedly the Gaeltacht areas, the only parts of the country which have preserved a quite distinct outlook and way of life, are slowly dwindling. Certainly English newspapers and journals circulate more freely and more widely among the people than they did fifty years ago, while broadcasting and the cinema bring in English and American ideas and manners. This is true also of most Western European countries, but since Ireland is English-speaking the effect is probably more profound here. On the other hand, the official policies designed to bring about a revival of Irish as the spoken language of the people, although they have been pursued less than half-heartedly and have quite failed so far in their ultimate object, have not been completely without effect. They have managed at least to preserve the language as a symbol of the distinctive Irish culture which has not yet come into being. And I think that the profound social changes that have taken place in Ireland since the beginning of the century showed a movement away from English culture in the first instance – although what direction these changes are taking today is another matter.

The society of pre-Norman Ireland, the Anglo-Norman society of medieval Ireland, even the oppressed Catholic and Gaelic society of the seventeenth and eighteenth centuries; all these have vanished. It was a natural thing for people who were struggling to achieve national independence to take as their model, when they tried to envisage a free Ireland of the future, those past periods of our history. It was a natural thing, but it is dangerous for us to follow their example. Our hopes and aspirations for the future *must* lie in making the best we can of what we have now.

What we have now gives us grounds for a modified confidence, confidence not that there necessarily will be in this country a nation which is distinctly and distinctively Irish, but that there can be. The present century, and the later part of the last century, have seen, and I think this is an important point, several different kinds of revolution at once in Ireland – political, social, economic – none of them quite carried through to a conclusion and all of them intextricably connected. Since there has not also been a full-scale cultural revolution, many people are left with the uneasy feeling that all we have achieved is a 'distinction without a difference' after all the struggles and aspirations of our people. This feeling, of course, is unjustified. It would be remarkable indeed if the builders of our Republic had not made any mistakes; but they have achieved an extraordinary proportion of the aims of traditional Irish nationalism.

Not only has the British government disappeared from the greater part of

Ireland, but the Ascendancy class which was associated with that government has also been swept away. The affairs of the country have been more and more coming into the hands of the descendants of the Catholic masses who were oppressed to subsistence level and below it in the early nineteenth century. This is the great change which is bound to affect the whole character of the country in the coming years. Not under the Irish high kings, nor under those Normans who were 'more Irish than the Irish themselves', any more than under Dublin Castle, were these people in control of affairs; but they now come into control of the heritage of the past of Ireland – the *whole* cultural past. The rural, traditional folk-culture, which is their background, embodies many fragments from the ruin of Gaelic Ireland. But they also inherit what remains of Ascendancy culture, the culture of the eighteenth-century towns and country houses; of the Irish 'Literary Revival'; of the learned professions, the sciences, fashion and art. Remembering how much in fact nationalism owes to the members of the Ascendancy class, remembering that they, for all their faults, were 'no mean people', what will Ireland make of this inheritance? There is a considerable tendency to disown it; but in plain fact we can't do without it, since the circumstances of Irish history left little opportunity for any other culture to develop to a high level.

Do not think that I am advocating or foreseeing for the coming years a mere continuation of Anglo-Irish traditions. As you will see, my intention is almost the contrary. But I am simply returning again to the theme that any view of the future that does not envisage our working with what we have, here and now, is unrealistic.

In most discussions of the problem of Irish culture today, what might be called 'the native tradition of culture' is given pride of place. Now, I am not trying to suggest that this tradition does not exist or that it is unimportant, but I am trying, since it is the immediate future that we are now concerned with, to put it in perspective. That tradition exists in a living state only in the Gaeltacht areas, where not only the Irish language but a distinctive outlook and way of life survive. Elsewhere the Irish language, however enthusiastically cultivated, has a more or less artificial existence. The obvious reason for the failure, so far, of the policy of teaching Irish in the schools to achieve its objects is that Irish is merely a 'subject', out of its cultural context. There is both a lack of a follow-through after school, and very often a lack of any real teaching of the language as a living tongue. The policy has had some limited success, in preserving the *status quo ante*, but if Irish is to be saved, it can, I think, in the immediate future at any rate, be saved only where it is spoken. As the spoken language of the people at large it could be revived now only by an extremely widespread popular movement of revolutionary fervour – of which there is no sign whatsoever – or by a Government ruthlessness which would be impossible in a free society.

Even the most sanguine supporter of the revival of Irish must therefore, I think, look forward to a mainly English-speaking Ireland for a long time to come, a period which can hardly be less than a century. The Irish language is one of our most valuable possessions, and it deserves strenuous efforts for its preservation and cultivation, but the sort of wholehearted effort which might have begun the process of its large-scale revival was not made, and that revival is something which we may not now hope to see in our time. If it is to be saved at all, effort must be concentrated on the Gaeltacht.

In the meantime, what of the rest of the country? – the remainder which, in terms of population, is ninety-nine per cent. Irish is spoken and understood by many people here – and may that knowledge of the language increase and flourish – but it is not the mother tongue, not the language of everyday life, not, in other words, the language of the culture of the people. It is an English-speaking culture. And in the long period ahead of us in which we must foresee its remaining English-speaking, what is to become of *that* culture?

Fear of the influence of the English-speaking world to which we belong has become marked in much recent thinking on cultural matters in Ireland. The fear in itself is probably healthy enough, but that it should lead to a wholly negative attitude of mind is to be deplored. We read protests every day at the influence of foreign – specifically English and American – culture on our people, and demands for greater efforts to keep out this influence.

If we pause to examine our position within the English-speaking world, and try to see what distinguishes us from the other English-speaking nations, one important fact stands out immediately. We are different from them in outlook, and that difference is rooted in religion and philosophy. Religion is one of the most important elements which give form to a culture, and in Europe as a whole there is a clear *cultural* distinction between Protestant and Catholic, and even between Protestant and Catholic parts of the one country, as between North Germany and South Germany. The difference is discernible in architecture and the arts, in the way leisure is spent, in social and business habits, in attitudes of mind generally. Ireland's position in this respect is unusual, because the culture of the greater part of the country has taken on the colour, as it were, of the culture of the Ascendancy class. But Ireland is also a mainly Catholic country, whose affairs, in the twenty-six counties, are now mainly in the hands of Catholics. One can therefore foresee a gradual cultural change which will reflect this changed state of affairs, and one can perhaps foresee Ireland acting to some extent as an interpreter of the Catholic tradition of European culture to the great group of English-speaking nations of which she forms a part. For Ireland is in a unique position, partaking as she does of the two main streams of European tradition, being in possession of the opportunity to interpret one of those traditions to the great English-speaking nations which belong, culturally, to the other.

We should therefore finally abandon the view, so far as it still lingers on, that the future can be a return to the vanished past. But we should accept, and indeed value, all that we have received from the past: the wider European culture to which we belong, and with which we have many historical links; the Anglo-Irish culture which comes to us from the past few centuries of our history; our folk culture and what remains of our old Gaelic culture. It is a blending of all these that will preserve our individuality as a nation and that will give us something to contribute to the world, in justification of our independent existence. It is not by the exclusion of foreign influences, but by having something positive of our own to offer, that our culture can survive. For this, the education of our people is clearly of the highest importance; they should be able to look outwards as well as inwards. The importance of our schools and of our National University – both of which have been neglected in favour of seemingly more pressing political and economic concerns – can hardly be exaggerated in any consideration of what is likely to be the shape of Ireland in the coming years.

24

The Dilemmas of Conservation

There is a natural temptation for those of us who are deeply concerned about the damage which is being done to our environment to rush about shouting 'Stop! Stop!' So much seems to be happening at once, and so rapidly – more floral or faunal species endangered every day, more landscapes marred, more pollution from noise, silage, combustion products, gases discharged into the atmosphere, radio-active waste in the sea, and so on. In the large scale of the destruction that is happening, perhaps indeed the only remedy is to cry halt, to reverse what we used to call 'progress', and to retreat from the comfortable but rather unpleasant world which technology has created for us.

But I would like to look into just one very small corner of this large problem, and not particularly in relation to the environmental and ecological emergency which confronts the developed world as a whole. As it happens, I have been engaged, professionally and otherwise, for a good part of my life in what might at first glance seem to be the opposite process – preservation, conservation – endeavouring to prevent or undo damage and decay. This work has been in places away from those parts of the world where most of the frantic activity is going on which everybody nowadays recognises as some sort of threat to our environment.

For example, twenty years ago, in 1952, I spent several months of the spring and summer in south County Kilkenny, in the south-east of Ireland, supervising conservation work on medieval ruins. It was then a quiet leafy countryside, with not too many motor cars; a lush river valley that had been well tamed by the Normans centuries before; where the air was clean and the processes of time and decay had a natural and almost acceptable quality. Again, in the middle sixties, I was up on the plateau to the north of the main Himalayan range, on the borders of Nepal and Tibet, trying to formulate some policy for preserving what could be preserved of the material culture of lamaistic Buddhism, surviving undamaged only in some pockets south of the frontier after the catastrophe of the Kamba War of 1959. Or, to take a rather different kind of example, I have from time to time been concerned unprofessionally with the problem of the Irish language – a problem which will probably seem fairly remote to most English people but which will more readily be understood by people in Wales and in many parts of Scotland.

All work of preservation, conservation or restoration is slow and requires pa-

This was given as a talk on BBC Radio 3 in 1972.

tience. It is also a kind of work which, more than many, demands reflection on its meaning. Consider 'Restoration', in terms of buildings. We are all familiar with examples, since for more than a century – certainly since the Gothic revival – it has widely been considered a good thing in Britain – and in Europe – to try to rescue some buildings from the effects of time, whether this involved only decay or whether it involved accretions and alterations by people who lived long after the original builders. The cathedral of Notre Dame in Paris is largely a restoration, as is the famous walled town of Carcassonne. Nineteenth-century France had the services of a skilled and imaginative restorere, Viollet-le-Duc, who has left his imprint on the townscapes of tourist France. But what is the restorer doing? Presumably if we interpret the word strictly, he is bringing something back to the exact state it was in at some earlier date. A moment's reflection, however, will show that this is simply not possible. In the first place we rarely have enough knowledge in sufficient detail to do this. In the second, many of the physical processes of change – weathering, aging, decay – are irreversible. If the surface of a sandstone carving has weathered back, say, an average of half-an-inch all over, not only has the character and quality of the carving been profoundly changed, but we can never restore the half-inch of sandstone. We can employ a sculptor to make a new carving, trying to re-created the old, but this simply is not restoration. Look at the nineteenth-century sculptures on the west porch of the cathedral of Paris, and observe how obviously nineteenth-century they are. The very best restoration cannot get beyond a very clever pastiche.

A friend of mine, Percy Le Clerc, who for many years was Inspector of National Monuments in Dublin, recently restored a twelfth-century abbey church in the west of Ireland, at Ballintubber, and made it available for worship, as a parish church. The approach here, very successful within its own terms of reference, was to attempt something which was more than conservation but which was a good deal different from simple restoration. The church was repaired and rendered structurally sound. It windows were re-glazed, chiefly with clear glass, although there were one or two windows painted by modern artists in a modern idiom. The nave roof was put back – for centuries the nave and transepts had been open to the sky – using traditional materials and such carpenters' joints as were known in the Middle Ages, but without any of the kind of 'antiquing' that producers of imitation Hepplewhite or Chippendale sometimes employ. The masonry of the interior was left unplastered but was whitewashed.

Ballintubber, to my mind and eye, is one of the most satisfying examples of restoration of a medieval building that I have come across. I think the reason is that the architect was fully conscious that he could not transport us back to the late twelfth century or successfully persuade us that we had been so transported. Its pleasing quality is its honesty, its truth, a quality which Ruskin would have understood. What it says is: 'Here are the remains of work done in the twelfth and thirteenth centuries, which we in the twentieth century have treated with respect and have looked after in such a way that people can still in some fashion enjoy them.' I find this more satisfactory than an attempt on the part of the twentieth century to efface itself altogether. Once it becomes clear that *this* carving or *that* moulding is not medieval work but a clever modern copy, then doubt begins to set in about the whole of what is being presented. This brings us back again to nineteenth-century restorations and to the whole question of the true and the false. The nineteenth-century *flèche* on the Cathedral of Paris may be elegant and pleasing enough in itself, but by not proclaiming more clearly its own age it does place a large question-mark on the building as a whole.

There are other practical problems which arise in architectural restoration and conservation. I take an example from my own work in Ireland, arising from the excavation of the Cistercian abbey of Mellifont, founded in 1142. The buildings here, constructed during the second half of the twelfth century, were destroyed by fire at about the beginning of the fourteenth. Their gutted shells were then pulled down, a foundation made with the rubble, and new abbey buildings constructed. These in turn were demolished after the Reformation, and a country house built on a part of the site. It was destroyed in 1641, rebuilt, abandoned about a century later, and then used as a quarry for an early nineteenth-century mill which stood in ruin at one end of the site when I was working there. The excavation disclosed remains of all these stages of the building on the site, one superimposed on the other in such a way that destructive choices had to be made here and there. The nineteenth-century mill in fact was removed in the course of the works. The final presentation of the site was a matter of choices determined by our view in the nineteen-fifties of what was valuable or significant at Mellifont.

This is a fairly extreme example, although I can think of much more extreme cases elsewhere. But it illustrates a point which I think is true of all conservation and is certainly true of all restoration. These involve policy decisions, all along the line. They relate to a philosophical difficulty. Just as it is not possible to step twice into the same stream, there is no such thing as the building to be conserved or the building to be restored: by our interference, by our modification, we are making something new. We are inevitably making it to fit our own tastes, prejudices and preconceptions, and what we produce will bear the marks not only of its period of origin but of its period of restoration or conservation. It may be objected that there is a sophistry in the argument, that in an important sense we can step twice into the same stream, and that in this sense there is a building there for us to conserve or restore. True. This indeed is the justification for the work and it is an argument which must be accepted. But it must equally be accepted, I think, that in this kind of work we are not 'restoring' or 'reviving' something which is past. We are instead making a statement about our attitude to that past and placing ourselves in a particular relationship to it.

Conservation, of the kind I have been discussing so far, involves intervention in the processes of change which affect the object we are interested in. Although conservationists speak of 'stabilization', in fact change cannot be stopped. It can be given a new direction and its pace can be changed, speeding it up or slowing it down. If we put up a notice at an ancient monument telling people that they will be prosecuted if they interfere with it, we are, perhaps effectively, slowing down processes of change due to human agency, and perhaps postponing for an indefinite period a drastic change such as demolition. We can do that and no more, and go away and leave the monument to the natural processes of decay – change proceeding at a pace not directly controlled by human-intervention, although it may well be indirectly controlled through human pollution of the atmosphere. But more commonly we interfere with the natural processes too, cleaning, killing harmful growths like ivy, grouting, flaunching and so on.

This brings us back to the kind of decision-making I have already touched upon. Do we want our Norman castle to be a romantic ivied ruin? This is perhaps an old-fashioned taste, but it is not unknown. It must be borne in mind that the ivy will in time pull and burst the masonry asunder. Or do we want it so displayed that all its architectural features are revealed nakedly or graphically to the scholar of Norman buildings? Or do we want something in between, to suit the general visitor? Or do we simply want to slow down gently the decay of the building, leaving it otherwise as little interfered with as possible? All of these, and many more intentions are possible. Each involves making a decision, but the decision is not dictated wholly by what Richard de Clare or Hugh de Lacy built eight hundred years ago. It is dictated as much by what *we* now want.

From these examples within one small corner of a very large problem, I think it is possible to venture out to larger considerations of conservation. For it seems to me that there are echoes of these small problems throughout the environmental debate which is now being conducted, and that in the end we are always brought back to decisions which are in the last analysis political. There are not only negative questions: what do we want not to lose?; but positive questions: what do we want to have?

It is part of the value both of the thesis put forward in the January issue of *Ecology* in the report 'Blueprint for Survival', and of the sharp criticism of that report made by the editor of *Nature* that they bring out this political implication. 'Fresh air is better for you than carbon monoxide' is a blank proposition which has a wide if specious appeal. 'Walking is better than driving about in a motor-car' is a proposition which still has an appeal, but a more limited one. 'We should depend for all our supplies on pedlar's packs, horse-drawn carts and barges, and sailing ships' is a proposition which would have a very narrow appeal indeed. Control of the environment is, in a broad sense, an activity in which humankind, one way or another, has been engaged as far back as we can trace the activities of our species on earth – helping, no doubt, to exterminate the mammoth and the woolly rhinoceros long before we almost succeeded in wiping out the great buffalo herds of the North American prairies.

People have always struggled against the rest of nature: it is in our nature to do so. This cannot be stopped, but it can be directed. The direction must inevitably be towards some social end: decisions about such ends are political decisions. This is why the editor of *Nature* can use political rather than scientific language in condemning 'Blueprint for Survival', calling it illiberal. This is why 'Blueprint for Survival' offers political rather than scientific or scientific prescriptions for saving the world. Some of these indeed, would seem to me to have an equal attraction for traditional conservative and for socialist temperaments. 'Make the polluter pay', for example. But the fact that political decisions, and therefore political ideologies, are involved does tend to blur the issue.

We very soon come up against the kind of either-or propositions which reveal our political stance in these matters. Hand-made shoes for the few, beautifully finished works of leather craftsmanship, or plastic imitation-leather shoes, rather nasty but serviceable, for the million – that kind of choice.

A number of years ago I was concerned with the material aspects of what remained of Tibetan culture. This civilization was unique, or at least highly distinctive. Its remarkable geographical setting, its focus in the lamaseries of Mahayana Buddhism (with more than a trace of older cults), its literature, its extraordinary political structure, its art, its complex symbolism, all render it a culture of great interest. That culture in some of its most distinctive features, has been profoundly changed by the Chinese armies of occupation since 1959. But should it have been conserved? It is very doubtful if the people of Tibet, with or without the Chinese occupation, would have gone on indefinitely enduring many of the inequalities and forms of exploitation on which lamaistic civilization depended. Should they be forced back into a slavery or vassalage which was not merely picturesque but was genuinely productive of spiritual and artistic achievements? The Chinese said No, not simply because they were a great power enforcing anew an old suzerainty over a subordinate state, but because they were Communists enforcing a view of the kind of society which should be established everywhere.

Similarly, on a much smaller scale and in a much less significant matter, I remember a conservation case in Ireland about twenty years ago. It concerned a group of traditional cottages, the last surviving in a particular region. These were made of mud, they were very small and cramped, they were wholly devoid of what the estate agents call 'modern conveniences' and they had roofs of straw thatch. There is really only one satisfactory way of maintaining such buildings, and that is to inhabit them. But should the families who had lived in them be deprived of the privilege of going into drab concrete-block cottages, of no artistic merit or historic significance, but with running water, dry timber floors, and slate roofs? Clearly not, and none of the gentlemen who were exercised about the preservation of the picturesque little buildings was prepared to go and live in cramped, damp and unhygienic conditions in the interests of folklore or social history. No doubt, in theory, other solutions were possible, but while the matter was being debated, the cottages, after the manner of their kind when abandoned, melted away to heaps of mud in a winter's rains.

What I have been trying to say is that even in small matters there are dilemmas at every turn for the conservationist. He is like the historian who, however hard he may try, if he does try, can never grasp the past in its fleeting reality. He is always trying to maintain that which, in some sense, has ceased to be, and to impede the activities of his busy fellows with what has become irrelevant to them.

But this work, whether it be concerned with ancient and historic monuments, as mine mostly was, or with the safeguarding of the natural environment or of forms of life, is necessary. It is necessary, I think, in the same way as governors and escapements are necessary in many forms of machinery, to keep the machine regulated and in control. This principle, I feel, could help to keep in perspective the politics of conservation. It is the application of moderation to the relationship between past and future. The future must not be allowed to run out of control through the reckless input of energy. It should be regulated by the past.

25

The Artificial State

In this divided city in a divided country there are obvious reminders of the situation at home in Ireland. Berlin and Belfast must be the only cities in Europe with a wall, patrolled by soldiers, running through their central areas. The visual similarity is striking. As one approaches the crossing point into East Berlin, 'Checkpoint Charlie', the affluent vulgarity of the West peters out along the Friedrichstrasse, into a drab and depressing no-man's-land where the scars of war are plainly visible still in the shattered masonry and fire-blackened and twisted girders. Then, at the other side, the side streets off Friedrichstrasse have the dead and abandoned look of streets going nowhere: they terminate in the blank Wall with its string of barbed wire and its catwalk for the watchful security forces. They are just like side-streets down to the Belfast 'peace-line'.

The resemblances are striking. The differences are even more striking. And then, beyond the differences again, there is a more profound comparison to be made between the German situation and the Irish.

Apart from the walls, and certain consequent visual similarities between a small part of Berlin and a small part of Belfast, the fact that both Germany and Ireland are partitioned, and that in both the partition is a live political issue, provides an obvious basis for comparison. But comparisons and analogies based on small aspects of large situations can often be very misleading. To take the smaller first, the Belfast wall was put up largely to prevent people from killing one another; the Berlin wall was put up largely, it might be said, to prevent people on one side joining those on the other.

The larger partition of Germany, like the dividing of Berlin, was imposed by the conquering United Nations, without reference to German wishes, at the end of the Second World War. It was imposed, of course, not quite in its present form, but as part of the division of the country into occupation zones for the armies of the victorious powers. It was the rapidly developing quarrel among the victors – the 'Cold War' – which made this into a simple division between the Russian-occupied zone on the one hand and the occupation zones of the other United Nations armies on the other. The division has now assumed semi-permanent political form. The two Germanies have their autonomous governments, each of an ideological complexion acceptable to the appropriate occupying power.

Written in Berlin and published in the 'Roots' column in the *Irish Times*, 4 December 1973.

201

But the foreign armies remain – no doubt as 'guests' and under treaty arrangements with the German government concerned in each case. However, the recent warlike alert of the American forces in the West, and the warlike use of German ports, without reference to the German government, show that the guests, on either side of the division, will still when put to it behave like occupying conquerors. (Although, since it seems plain that the recent alert was designed to defend the president against the Congress of the United States rather than Western civilization against any external threat, perhaps it should not be taken too seriously.)

This provides a ready parallel for the Irish situation. Partition in Ireland too was imposed by an external force – by England, in 1920 and 1921. Yet, as soon as we examine the circumstances of the two cases, we see that they are quite different, and the parallel straight away breaks down. Partition in Ireland was not imposed without consultation with the Irish, nor as part of a new conquest. On the contrary, it was imposed as what seemed to be the easiest way out of a situation in which a vociferous and strong-willed Irish minority had opposed with violence and the threat of violence the measure of devolution that was embodied in the Home Rule Act of 1914. It was imposed, but it was imposed in response to Irish expressed desires and as part of the processes of undoing conquest and of colonial withdrawal. When we consider the historic circumstances, the partition of Ireland and the partition of Germany appear as quite dissimilar events.

There is another aspect to partition. What is being, or has been, divided? Are the entities strictly comparable? West German maps and atlases today, while of course they show the existing German frontiers, tend also to show as a dotted line, expressing some form of irredentism, the pre-War frontiers as well.

I have before me as I write a two-page opening in the 1972 edition of a current atlas, at the map showing 'Deutschland'. To the chosen scale, this could comfortably be fitted onto one page, but two are needed for the eastward extension of about 600 kilometres necessary to include the dotted-line frontiers which encompass a great deal of what is now western Poland, as well as the old East Prussia, and even the enclave surrounding the 'free city' of pre-War Danzig. These, in other words, are not the frontiers established by Hitler. Austria is not 'claimed', nor the Sudetenland. The dotted line shows the Germany of Versailles, and it is something of a mystery, since the Versailles arrangements were so universally denounced in inter-war Germany, why these precise limits should be chosen for perpetuation.

However, the point is that someone had to choose them. When one speaks of 'Germany', unless the reference is specifically to one or other of the existing German states, one is speaking of something very real but not immediately definable in terms of boundaries on a map. After all, in any ethnic or cultural definition, Austria is as much a part of 'Germany' as Prussia is. As it happens, Austria now exists on the political map as a separate state – with a very unhistoric shape – while Prussia has no political existence at all. 'Germany', if by this expression one means the lands in which German is spoken and which share the cultural experience that goes with the language, was united in modern times only under Hitler. And, of course, the nature of Central Europe is such that there is no clear-cut dividing line between German-speaking lands and Slav-speaking lands, so that any such ethnic unification must inevitably include within the unifying boundaries a great deal that properly pertains to other ethnic entities.

It is, in other words, very difficult indeed in some parts of the world to devise a state whose boundaries will coincide neatly with the limits of a nation. Yet this is what 19th-century romantic nationalism demanded. So powerful was the demand that at the end of the Second World War the problem was solved in Eastern Europe by redistributing the population to suit the new frontiers. The dotted lines in the 1972 atlas showing the extent of East Prussia and the Free City of Danzig might as well be defining the territorial claims of Nineveh and Tyre.

Here there is an immediate apparent contrast with Ireland. Our situation is obviously different, because Ireland is an island. Irish nationalism has never had to pause for a moment to work out where the frontiers of the Irish nation should be. It had clear historical precedent: the kingdom of Ireland, which for long had its own parliament and which was a distinct entity in the seventeenth and eighteenth centuries, included the whole island, and no more. Under the Union too, Ireland remained a distinct administrative entity, unified from the centre to the sea.

Irish nationalism, in spite of being as ethno-centric as other nineteenth-century nationalisms, observed the strange law which applies to conquered and colonized territories, and accepted the definition of its conquerors; just as West Germany has sanctified the boundaries laid down by the Versailles victors; just as new African nations treat as sacred the arbitrary line drawn on nineteenth-century maps by European colonial powers dividing the share of one from the share of another.

The sea is a more significant divide than a mountain range or a river. The sea around Ireland is a formidable barrier, even in its narrows. It does contain an 'Irishness' which is apparent whether one crosses from Stranraer to Larne or from Fishguard to Cork. But it has not prevented the movement to and fro of ethnic groups, and in defining an island it does not define a homogeneous human mass. 'The kingdom of Ireland', coincident with the island, is a concept which did not depend for its validity on any such homogeneity or on the will or consent of the inhabitants of the island. 'The republic of Ireland' is a concept which, by definition, must depend upon the will and consent of the inhabitants, although not necessarily on their ethnic homogeneity.

It is a concept which requires politics of the kind appropriate to central European situations, as in Czechoslovakia or Yugoslavia, where there are deep divides which do not at present take the political form of separate states. The mistake made by generations of Irish nationalists is that of thinking they are trying to restore a 'natural' nation when in fact they were trying to create an 'artificial' state. The artificial state seems to me to be a worthy endeavour, but it requires working with different models.

26

Cars and Culture

The West German ban on the Sunday use of private cars is saving more than fifty lives every weekend. It also makes the air of this great city really breatheable once a week. People on the whole seem to have found it, for the moment anyway, more of a relief than otherwise to be relieved of the Sunday chore of taking the family out into the suburban traffic jams. At the same time, government statements have indicated that this is only the beginning of the energy crisis and that a good deal of distress, including some unemployment, may lie ahead. West Germany and Berlin had become almost as committed to the motor car as had the United States of America. In this particular respect – the use of cars – Ireland does not lag as far behind the rest of the developed world as she does in others. Perhaps the crisis, which in some sense looks like being a permanent one, will cause some heart-searching for us as well about the whole question of development and of the scrapping of so much of our traditional life in favour of a new world which is already loud with the ringing of alarm bells.

For us, as for other nations in the West, the arguments have been overwhelming for the subordination of our beliefs, traditions, customs, ideals, idiosyncrasies, prejudices and affections to the single aim of a steadily increasing Gross National Product. The 'standard of living' must steadily rise, even though this standard no longer relates to food, shelter and a decent way of life, but to the accumulation of gadgets and gimmicks and to the kind of conspicuous waste involved in having three-car families in Dublin or Cork suburbs; even though the standard no longer applies to the community as a whole but to a large parvenu middle and upper-working class, which is prepared to cut its own roots and to ignore increasing distress at a lower level in pursuit of the tinsel rewards of affluence.

We enter into this competition without reflection, in spite of the example of other societies which are far ahead of us in the progress of technological surfeit and which have problems profound enough to give anyone pause. We enter it although there is abundant evidence that the orgy of greedy wastefulness and of expensively titillated boredom in the advanced societies of the West is paralleled by massive breakdowns and great suffering and deprivation in the undeveloped and exploited societies of the Third World.

Written in Berlin and published in the 'Roots' column in the *Irish Times* on 11 December 1973.

There have of course been many prophets of doom, especially in recent years, trying to point out that the old idea of progress has been transformed into a crazy obsession and that in committing ourselves to explosively expanding consumption and rejecting older values we may be throwing out the baby with the bathwater. The prophets of doom have been listened to, have indeed enjoyed a vogue, but not to the extent that their views are permitted to have more than the most superficial effect on our social actions.

People who study the past usually eschew prediction of the future. Those on the other hand who attempt to predict the future generally try to do so without reference to the past beyond what is very recent; in other words, they try to make their predictions on the basis of the present. This, perhaps, is why so many visions of the future are prophecies of disaster, because some recent developments which strike the prophet as significant are projected into the coming decades or centuries, very often as an exponential curve expressing increasing numbers of births or density of pollution or whatever the chosen area of emphasis may be, leading ultimately to catastrophe. Such exponential curves, leading to the point of catastrophic breakdown, would be difficult to draw for events in the past, and therefore there are some grounds for hoping that they need not set the pattern for the future. Calculations based on current trends extrapolated, like those made, fairly recently, at MIT for the Club of Rome, which forecast global collapse within a comparatively short period, usually ignore the factor which in various kinds of systems, is called 'negative feedback'.

In human systems too, feedback operates. Human societies are to some extent self-correcting, however tardy, clumsy and partial the process may be. Self-correction is already, I believe, in operation in Western societies today – and it is to be hoped that Ireland, which has been a latecomer to Western affluence, will not feel it necessary to go through the whole series of destructive mistakes which the earlier arrivals have made before arriving at the point of correction too.

Self-correcting feedback, however, operates not only within the Western systems but within the whole global system which they have dominated. For all the grimness of its possibilities, in the short run, for the developed West, there is a certain beauty in the present crisis, because it shows neo-colonialism suddenly going into reverse and makes plain what a great many people in the West would have ignored or denied, that our affluence and comfort are directly derived in part from the exploitation of other parts of the world. Admittedly the oil-sheiks are not candidates for sympathy. It is just because of the peculiar situation of Mid-East oil – that it happens to occur in largely desert countries and that its exploitation has occurred, socially speaking, almost *in vacuo* – that it has been possible for the exploitation to go so readily into reverse. The superpower confrontation in the Middle East, which rules out Western military retaliation, adds to the special conditions.

Because, in microcosm, as it were, the oil-sheiks have already won the affluence race and have achieved what appears to be the ultimate aim of the law-and-order-abiding householders of the Western world: gold-plated Cadillacs fitted with wall-to-wall carpeting, air-conditioning, colour television, cocktail cabinets, deep freeze, houris and blue movies. They have discovered the capitalist secret that the more anti-social one is the better it pays, and, like the property specula- tors (the owners of Centre Point in London, to take a good example) that it is possible to make more money by not providing a service than by providing it. Not selling oil turns out to be more profitable than selling it.

The crisis has a beauty too (the kind of beauty which a good mathematical proof possesses) in its *quod erat demonstrandum* of the Common Market. The cant about the ideal of European unity vanishes. The rules of the Community vanish, insofar as they conflict with the various national self-interests. The greed which united the Nine now drives them apart, or at least drives eight of them apart from the Netherlands.

But the main beauty of the crisis is that, while it will undoubtedly give rise to much suffering and distress, as must anything which causes a sudden revolution- ary change of direction in the affairs of great and complex societies, it has come much sooner than might have been expected and therefore will in the long run spare much more suffering than it causes. And it has struck at one of the chief agents of destruction of the civilization our forefathers built with much effort and thought: the misuse of the motor car.

It seems very likely that people of future generations (and I optimistically believe that there *will* be future generations) will look back with incredulity on the society that committed itself so wholeheartedly to such a monster as the mo- tor car in its present form. Belching out poisonous gas, killing hundreds of peo- ple daily, demanding roads, space and raw materials at fantastic expense to the world at large, and proving insatiable in demand for ever increasing supply of these, this monster has been altering, generally destructively, the face of both town and city in order to cater to the laziness and self-importance of a small proportion of the human race. It is not the internal combustion engine as such that is the monster: it is the social mosntrosity that has been made of it in the West.

The action of the Arab rulers may provide no more than a temporary check to the crazy career of our advertizing-dominated culture; but there is a possibiliy – no more – that it may do much more and that it may have come at the right time to make clear how unreal our never-satisfied consumer world was becoming and to give us a chance to pause, perhaps to change direction and perhaps to reassess the values of our own culture.

27

A German Boom City

Here in Frankfurt the old city centre was largely destroyed by the bombing raids of the Second World War, which caused the destruction of eighty per cent of the buildings in much of the inner city. The old city had preserved memories of the medieval imperial past – it had been the coronation place of the Holy Roman emperors – and was described by Goethe as the 'secret capital' of Germany.

The memories were embodied in streets, squares and buildings in a mixture of rather heavy late medieval and equally heavy Renaissance styles, like a good operatic setting. Its destruction is much regretted by those who remember the prewar Frankfurt but is more or less forgotten by those who have been struggling down the years to make, not just a living, but a 'standard of living' in this boom-town of Germany's 'economic miracle'. The rubble and ruins were cleared away more than twenty years ago and a new city grafted on to what was left of the old. In the inner city the tracks of the falling sticks of bombs can be traced by the twenty-year-old apartment blocks inserted among housing of the earlier part of the century, or of the palmy imperial days between the Franco-Prussian War and the Great War. Where the bombs fell, usually only the churches remain ruined (although tidy). In all else, life has long since reasserted itself.

It must be at least fifteen years since the last major gaps left by the bombing were filled by the frenzy of postwar rebuilding. As might be expected in such circumstances, the rebuilding was undistinguished architecturally – utilitarian and often not much better than shoddy – and has been accompanied by the visual squalour to which our late-twentieth-century eyes are accustomed: strident advertisement hoardings and signs, wires, cables, poles and all the litter and clutter generated by an economy of waste. A second wave of new building is now occurring, and is causing problems here which are familiar in New York, London, Dublin and most of the cities of the Western world. Deep excavation in many of the main streets for a new underground transport system is causing disruption to traffic and commerce, while large parts of the inner suburban areas are being cleared by property developers for the erection of new office blocks.

A new crop of skyscrapers, sheathed in glass, is rising like mushrooms through the haze of atmospheric pollution. Great yellow machines snarl and bang, claw-

---

This was written in Frankfurt am Main and was published in the 'Roots' column in the *Irish Times*, 6 November 1973.

ing into the earth, or pulverizing the stone and brick of buildings the bombers missed. The familiar combined assaults of the motor car and the property developer show signs, here as elsewhere, of doing serious damage to the life of the city. In places these assaults are intimately combined, for in the commercial heart of Frankfurt most of the developers' high-rise glass boxes are not in fact office blocks but car parks.

These of course have not diminished the traffic in the streets below, for there is a kind of Parkinson's Law relating to the motor car, to the effect that enough cars will come to jam the space provided for them.

Frankfurt is a city more singlemindedly devoted than most to money. It is the Federal republic's financial centre, and almost all the new shining skyscrapers bear the names of banks. And, largely because of the wartime destruction of its historic centre, it is a no-star city in the *Michelin Guide*. In spite of this, there are movements of resistance to the developers. There has been considerable agitation about some threatened properties. Some weeks ago the *Frankfurter Allgemeine Zeitung* in a special article discussed several cases of old or threatened buildings, among them a house known as the Varrentrapp Villa, in the inner suburb known as Westend. This, which has long been vacant, is threatened with demolition but is being defended by a special action committee of local residents. The Varrentrapp Villa is a large bourgeois house of the 1880s, quite typical of its kind and of its time. In this particular instance the good burgher's fantasy, or his architect's, took the form of a Romanesque castle, so that the large square comfortable building is fitted out with appropriate embellishments. It is not what would usually be regarded as a work of outstanding architectural interest, nor are several other houses in Westend which are being hotly defended by local groups.

There is nonetheless a sound instinct at work in the agitations. The motif which runs through the complaints of the protestors is that the places in which they live, and in which their forebears lived, are being invaded and destroyed or transformed out of recognition by strange, nameless, unseen people, whose agents come to smash down the old and to overwhelm mellow neighbourhoods with monstrous alien towers. It is a non-political, non-analytical, bourgeois instinct: 'A Frankfurter's home is his castle'. The case is put in terms of cultural, including aesthetic, values, but it seems to arise in the first instance from a simple instinct of self-protection.

A different case against the speculators is put in an agitation, run at quite a different level (since it is not 'respectable') by left-wing groups. Their point is that office blocks are being built not only in a diversion of effort which could supply new housing, but at the expense of old housing which is being unnecessarily destroyed. The agitation is at times noisy but it is likely to remain ineffective, since the chief sufferers from the housing shortage are alienated not only from the middle classes here but from the native workers.

They are the new proletariat, or slave-labour force, of the richer Common Market countries, the immigrants who do the dirty and low-paid work. They include Italians, but mostly come from outside the EEC: Greeks, Turks, Yugoslavs, Portuguese and Spanish. The Irish are not yet included, but otherwise the underdeveloped fringe of Europe is fairly comprehesively represented.

It is remarkable how consistently this pattern appears at present in the cities of our Western world. It is felt as a threat to many millions more than are directly aware of it. The reaction to the threat, naturally enough, sometimes takes the form simply of a desire to put the clock back. But the rational objections to the forces which are at work in our cities are by no means those merely of blind conservatism, or resistance to change. Germany, in a sense, has now lived through the space almost of a generation as a country without a history. The Nazi years and the War being impossible to live with in the late 1940s and the 1950s, the Germans simply cut themselves off from their past and concentrated on the present. But they too find that they cannot live without their past. Whatever about individuals, communities – cultures – cannot live wholly in the present. It is like being in space: the condition of weightlessness cause disorientation.

In terms of population, Frankfurt is comparable in size to Dublin. It has not yet reached the stage of crisis of many major American cities, the stage which, largely because of the effects of property speculation, London is fast approaching. But the population of the city itself is an inadequate measure of its problems, or even of the scale of what is involved. For Frankfurt is the centre of a rapidly agglomerating conurbation. From Mainz and Wiesbaden on the Rhine to Frankfurt and Offenbach on the Main there is a series of large, and barely discontinuous, urban blotches on the map, which soon will run together to form a continuous amorphous entity held together by the technology of conspicuous consumption and waste, and echoing day and night to the wail of ambulance and police sirens and the sound of jet-aircraft engines. The ubiquity of the motor car has made it *seem* possible for everybody in the Western world to emulate Boyd-Roche's bird and be in two places at once. It makes it seem possible for our cities to be occupied by people who actually live somewhere else: the office towers in one corner of the landscape, the dwelling towers in another. Indeed, to achieve this, it is necessary for everyone to occupy *three* spaces simultaneously, the third being the motor car itself, sixty to a hundred square feet of city occupied all day every day by each commuter.

Of course there is a flaw. All this only seems to be possible. In fact it is not. But what is being destroyed in pursuit of this illusion is not simply the heritage of the past. It is to a large extent the technology of the recent past (like, to take a very small example, Dublin's Harcourt Street railway line). We are all acting as if we had full confidence in the *permanence* of our highly complex present-day technology and are therefore willing to tear down everything that seems to impede it. And perhaps one of the arguments for not discarding our past completely is that parts of it may come in useful in the future.

28

The Archaeology of a Poem: Seamus Heaney's 'Seeing Things'

Like Sigmund Freud – another twentieth-century writer who combined insight with clarity and beauty of expression – Seamus Heaney is an archaeologist of the imagination and an excavator of the soul. In Freud's rooms at Berggasse 19 in Vienna, artefacts of ancient civilizations cluttered the shelves and tabletops. Before Dr Freud turned to thermodynamics for his lifelong elaborated metaphor of humanity's inner life, his model was the Near Eastern tell: the layered accumulation of the débris of experience, with consciousness and culture emerging from the earth of unreflective existence.

Dr Heaney's desktop may or may not be cluttered: he has a singularly uncluttered mind. But he too has reflected much on the stratifications of time and, more interestingly, on other hierarchical layerings – of modes of being, for example. As one who has worked for many seasons on the palimpsest of palpable earth, I find his procedures have a natural appeal. 'I'll dig with it', he says of his pen, which is 'snug as a gun', but he promises, not so much to beat the sword into a ploughshare – although that too – as to go

> down and down
> For the good turf.

This has led to superficial comment in some literary journalism, where occasional snide remarks in the past few years about Heaney's interest in bogs and the like reveal a tendency to try to relegate him to a Celtic fringe, too far from the Home Counties to be truly serious. No doubt the Nobel laureate in literature will mend that. Heaney is indeed a long way from the Home Counties, but Tollund Man doesn't speak to him in a Derry accent.

He begins, like an archaeologist, with the material culture; begins, of necessity therefore, with the material itself, a very difficult thing to do. He has the rare and remarkable ability to make the reader feel the dense incomprehensible reality of a drop of water on the rim of a bucket in a country kitchen as if it were a special creation. Claritas. The unbearable intensity of being. It is a candour of vision, recalling:

Previously published in the *Recorder* (New York), vol. 9, no. 1, Spring 1996.

> Vides ut alta stet nive candidum
> Soracte, nec jam sustineant onus
> Silvae laborantes, geluque
> Flumina constiterint acuto.

or:

> Maidid glass for cach lus
> bilech doss daire glais . . .

or:

> Ships, towers, domes, theatres and temples lie
> Open unto the fields, and to the sky;
> All bright and glittering in the smokeless air.

The difficulty of doing this is perhaps expressed by Wittgenstein's remark:

> 'A thing is identical with itself'. – There is no finer example of a useless
> proposition, which is yet connectd with a certain play of the imagination.
> It is as if in imagination we put a thing into its own shape and saw that it
> fitted.

This is what Heaney can do; but it is only the beginning. 'Seeing Things', the title poem of his 1991 collection, is in three parts, the third and longest being a kind of envoy. Parts 1 and 2 both describe, and bring into imaginative reality, moments in a travelled life. The first recounts the commital of the poet and some others to a boat making the short crossing from Inisbofin to the mainland on a Sunday morning. Why Sunday morning? No doubt that's when the trip was made; but it is also a time out of time, a pause, a change of mode, a recreation of the soul. Inishbofin is a real place, in County Galway, with two hotels, where they take credit cards. But in the realm of imagination it is an island in the ocean St Brendan sailed, beyond the end of the world. It is 'the island of the white cow' (and it is white cows, with red ears, that graze on the enchanted isles of the Otherworld). And it has a unique past. This is where imperial Ireland vanished over the sunset horizon of history after the Synod of Whitby in AD 664. At that meeting, as Arnold Toynbee put it, 'the issue at stake was whether the future civilization of Western Europe should derive from an Irish or from a Roman embryo; and on this issue the Irish were defeated ...' The vanquished monks left the North Sea island of Lindisfarne and settled, some of them in 'Mayo of the Saxons,' the others on Inishbofin.

The voyage with which the poem begins, is, to change the frame of reference, the crossing of the Styx: a return from the Underworld; which is the underlying theme of the work. In this it refers back to 'Station Island,' the title poem of the collection Heaney published in 1984; for Station Island in Lough Derg, County Donegal, is where, in the lore of medieval Europe, it was possible, through undergoing a great ordeal in the entrance cave, to make the pilgrimage to hell. That poem too opens with the stillness of Sunday and is marked by the apparition of

Orpheus with his lyre – who is also a neighbour, and is also the mad and wonder-
ful Sweeney, protagonist of a cycle of early Irish tales and of another cycle of
poems by Heaney:

> ... Sunday,
> the silence breathed
> and could not settle back
> for a man had appeared
> at the side of the field
>> with a bow-saw, held
>> stiffly up like a lyre.
>> He moved and stopped to gaze
>> up into hazel bushes,
>> angled his saw in,
> pulled back to gaze again
> and move on to the next.
> 'I know you, Simon Sweeney,
> For an old Sabbath-breaker
> who has been dead for years.'

The dead. The poet encountered them on Station Island. Tom Delaney (described, not named), an archaeologist, who was to die at the age of thirty-two. A
cousin, to be murdered in the Ulster blood feud. Here, in reading the poem, I
must intrude a personal gloss, being for a moment spun into the gyre of lives and
meanings. A July evening twenty or so years ago. Tom was a friend of mine too
and came more than once with his small family to stay with me in the County
Clare, where I was excavating on Holy Island, on the other Lough Derg (on the
Shannon), leaving his own digging in Carrickfergus to escape the week of the
Twelfth in the North. They arrived when the day's work was done, but I set out
to row his wife Máire and their new infant daughter Sarah to visit the island. The
boat, just delivered and not properly caulked after the winter, began to fill just
over the deep of the sound, and with cautious urgency I had to pull back to the
shore. The boat sank as we disembarked. It is perilous to change the element we
live in.

But the opening lines of 'Seeing Things' give us the concrete: the smell of
diesel exhaust, the kick of the starting engine, the alarming dip and skittishness
of a small boat as a man's weight comes down on it (conveying both the resilient
buoyancy of the water and the panic loss of stability). They were 'handed down'
into the ark 'one by one', to sit

> ... in nervous twos and threes,
> Obedient, newly close, nobody speaking ...

Then the perception deepens, as the poet peers over the gunwale through the 'deep, still, seeable-down-into water'. 'Seeable-down-into', an impedimental phrase, refracts: we are pushing down from air into liquid. But then he imagines himself looking

> from another boat
> Sailing through air, far up ...

This is like the near-death experience so often reported, where the person on the point of losing life has the sensation of being above the scene, looking down on the deathbed. Here, it is the view of a company, a people. Charon has counted them; they are, Biblically, 'numbered.'

And at this point the theme appears, a metaphor that runs through Heaney's work and draws on layers of imagined systems, from the buried dreams of many civilizations. It is the theme of the transcendental; overriding the bounds between one medium or sphere and another; which, in a sense, is what 'Seeing Things' means. There was once a widespread legend along the west coast of Ireland, of a lost city beneath the waves, visible every seventh year, a fatal sight. Mr and Mrs Hall reported, from their tour of 1840, that the city had last been seen on a Sunday morning in 1823 by a boat's crew of fifteen, who perished. While they were drowning at sea they were seen by their neighbours on the shore apparently at Mass in their company. Seeing things. And there are many stories of saints, like Brendan, Barra and Scoithín, to whom the watery deep, their element, was as a plain covered with flowers.

But the reference in the poem is not so much to submarine worlds; rather to the air above and to another legend which is the subject of a different passage in Heaney's 1991 collection:

> The annals say: when the monks of Clonmacnoise
> Were all at prayers inside the oratory
> A ship appeared above them in the air.

The ship's anchor caught in the altar rails and a sailor came down the cable to free it but got into difficulties. The abbot had the monks help him: otherwise he would drown. So he

> ... climbed back
> Out of the marvellous as he had known it.

The humanity of the act is the colour of Heaney's vision: he has restored a holistic mystical truth to the disintegrating Swedenbogian 'correspondences' of his Symbolist predecessors.

The second part of the poem begins not with the concrete but with the abstract; not even with an English abstract noun but with the Latin word 'Claritas', standing alone. Pliny refers to 'claritas sideris Veneris' – 'the brilliance of the

Morning Star' – and the second part of 'Seeing Things' has something of the clarity of that other poem of brilliant epiphany, 'Mossbawn Sunlight'. 'Claritas', the opening statement of part two, for Heaney is a 'dry-eyed Latin word'. It comes immediately after the note of acute pathos that ends part one. We are going for the dry power of knowledge now, to reach the shore, not for life which drowns in emotion. The poet and his company are submerged 'up to our eyes' in *air* (but imagining, and seeing through, water). The theme begins to be universalized. We are shown a relief of the Baptism of Christ on the facade of a cathedral in the blazing sunlight of Mediterranean Europe. The significance of baptism was drowning; dying to the world of sin and imperfection, followed by rebirth.

The Baptism of Christ makes its appearance in the art of the fifth century, its iconography already fully worked out. The Jordan was reputed to have two sources, and these are represented by two personages (derived from river gods) pouring out water from urns. Christ stands in the river while St John pours water over him from a dipper, a dove descends from heaven and the right hand of God appears from behind the clouds to signify divine approval. The Baptism is depicted on some Irish high crosses—the broken cross at Kells, for example, where the two sources are rather clumsily represented by disc-shaped features.

In due course, through the centuries, the iconography was tidied up, and in particular the different dimensions of heaven, air, water and earth were sorted out hierarchically. 'Lines which are concentric and sinuous represent the sky, those which are horizontal and undulating represent water', as Émile Mâle wrote about the conventions of medieval art. You can see the right hand of God emerging from concentric segments of circles (the sky) on the underside of the north arm of Muiredach's Cross at Monasterboice (but the inability to distinguish right from left goes back a long way in Ireland: the Dextera Dei, God's right hand, at Monasterboice is a left hand).

The poem shows us this iconography in its developed form, on 'the facade of a catedral': a Romanesque relief; and this kind of sculpture is itself a figure for what Heaney is doing. For it is low relief, a suppression of sculptural quality, and therefore a kind of contradiction, or rather, resolution of contradiction: *Aufhebung*. Greek sculptors working on pediment or frieze still thought in the round, and the reliefs for, for example, the Panathenaic procession depicted on the Parthenon frieze, or the procession of noble persons on Augustus's Ara Pacis, overcome their mural situation and consequent lack of rear space by forming a strip series without great need for foreshortening. Those who *painted* walls, on the other hand, as at Pompeii, attempted an illusion or at least suggestion, of aerial space not by working in three dimensions but by flattering the beholder's eye with recollections of distant landscapes and arching skies. And there were many compromises; but the sculptors of the Romanesque tympana and porches, masters superseding the Late Antique tradition, could turn from series of prophets or saints or apostles in frieze-like arrangements to attempt set-pieces in which they emulated the painters' graphic skills – making the stone, as it were, dissolve, offering us perspectives and chiaroscuros that lead the eye through their intractable medium into an imagined space.

This is what the poet has observed, and he has also discerned, among other things, how sunlight seems solid and permanent, stone diaphanous and translucent. Fish are depicted among the wavy lines that delineate the Jordan, and Heaney sees through the sculptor's stone, and beyond it, to the delicate renderings of water's refracted transparency in the sculptor's remote models in Byzantine mosaics and Roman murals. And beyond that to the enchanted world below the Inishbofin boat, until it is 'the shadowy, unshadowed stream itself' that is the medium of life, while the shimmering air on the cathedral steps is the medium of drowning.

And the wavy strips of stone that are the sculptor's sign for water become 'the zig-zag hieroglyph for life itself.' So the theme is further universalized, beyond Christendom. The horizontal zigzag line is the Egyptian hieroglyph that represents, in the alphabetical series, the letter N. But water is life. The Nile, pictographically shown by the zigzag, was the life of Egypt, as the Liffey (according to Joseph Campbell, discussing *Finnegans Wake*) was 'also the river of the energy of life that is ever pouring through us and all things into the void from which it simultaneously rises.' Which recalls the Second Law of Thermodynamics in Robert Frost's 'West-running Brook':

> It flows between us, over us, and *with* us.
> And it is time, strength, tone, light, life and love –
> The universal cataract of death
> That spends to nothingness ...

Parts one and two of 'Seeing Things' form a kind of palindrome (mirror images of meaning rather than verbal form), two half shells of a walnut whose kernel is the interlocking duality of the first phrase of the second part and the last of the first. 'Claritas'; and how the poet, from his imagined boat in the sky over the Inishbofin expedition

> ... could see
> How riskily we fared into the morning
> And loved in vain our bare, bowed, numbered heads.

'In vain'. Here, in the heart of the poem, the fourth dimension is introduced (although we are already outside three- and into multi-dimensional space): time; 'numbered heads.' And memory. hrough all the layers of being, with their translucencies, opacities and refractions, we focus on the tender fragility of our human life, with the 'claritas' of 'little antic fish ... all go.'

And the third movement, separate, is the personal memory, powerfully evoked, of the event that stimulated the claritas of this reflection, the accident that almost drowned the poet's father, when a horse drawing a potato-sprayer reared so that

> ... the whole rig went over into a deep
> whirlpool ...

We may hear an echo here of Eliot's Phlebas the Phoenician:

> ... He passed the stages of his age and youth
> Entering the whirlpool ...

This part is introduced by a framing, and reassuring, formula: 'Once upon a time ...' We expect, and receive, the conclusion to the piece, '... happily ever after'. Between the two formulae, between the two elements, air and water, we have a moment of undirected activity, a moment of chaotic motion, a loosening of the restraints that separate one medium from another, life from death, time from memory, us from our imagined selves, being from nothingness. There is confusion, anguish, pity, terror, love, in the two modes of time, before and after: first 'my undrowned father', then:

> ... scatter-eyed
> And daunted, strange without his hat ...

This is also inverted: after and before; for the father, who is, after, dead, is undrowned after his drowning, without his surrogate hat, which is

> ... merrily swept along
> The quieter reaches.

The poem is a fugue, its counterpoint returning us by 'a commodious vicus of recirculation' to that moment of peril, poised between one mode of being and another, which is our human life. The claritas is powerful, sexual in its energy (Heaney is like Yeats in this, and like Rilke), and the simple little poem, like a pebble dropped in a pond, sends shining rings ever outwards. He has achieved Rilke's intention:

> ... Dann, stark und breit,
> mit tausend Würzelstreifen
> tief in das Leben greifen –
> und durch das Leid
> weit aus dem Leben reifen,
> weit aus der Zeit!
> [Then, with all my strength,
> through a thousand tangled roots
> to search deep into life –
> and through grief
> to fruit far from life;
> far from time!]

29

Irish America

A touch or two of schmaltz, a chilling glimpse here and there of the mailed fist, and the uneasy presidential visit was over, the American president winging his way onward to the world of global power struggles. He – and we – in the course of the few days had a brief view of three Irelands.

One was the young Ireland whose concern about oppression and poverty in the Third World is reinforced by its own bleak prospect in an economy that is characterised by greed, callousness and increasing dependency on the rich and powerful of the earth. This is the Ireland of involvement in missionary and social work both at home and abroad. It is also increasingly represented by various sects and factions of the Left, although these are, for the moment less significant. With its placards and slogans it was kept at considerably more than arm's length by the president's heavy squads.

The second was the Ireland of the political and business establishment. Every country has to have, or is bound to have, its caste of functionaries, tycoons, executives, placemen, and the like, and from country to country the variations are minor. It was with this Ireland, of course, that the visitor was in close and direct contact. The absence of bishops on the main occasions may be an omen. It is certainly worth pondering.

The third Ireland was represented by Ballyporeen. Ballyporeen, ideally situated for this representative function, slightly off the main tourist routes (up to now) but in the heart of Munster, appears to be one of those places that have preserved, as if in amber, the values of the rural Ireland of fifty years ago. I don't mean to suggest that Ballyporeen is not, in other respects, as up-to-date as anywhere else. I mean that, to the America that generations of ordinary Irish people looked to with hopes of dignity and freedom, Ballyporeen could show the face of the Ireland that Irish-Americans of President Reagan's generation would like to imagine or remember.

This is a quite complex relationship that is of the greatest importance for understanding modern Ireland. For two hundred years or more America's effects on our country's development have been profound, if often indirect. They are perhaps as important in their influence on mind and imagination as in any other way.

After the centuries of migration there are about nine times as many Ameri-

---

Previously published in the *Irish Times*, at the time of President Reagan's visit to Ireland.

cans who claim Irish descent as there are people on our island. They include descendants of those (a large proportion of them from Plantation Ulster) who emigrated to the colonies before the Revolution, as well as people, reared and educated in Ireland, who crossed the Atlantic ten or twenty years ago. To generalize about the forty-odd millions would be rash – except to note that they are all primarily *Americans*.

But to visit Irish America, especially to live for a while among Irish Americans, is to learn something about the culture from which they and we came. There are reflections, as in the curved mirrors in a fairground, that are at once distorting and disturbingly revealing.

When this series was being prepared, in the spring, I visited Pittsburgh, Pennsylvania, for the St Patrick's Day weekend. The city had, for me, the advantage that I have lived there for a year, have visited it a number of times, and have friends, including a number of American Irish, or Americans closely interested in Ireland, who were willing and able to open their minds.

Pittsburgh is a middle-sized American city, of the same order of size as Dublin, but wholly different in character. It is founded on coal and steel (and transportation: at the head of the Ohio river, it was an important port in the supremely important navigational system that opened up the heart of the Continent in the last century). Like other towns dependent on 'smokestack industries' it has been slow to benefit from the American economic recovery (if indeed it is an economic recovery) of the past few years. But the air has been cleaned of smoke and soot, and glittering new skyscrapers mark what Pittsburgh calls its 'renaissance'.

The city is dominated, numerically, by East European ethnic groups. There is a large black population, mostly poor and (in every sense) depressed. There are other 'minorities' in this characteristically pluralistic city, including, somewhat surprisingly, quite a large colony of Indians (Indians from India).

But the Irish, and the Scots, have been in Pennsylvania since long before the Revolution. They were in the woods when Washington reconnoitred Pittsburgh (then Fort Duquesne) in the French and Indian War. They were on the river flatboats. They came in the pre-Famine and post-Famine migrations, worked in the mines and mills, built the railroads, thronged into the Union armies in the War Between the States. They came in smaller numbers since then, but there are quite a few, even now, who were born and grew up in Ireland. The Irishness of all these people is the background to an experience which is American.

Pittsburgh puts on one of the biggest Patrick's Day parades. It is a holiday occasion. People come downtown with their children, wives, girl-friends, and enjoy a day out. There's lots of that harsh 'Kelly green' that has now come to symbolize Irishness. In card-shops, confectioners, pubs and elsewhere, there is some display of leprechauns, shillelaghs, and 'top of the morning' or 'begorrah' greetings. 'Kiss me: I'm Irish', however, is commoner. In the busy American pluralism, where each ethnic community has to have its readily recognized symbols, these are just the codes for 'Irish'. And it is a gesture of goodwill for others to adopt them for the day. After the parade I was bought a beer by a Greek-

American district attorney, wearing a vivid green favour, who was professionally and perceptively interested in the crime problem in Dublin.

There are some in that city, with Irish names, who have never set foot in Ireland (or for that matter in Europe), but retain a keen and enduring interest in Ireland and its welfare. The interest is neither wholly sentimental nor wholly uninformed. There are half-a-dozen or more Irish-American societies. Most of them take the trouble to diffuse up-to-date information about Ireland and Irish affairs. This is largely for the benefit of those of the American Irish who continue to maintain, in their homes, beliefs, customs, an outlook that derives from the country of their ancestral origin. The American 'melting-pot' never quite melted down all the 'ethnics', and it is no longer felt that it should. And the Irish have done extremely well, rising through the American class system to a secure, indeed commanding, position in many areas of life.

There is, in other words, a very large body of people across the Atlantic that takes a keen and moderately well informed interest in our affairs. Not all American Irish do, by any means. But enough do. They are not a homogeneous body. But they have in common not only this interest in us, but also the great confidence engendered by their own successful history in a very hard world.

30

Some Ulster Protestants

There has been a fashion for some years now for what is known as 'oral history'. It is felt to be somehow more democratic than the kind that works with archives and documents. It is the record not merely of the recording class, the people who keep documents because as often as not they keep control. It gives access to the *real* people.

Well, there is some truth in this. There are some people whose story is told, not written – unless it is to be taken down and written from their telling. The famous Blasket autobiographies, *An tOileánach* and *Peig*, are oral histories of a kind, and classics of a kind, giving us an unforgettable picture of a way of life that is no more. But oral history has real defects. It depends on memory, and memory is fallible. We constantly rearrange our own past in our minds, when we are not thinking about it at all, and when we are called upon to recount some episode we present a version which is pre-edited. It is astonishing how we re-order what might seem to be the most innocuous events; as soon becomes clear if there happens to be a contemporary written record by which the verbal reminiscence can be checked.

Nonetheless, talking to people can tell us a lot about them and about their society. I have recently paid two visits to Ulster, one in the marching season of July, the other more recently, to talk to people. The people were Protestants, and they would mostly fall into the broad category that we would loosely describe as 'middle class'. We have had a good deal of information supplied to us in recent years about the views, attitudes and 'tradition and identity' of loyalists, of working class background. It is among working class people that Ulster 'extremists' are largely to be found. It is from their ranks that the UDA and the UVF are mostly recruited, and it is they who give their support, in parts of the northern province, to Dr Paisley and the DUP rather than to the official Unionist or Alliance parties – although in other parts many working class Protestants vote Unionist, and some vote Alliance.

Extreme views command attention, and extremists are vociferous in expressing their views. But we have become familiar with the idea (possibly erroneous) that there is in most countries a 'quiet majority'. At any rate there are lots of quiet

This is an account of conversations, suggested by Douglas Gageby, that appeared in three parts in the *Irish Times* in 1986.

people, whose views don't come to us every day on television and radio, or in the papers.

In talking to people, in fact, I met quite a few who didn't want their names to appear in the paper – not necessarily for the reasons that might first spring to mind. Some are simply modest, or retiring. Many, however, are undoubtedly uneasy at the thought of having public attention drawn to them, although they were quite willing to express their views anonymously, for the record. One or two, because of the nature of their work, wouldn't talk, even anonymously, for the record. This caution was striking. Almost everyone was willing to talk at length: there is some need for expression. Everyone in the North has quietly or otherwise absorbed the impact of cruel, violent, sudden and random events, and has had to find some meaning for them. The cumulative effect of a number of conversations in different parts of the province has shown me that there is a considerable difference in mentality at the moment between middle-class Protestants and middle-class Catholics on the whole (and I don't simply mean what is obvious, that by and large they have different political opinions). But what they all have in common is having had to react to the 'Troubles', to re-examine their views, perhaps to examine their consciences. Throughout Ireland we have had to do that. Naturally, however, it is particularly the case in the North.

There are, as I would read it, three main constituents in Protestant Ulster. These derive, firstly from the Plantation, where the settlement was drawn from both England and Scotland, affecting six counties including two (Cavan and Donegal) which are now in the Republic. The second came from the dense settlement, in the seventeenth century, of parts of Antrim and Down, chiefly by Scottish Calvinists. The third, which is very important, derives from the after-effects of the Industrial Revolution and the consequent integration of east Ulster into the economy of northern Britain. It maintained a fairly steady movement of people, over most of the past two centuries, between Ulster and Britain, and accounts for much of the settlement around Belfast.

Mr Leonard Troheir, a bank manager who lives at Craigavad, near Bangor, County Down, told me about his surname, for example:

> Troheir: my grandfather originally came from Cumberland. Yes. And in that area, St Bees and Whitehaven, and down that coast there are Troheirs. He came over here and he settled in Castlewellan, which is near Newcastle, and he started up what's known as a boot factory. He called it a boot factory. It was just really a loft over a boot shop. And they made clogs. And then he was very ambitious, and he formed a company with some folk over in Liverpool, a little shipping company called the West Coast Shipping Company. That shipping company developed from the nineteenth century up until the Second World War. At that point they had about eight or ten little steamboats. They were working all around the British Isles. They originally started off: Belfast across to Liverpool – that sort of thing – but gradually they worked all round the coast. They were little coasters, and

during the War they were all torpedoed, except one. Of course, my grandfather was dead at that point, but the shares reverted to my father and the
family, and whenever they were torpedoed, of course they thought that
they had lost all their money. But after the War was over they got a great
sum of war damage money in payment for the ships ... Ships at that time
were very expensive to build, so they decided at that time that they would
wait a few years until prices would be down. But of course prices escalated
and they never got the ships built, and the money was divided out among
the family.

A striking number of the people I talked to could illustrate the frequent and
constant intercourse with Britain through their own immediate ancestry. Michael
Longley, the poet, who, with his wife Edna, entertained me, is English a couple
of generations back. As is that other, elder, Ulster poet, John Hewett – but some
distance further back. Come to think of it, my own maternal grandfather was
born in Liverpool, although as the son of Irish exiles. Before independence, at
the beginning of the present century, Dublin too had a close settlement relationship with Liverpool, and Lancashire craftsmen came over, for example, to industries like Guinness's brewery. In the North, such links are maintained, strength-
ening, generation by generation, the British connection with east Ulster.

I have one daughter – Mr Troheir told me – She is twenty-seven. She has
been to university and has a B.Sc. in Psychology. And then, when she was
doing her thesis and she had to write about animal study – they usually
write about rats or white mice or something like that, and experiment
with them – she was keen on horse riding and she asked the professor
could she write about horses. She did a great study of horses and it was
very well received. She got an honours degree. She found out that the
only university in the world where they do a degree in Equine Study is
University College of Wales in Aberystwith. She went over there and got
an M.Sc. in Equine Study. She's the only person in the whole of Northern
Ireland – maybe in the whole of Ireland; I don't know – with a degree in
Equine Study. But nevertheless, with all this, she's unemployed; she's on
the dole, she can't get a job. She's had various jobs in research but at the
moment she's unemployed. It's not like the South of Ireland where, perhaps if she was down there, she'd get work round the Curragh or some
place. She's tried to get a job down there. She has tried, but, well, you
know the unemployment situation down there is very bad.

Mr Troheir went on to say that the unemployment situation in the North was
very bad too, but that it seemed just now as if things might be getting a little
better.

> As you know the bank rate is gradually coming down, which makes it easier for companies to borrow money ... Trade's generally picking up a little bit.

I talked to him about industry in the North.

> As you know, the big industry in Belfast is ship-building. Only today I was down – the bank has an office down in the actual shipyards, Harland and Wollfs, and of course a lot of the customers are shipyard workers coming in – and now they're still paying men off. They're trying to streamline the shipyard. They can't beat the Japanese for price. Although Belfast-built ships are known throughout the world. You know the Titanic ws built there (he laughed) and they've just rediscovered it miles down.

Leonard Troheir comes from north Belfast, where his father was a traveller for shoes. He had two sisters and he went to a public elementary school.

> ... A model school, which had very high educational standards. You had to pay fees at this school. The idea was that the fact that you paid fees kept the lower class of people away from that school. The children paid something like three-and-sixpence per quarter, but the fact that you paid just brought it that little bit higher in the social scale. And Mod School was renowned for lifting scholarships, and there was a scholarship class at that school. You came in early in the morning. Whilst the other pupils perhaps started at nine o'clock, you started at half-past eight, so that you had your homework asked and there wasn't valuable teaching time wasted. And you worked a little longer in the afternoon.

His father was anxious that he should enter a bank, and that is what he did, having attended commercial courses in the Technical High School. He passed Matriculation, sat for the Civil Service examinations, and then entered for the old Belfast Savings Bank, and has been in the bank ever since.

> Yes, we were a church-going family. My father always set the standard. We were originally Church of Ireland, and when my father got married and moved to north Belfast, the church was some distance away, but there was a convenient Methodist church; so we all went to the Methodist church, and very regularly every Sunday morning we went to the Methodist church. When I got married and came down to live in this house, here in Craigavad, which is eight miles from Belfast, we went to the Methodist church at Bangor, which is another six miles down the road. Lately, we found that we were going six miles, and we were only going there on Sunday. Whilst we knew the congregation, the people who sat round us, we didn't really mix with them the rest of the week. So, there's a local

Presbyterian church just up the road, and one Sunday morning we were a
little bit late for Bangor: we called into the Presbyterian church, and we
got a very nice reception – a nice young minister. So we've been there now
for a year, and we like it very well indeed.

Craigavad is a well-to-do area, quiet and easily protected. Mr Troheir's house
looks northward over the waters of Belfast Lough. There is golfing. There is
fishing on the Lough. People have yachts and smaller boats. Numbers of the
houses have been used by the Secretary of State's office for housing officials. But
no one in Northern Ireland wholly escapes being touched by the Troubles. In
Leonard Troheir's case, he has had armed bank raids to cope with, when he
managed a branch in the city. And, as he mentioned, there is no family that has
not been touched, in some of its members, by death or injury.

If our society in the Republic suffers from being too homogeneous, as I think
it does, we might expect to find a greater liveliness in Northern Ireland. But, the
Troubles aside, things seem to be just as static there. About ten years ago the
Canadian anthropologist Elliott Leyton published a study of the Protestant community in a County Down fishing village, under the title *The One Blood* (subti-
tled *Kinship and Class in an Irish Village*). Aughnaboy, the fictitious name for a
readily identifiable place, is a Protestant village in a Catholic countryside. The
findings about its kinship and class could be applied with little change to villages
elsewhere in Ireland, north and south. The religious difference, and the tensions
arising from it, affect in Ireland only limited areas of life. Dr Leyton, in another
study of the County Down area, where he dealt directly with the Orange-Green
or Protestant-Catholic tension, suggests that we have not two communities or
two cultures, but a dual community of a type known in other parts of the world,
in which complementary relationships operate in much of daily life, shared relationships in other areas.

In visiting Ulster to talk to Protestants in the province, middle-class people
like those who live in the Dublin or Cork suburbs, I thought it was worth while to
look at an area in the Republic, in Ulster, where there is a reasonably high Protestant population. In Rathmelton, County Donegal, I stayed with the Church of
Ireland rector, the Revd Brian Smeaton, an old friend, and his wife. Brian is a
Wicklow man, who worked in a bank before entering the church, and then served
for a number of years in Belfast before moving to Rathmelton. This is Plantation
country, and Rathmelton is a Plantation town. There is a sizeable Church of Ireland congregation and there is also quite a large Presbyterian community. There
are in fact two Presbyterian churches in the town – three, if the old meeting
house, which is an historic monument by now, were to be added in – although
here is only one minister.

The previous minister, Dr Scott, served here for half a century, from the
1920s. His predecessor also served for half a century, having begun his ministry
by travelling to America to raise the money to put up a decent church building,
and having come back with success. The place has quite early American associa-

tions, since it was occupied from an early date in the Plantation and had a Presbyterian community in the seventeenth century which survived Anglican persecution, and was involved in the establishing of Presbyterian churches in the eastern United States.

Mrs Scott, the widow of the former minister, talked to me at some length about the Presbyterian history of the place, including her late husband and his predecessor. She is, she told me, a 'real republican', meaning that very accurately: she looks back to what republicanism meant in the eighteenth century. She and her late husband were both County Antrim people. She married at eighteen; he was called to County Donegal, and she has lived on the shores of the Swilly ever since.

Mrs Scott represents a particular, liberal, tradition in Ulster Presbyterianism, and is proud of it. In her conversation, she associated herself, again and again, in talking about her background, with her husband. They were obviously not only very close, but they came from very similar traditions: non-Orange, non-covenanting, to take the negatives; plain-speaking and plain-dealing, to take the positives. Her husband was a man who practised a Christian ecumenism. Just when the Troubles were beginning in the North, he took part in what must have been very nearly a unique ceremony for this part of the world. He joined with the then Church of Ireland rector in the burial service of his friend, the parish priest. 'And just a few miles away', as Mrs Scott put it to me, 'they were fighting one another in the streets of Derry.'

Her house is a history in itself. What is now the kitchen is the original Plantation cottage. A Georgian enlargement was succeeded by a Regency extension to the charming drawing room. And there are twentieth-century additions to make a house which has character, elegance and, in its fittings and decorations, many evidences of a distinctive Ulster past.

Mrs Scott is and always has been active in the affairs of the community. But it is necessary, she says, to get out of the community every now and then. Otherwise Rathmelton begins to become the centre of the world, if it doesn't become the whole world, and it's not big enough for that. Her son works in Dublin; she comes there from time to time and attends the Presbyterian church at the end of Highfield Road in Rathgar. She goes to Germany and Austria and has long-standing connections there. Just before the War she helped organize the escape and passage of Jewish girls from Munich and Vienna. Getting them into the twenty-six counties was difficult. The authorities tried to block it on the grounds that Irish people needed jobs. It was easier to bring them into Belfast, and then across the border.

She still has many connections in east Ulster, where she and her husband come from. Before the Troubles began, reunification of Ireland was a regular topic of light-hearted conversation, or banter, with them. She would put the view to them that 'one of these days we'd all be together in a united Ireland', and this was received in a good-humoured way. People were quite prepared to believe that she might be right, and even that, perhaps, in the end, it might not be the worst thing that could happen. No more. This is a matter which cannot be treated in a light-hearted way any more, nor would it be taken as a friendly act to talk in that way. Too much blood has been spilt. Everyone has been hurt, one way and another, and there is great bitterness.

Mrs Scott herself sees unification recede. She has plenty to keep her busy, looking after the affairs of Rathmelton and Donegal, keeping in touch with her family, keeping a window open on the wider world. She has the calm of a person of good will who does what has to be done, that is to hand, and does what is practicable to improve the world, leaving aside what can't be done. She is critical of much in the way we run our affairs in our state, and quite critical of the *Irish Times* for its, at times, unrealistic attitude to the North, as she sees it. But this, it seems to me, is in the way one is critical of one's own club.

Liberalism was once quite a force in Ulster Protestantism. It is difficult to say if it still is. Several of the people I talked to – in the professional classes, and, particularly, public servants – referred in one way or another, approvingly, to Armour of Ballymoney. But I had a feeling that this was both a cliché and a guarded evasion. Ulster Protestants are by no means immune to the Irish fault of giving the answer that is expected to please. In fact, it has been quite interesting to note, in dealing with the middle class people who conduct the affairs of Northern Ireland, that they display many of the characteristics that are stereotypically just plain 'Irish'. To offer a second- or third-hand connection with Armour of Ballymoney seemed to be a regular placatory gesture to the southerner who was not himself displaying hostility.

Country people were less apt to put up a polite smokescreen. A few miles west of Enniskillen, a farmer, although guardedly, told me of the tensions in the Border country and indicated (what I knew from previous conversations with people from that region) that there is a real sense there that the most deadly kind of civil war is already happening: the Protestants have been marked for extermination. This was a wary conversation and the man didn't want to be quoted or identified in any way. This kind of wariness, and half-hostility and suspicion, I find, paradoxically, more open than non-committal references to Protestant liberals or Irish patriots of the past.

The most rewarding discussion of liberalism I held with Edna Longley, after dinner in her house in suburban Belfast. Her husband Michael was there too and between them they offered the welcome and warmth that I have invariably found in the North, and the animated and argumentative conversation that one expects at any good dinner table in Ireland. I certainly expected it there, since it was not the first time they had so entertained me.

Michael, a Belfast man, is of English background by parentage. Edna is not a northerner. She was born in Dublin, the daughter of an eminent professor who gave up religion of any kind early in his career. She met Michael at Trinity and came north. She is now an Ulster Protestant by the framework of her life rather than by local origin or by faith. They are both liberals, but of slightly different kinds: their political opinions are by no means identical. Nor, should it be said, are they typical, if anything is 'typical', of the views of Protestant middle-class Ulster.

One of the things that seemed to me important in what Edna said concerned the place of Trinity in the life of several generations of Protestant Ireland in this century—Trinity before the lifting of the Catholic archbishop of Dublin's ban. It might be said, perhaps, that there were really two groups of educated middle-class Protestants in the early and middle years of the century: those (almost all from Ulster) who went to Queen's and remained, as it were, outside the Free State or Republic, although at Queen's they met a number of (fellow-Northern) Catholics, and those who went from North and South to Trinity, meeting there a small number of Catholics, but a large number of English and other non-Irish people. The small and scattered Protestant communities of the South, in Trinity, were reinforced morally, matrimonially (very important, in view of *Ne temere*, for people from tiny enclaves of Protestants from parts of southern Ireland) and nationally. It provided an intimate, secure, common ground and formed a society of kindred spirits, or at least kindred experiences, that would last through life.

The English who hadn't managed Oxford or Cambridge were the foil: doubly outsiders. The Irishness of the insiders was appreciated, and Trinity was an important unifying force, binding northern to southern Protestants; providing for the North a significant body of people who knew the South quite well and could contemplate it without horror. This has gone. The link is not quite broken but it is no longer substantial. Trinity has large numbers of Catholic students and comparatively small numbers from the Protestant North.

Michael Longley, I think, would say: unification perhaps some distant day, but not now, not soon. Edna, if I understand her rightly, would put the question aside altogether for the moment: there are other questions to deal with.

There are other questions to deal with. Rational and liberal people find that the particular kinds of violence we have had to face in these past fifteen years are not so much counter-productive as irrelevant to our long-term problems and aspirations. But we don't enjoy the luxury at the moment of looking too much to the long term.

Jimmy Millar is the representative of an engineering firm that specializes in cleaning out industrial plant. I met him in Belfast, in July, in the marching season, and he talked freely and cheerfully about his life and his views. An outgoing and gregarious man – 'I like to make at least one new friend every day' – who came up the hard way to occupy quite a good job, which he enjoys, he is an Orangeman and a Mason. (Perhaps partly because he is a 'joiner.') And he is a unionist. Yet, in pure and remote theory, he is not wholly opposed to the idea of a united Ireland. But not now, or in any immediately foreseeable circumstances. Perhaps in the context of some sort of renewed union with Britain.

He visits Dublin regularly on business and enjoys it: Dublin offers the amenities of a capital, and a life-style different from that of Belfast. A good place to visit. Jimmy's brother joined us, a somewhat quieter personality, but also quite willing to talk about himself and his family. His job is with the shipyard: he is an expert on certain types of repair to ships' engines, and he too comes to Dublin from time to time in the course of his business. He admires some things about the South: a capacity to work and to get things done. If the Irish could get together they would be the best people in the world. He has a son who is a very promising athlete, still at school, and he talked about sport. Here, although politically a unionist, he tended somewhat to be an all-Irelander. Both brothers struck me as being proud to be Irish – in a way that is becoming rarer south of the Border.

The influence of the shipyard reaches throughout the working life of Belfast, especially Protestant Belfast. The linen industry is all but gone, but shipbuilding and its ancillary trades affect the world of business, finance, education. In the Belfast College of Science and Technology, Catholic and Protestant students tend, I was told, to follow somewhat different courses, with the shipyard apprentices being mainly Protestant. Most of their work is in technical subjects, which allow them to retain intact and unsullied their tribal hostilities and prejudices: two hostile groups in a state of precarious truce. They have to take some humanizing courses, in sociology, psychology and other social studies. The youngsters readily understand what is being explained to them when the results of the latest sociological studies of prejudice are outlined. Prejudice they understand thoroughly. But the concept of 'tolerance' they find mystifying: it would upset all the right ordering of normal life.

I talked to two teachers in the more humane branch of second-level education – in ordinary secondary schools – to learn something of their views on Ireland, on life and on the world. Ross Ewart teaches history in the Belfast High School, which is on the way from Belfast to Carrickfergus.

> I think there's a greater interest and awareness in Irish history in Northern Ireland now than there was – he told me. – The BBC broadcasts an increasing number of Irish history programmes on the radio for schools, and most schools, if they pursue some form of Irish history, must inevitably present some view of Irish history during the course of that. In my own school, and in the contacts which I have had with other teachers ... I'm aware of an interest in Irish history, specially at more senior level ... At 'A' level the Northern Ireland GCE Board provides a special subject on 'Ireland 1912 to 1923', so I think there's a relevance now between what is happening in Northern Ireland and the events of the past, perhaps even an attempt to mitigate the failings of previous educationists or academics who sought to protect us from Irish history, or even to pretend that we were no part of Ireland and that Northern Irish schoolchildren should be taught the benefits of British history, British Imperial history, and to avoid any sort of Irish history.

Ross, who is, I think, just under thirty, was born on the Ormeau Road in Belfast. When his father, who was a member of the Masonic Order, died, he went, with his own assent, at the age of ten, to the Masonic School in Dublin, and spent seven very happy years there. He came from a very warm home background, but was full of praise for his teachers in Dublin. He wanted to teach, and was advised to go to Trinity, which he did.

> By the time I went to Trinity, perhaps I was one of a breed of people that Trinity was beginning to lose, because there was some concern, especially among the clergy, in Trinity, that the Ulster or Protestant identity of the university might begin to be submerged under the influx of mainly Southern Catholic students since the Archbishop of Dublin's ban on Catholic students entering Trinty had been lifted.

He found it hard, on returning to Belfast (after teaching for a year in Limerick) to adjust to being without his friends 'of the Dublin type.' He enjoys travelling, but:

> I don't see myself having any real inclination to leave, or break out of, the environment in which I live at the moment. Sometimes I find life in Northern Ireland perhaps rather parochial, and feel that life in England, or across the water, would be more conducive – I've always admired English people, for example. I suppose it's a natural conservative instinct in me to accept the system in which I live and to respect those who govern us and who hand down the laws which guide us in our everyday life. But I don't see myself having any real mission in life, other than to live from one day to the next, to perform my job, to travel, to see the world perhaps, but not to move beyond the British Isles.

He is a Methodist by birth, but:

> I'm not a regular church-goer, and I don't have any really firm ideas on religion. I do believe in the existence of a Supreme Being ... I feel that in many ways the clergy in Northern Ireland have failed to lift us out of the sorts of problems that we are trying to resolve every day of our lives. If the clergy could divorce themselves from political actions, perhaps we could feel that there was more for us in religion ...

Comparing the Republic with the North, he said:

> ... I think the political systems were very much the product of our history, in that both the Southern Irish political system and the Northern Irish political system were the creations of a British parliament, a British administration; and each has evolved from its origins in slightly different ways. I think that perhaps the social systems are equally conservative, but in different ways ... there's a conservatism about the Protestant ethos in

Northern Ireland in the same way as there's a conservatism in the Catholic ethos in the South. No matter what way one regards it, equally, Protestantism influences life in Ulster in the way that Catholicism can influence life in the South of Ireland. And I don't think I would want to sacrifice Protestantism in Ulster or Catholicism in the South of Ireland for each other. Either way, I think, both are going to have to change, to the demands and to the changes which are occurring right across the world.

On the present political situation, which he was keen to talk about, he said:

I would basically start from the viewpoint that direct rule has consistently proved in various opinion polls to be the least unpopular type of administration that Northern Ireland can enjoy. It's sometimes rather galling for an Ulsterman to feel that he is being dictated to by an Englishman. The scenes at Windsor Park when Northern Ireland is playing England are enough to make one realize the partisan nature of the Ulster Protestant. But I feel that, with my own views on the existence of Northern Ireland in its connections with Great Britain, that direct rule is perhaps, for the moment, the most effective form of administration. It is not the ideal ... If I had been asked in 1973 what I thought of the power-sharing agreement, I would probably have been rather lukewarm about it; but I think events tend to catch up with people, and I feel that if some solution could be arrived at where both Protestant and Roman Catholic politicians could sit down and could agree, perhaps, to deal with the social and economic problems of Northern Ireland, and to leave aside the political question for a number of years, that perhaps might be a solution ... I would consider myself to be a unionist with a small 'U'. I would like to think that the people of Northern Ireland could live on much better terms with their fellow islanders ... I have been impressed with the arguments that have been put forward in favour of a confederated British Isles, but I think it would be too much like wishful thinking to consider that the people in the South of Ireland would be prepared to sacrifice their independence ... By virtue of my interest in politics and in Irish history over the past seventy-five, eighty-five, years, I feel that the time is going to have to come when some attempt is made to sit down with representatives of Sinn Féin to discuss with them what they're prepared to accept. I think it is ridiculous for the Government to suggest that Ulster politicians should sit down and discuss with Sinn Féin at local level the sorts of problems which government ministers are not prepared to discuss – when they are the very people who legalized Sinn Féin as a political party.

David, as I shall call him, since he decided that, on the whole, he didn't want to be identified, is also a teacher, of Spanish. He is thirty-six years old, and married. He was born in Larne and brought up a Presbyterian, but says he feels he is not a typical Ulster Protestant. He seeks a quiet life, to pursue his interests in his family, his home, his job, travel and sport:

> The dominating influences in my life are not political. The dominating influences in my life are my wife, my house, my friends – I have a large circle of friends – and sport. I love sport, not just rugby, but squash, running, swimming: I love it, and that is what dominates my life. My social life is what dominates. I'm a man of simple tastes. I don't want to hear about people being shot and things blown up. I don't want to spend my life talking politics. I want to vote for people who will make my life more pleasant – for economic reasons and not for political reasons.

David is widely travelled, on both sides of the Atlantic, but knows Spain particularly well:

> I admire Juan Carlos tremendously ... I was in Spain under Franco, in 1972, and found it appalling. Total censorship ... censorship of everything, political opinion, cinemas, theatres, everything ... But I admire tremendously what Juan Carlos has done in changing the nation. I go to the country and see happier people, more relaxed people ... My opinion is the country is much better ... It's a very interesting country, because of the range of political opinion. Perhaps I admire Juan Carlos so much because he is trying to achieve what I would like to achieve: open-mindedness; democracy; working – working; totally diverse opinions being allowed to reside together. He has achieved with the Basques, the separatists, an incredible amount. His idea of giving them autonomy, their own autonomous government, has worked very well – while still retaining their Spanishness. People think of the Basque country as a terrible place: I can tell you it isn't. The people there are lovely. They have their ETA as we have our IRA. I suppose foreigners think of Ireland as being a country of terrorists. You and I know that it isn't. Well, Spain isn't a country of terrorists either.

He still resents having been separated, at the age of four, from his Catholic friends in Larne – the doing of the Catholic church authorities he says. But at Larne Grammar School, Catholics, being the exception, 'were tolerated rather than treated as equals.' The Catholic minority in Larne 'had to keep their heads very low.' He detests bigotry and was involved in a row about the presence of the Orange Order at church, and, last time he was at church in Larne, walked out because the minister preached against Catholics. He says, however, that his knowledge of religion and of the Presbyterian church is 'pathetic', and that this is not untypical.

I remember when I was at Queen's University talking about Ireland and a

United Ireland and saying I would quite like it. It's a very small island. For me, it's too small to be divided. But that was before the days of the IRA bombs. Now there is no way that I could vote for a united Ireland.

He is very pessimistic now about the North, and constantly thinks of emigrating. He admires Mother Teresa of Calcutta more than anyone in the world, and thinks that, by a levy on income, we should all contribute vastly more to the Third World. He still feels that the Irish are the friendliest people in the world – open and trusting.

> When I go away and people say 'what are you?', I say I'm Irish;

and

> If Ireland did not have bigoted politics, it would be the best place in the world.

David is, I think, less unusual among Ulster Protestants than he says. In fact, in many conversations, I found some quite consistent, if at times faint, recurring patterns. Notably there is a turning inward, and there are elements of that kind of dependency that patients develop in a hospital ward. But most persistent, and deep, unless my perceptions deceive me, was a sense of rejection. Not the rejection by England that is so often referred to; but rejection by Ireland.

31

The End of the Wall

The Berlin Wall has been coming down, to make paperweights and conversation pieces in Texas and California. Its demolition, when it began last year, was hailed in the United States, where I then was, as marking the victory of freedom over dictatorship; in particular, of the free market over the communist-dominated command economies of Eastern Europe. More generally in the West, it was greeted with relief as signifying the end of the Cold War.

The Wall, however, was more than a symbol. It was both a closely guarded frontier and an actual physical barrier that served a purpose. The Wall, it must be remembered was not coeval with the Cold War. It wasn't built until 1961. Some historians would go so far as to trace the Cold War all the way back to the Great War of 1914–18 and the Allied armed intervention in Russia that immediately followed the separate peace the Bolsheviks made with Germany after the October Revolution of 1917. None would place the Cold War's beginnings any later than the spring of 1947, when the Truman Doctrine was enunciated.

In fact, if the demolition of the Wall has now been greeted as a triumph of freedom, its construction nearly thirty years ago was also hailed as a victory for the West. By the odd arrangements that the victors of the Second World War made in Europe in 1945, each side in what was to be the Cold War gave a hostage to the other in Berlin. West Berlin – the American, British, and French zones of occupation in the city – was isolated within the zone that the Red Army had conquered and occupied in eastern Germany as a whole, far beyond the border of the American, British, French (and Belgian) occupation zones in western Germany. East Berlin, however, was a short subway ride from the fleshpots of the West.

In the 1950s, before the Wall, East Berlin was a bleak and depressing place. So was the eastern zone as a whole (the German Democratic Republic). In the West, the tremendous destruction and devastation caused by the war had marked the landscape for more than half a dozen years. But within that period, the Germans shoveled the rubble into small mountains that lined the sides of the streets in cities which had endured a series of a thousand-bomber raids. I remember coming into Cologne by train from the south in 1951. The railway curves into the city, elevated on embankments and bridges, and at the time presented a view of the aftermath of Armageddon – miles of skeletal ruins. Interested in the Roman-

Previously published in the *Irish Times*, 24 April 1990.

esque, but using pre-war texts to guide me, I went visiting medieval churches that no longer existed. In one shattered and roofless building the whole space of the nave was occupied by graves, marked by little crosses, of men, women and children, all of whom had died on a single night, victims of 'Bomber' Harris's plan to defeat Germany by breaking the will of its civilian population through terror exercised from the air.

Then, quite quickly, the Germans set about replacing the rubble mountains with new buildings. While the 'economic miracle' was in process, I remember finding the new streets uninspiring as they went up, because the architecture was both dull and repetitiously monotonous. But the achievement was remarkable and impressive; and now the buildings of that day, in their turn, are being replaced.

Everywhere those hastily runup buildings, now forty years old, mark the extent of the aerial bombing or the artillery bombardments of the war. Last September, just as the great exodus from the East was beginning to gather force, I happened to be in a car on the roads of northern Germany, close to the border of the Democratic Republic, with two women in their 40s, both medieval scholars, one German, one English, who had been friends since their student days. The conversation turned on why some of the small towns we passed through had lost their medieval hearts to be replaced by this rather gimcrack architecture, and some hadn't. In that area it largely had to do with the flight paths of the British and American bombers heading for Berlin forty-five or forty-six years ago: when they ran into heavy flak or fighter opposition, they often dropped their bombs well short of the target. I made some remark about the enormous casualties suffered by the bomber crews.

And it suddenly emerged that the two women, although old friends, had never talked to each other about the war. And it then further emerged that the German – educated, and of the generation that has now moved into control, at the middle level and upwards – while she knew about the Hitler years and the war, and the concentration camps, knew quite little about what things were like just after the war; what her parents' generation thought when it was all over. She herself would have been born shortly after the war ended, and she grew up in the new, revived, burgeoning, democratic German Federal Republic.

The questions she asked are quite important now. What was it like? For the Cold War came on the heels of that other war, the ferocious struggle that devastated Europe between 1939 and 1945. One answer to one of her questions is that, after the final defeat in 1945, many Germans who had come through the years of destruction were bitter; because they had been defeated; because they had been subjected to such tremendous destructive power, which destroyed and then divided their country. A similar bitterness had bred Nazism a generation earlier, after the Great War. They resented defeat. The young people, who had been at school in the war years, showed a widespread reaction that took the form of pacifism and resented the new stirrings of the Cold War. '*Ohne uns!*' and 'Ami go home!' were the graffiti on the ruined walls among the rubble.

The occupying power in the West looted freely and treated the Germans harshly for a year or two, although from the very first moment of the occupation some provisions were made (notably by the Americans) for the different conflict, with the Russians, that so many foresaw. The East-West hostility, never fully subdued even at the height of the wartime alliance with the Soviet Union, meant that from the beginning of the postwar period West Germany was regarded as a potential ally for the future.

In the east, on the other hand, the Russians had had a much more terrible experience with Germany than had the British, or even the defeated French, not to speak of the Americans (who had no experience of war on their soil since 1865). Stalin, at the end of the war, turned loose his troops, who had endured unspeakable hardships, on those parts of Germany they occupied. East Germany was punished, along with the conquered and confiscated lands in East Prussia and in western parts of what is now Poland.

The whole female population, from fifteen to fifty-five, was raped, singly and multiply. Industrial equipment was carted off to the Soviet Union. The country was stripped, as if by a plague of locusts, of everything that wasn't nailed down and of a good deal that was. They stole the very lavatory seats out of private houses and apartments. Populations of millions of people were driven out of their homes to fend for themselves as best they could – those who survived – by making their way westward into East Germany or beyond.

Good enough for them, still say a great many people. The Germans deserved it. The Second World War is the most mythologized of wars, and revisionism has hardly touched the propaganda of fifty years ago. It is still presented as a great crusade of good against evil. It wasn't that. No war is. It has been possible to present it as that in the first place because of the horrors that were revealed at the war's end: the murder of millions in foul death camps by evil and perverted people serving an evil and perverted politics.

The evil is undeniable, but its sources have been insufficiently examined. It is difficult, looking back over the *whole* history of the past 150 years, not to see it as a European evil. It is an evil that was afoot in the enterprises of the vile Leopold II in the Belgian Congo, and in the villages of the Jewish Pale of Settlement in the Czarist Empire, a full 100 years ago, and that had already spread like a plague by the beginning of this century. This century, after all, has been one of the blackest in history.

The war was not fought to prevent the horrors of the death camps. It wasn't even fought against Nazism. None of the 'United Nations', as the western allies called themselves, entered the war for any of those reasons; Britain and France declared war because they saw their national interests threatened; most states took part in the war because they were attacked or invaded. It is in retrospection, and because of what was revealed at its end, that the war has for so long been seen, plausible enough, as a crusade against evil. But there is an urgent need for revisionism in its study, otherwise we are in serious danger of failing to understand modern Europe.

As it is, Germany continues to be blamed and feared, not unjustly, but disproportionately, for the great evils that occurred. Austria was not unwillingly swallowed up in the *Anschluss*. And Germany had allies, not only in the war itself, but in the crimes that took place while the war was going on, notably the attempted extermination of Jews, gypsies and homosexuals. Semi-fascist, anti-Semitic Poland (under Colonel Beck), shortly to be a victim itself, seized its hyena's share of Czechoslovakia when Hitler extinguished the country's independence, just as the Soviet Union was to take its share of Poland when the Germans invaded that country a year later. The Polish Resistance stood by while the Germans destroyed the heroic uprising of the Warsaw ghetto, just as the Red Army was to stand by a little later while the Germans destroyed the heroic uprising of the Polish Resistance. In the attempted genocide of the Jews, the Germans had the collaboration of French, Romanian, Bulgarian, Austrian, Ukrainian and other anti-Semites, along with the applause of South American anti-Semites and the tacit approval of many people in the very countries that were fighting Germany.

German bitterness after the Second World War – although it was real – didn't, however, persist the way German bitterness after the First World War did. The revelation of the horrors of the extermination camps, in 1945, silenced protest at the great evils the Germans, in their turn – including many innocent people – had to endure. But great evils there were. 'We are all guilty' is a good slogan for breast-beating liberals. Every responsible citizen is in some degree guilty for the evil that society does; Germans in larger numbers had acclaimed Hitler and therefore in some measure were responsible for what he presided over. But only in some measure. The rest of us, perhaps in some smaller measure, were responsible, too. And the Germans have worked their passage. Part of what we have been seeing recently is their declaration that, after years of standing in the corner with their face to the wall, they feel the time has come when they can turn around and face the rest of us. They can.

The Wall was the weak section of the Iron Curtain because it divided Germans. The Iron Curtain is interesting because, like so many frontiers of its type, it represented a long history and didn't just spring into being out of nothing after 1945. It marked, very roughly and crudely, that most important European division between German and Slav. Long, long ago, the Germans pushed beyond the line of ethnic division; but beyond the Elbe, German settlement has had something of a colonial character. The three great cities of Central Europe, the three capitals of modernism, Berlin, Vienna and Prague, were, in their formation, German cities on the frontier of German expansion into the lands of the Slavs.

The German contribution to Europe, which is immense, had its base farther west. The Roman Empire included, for a period, large parts of western Germany, and our European experience, since the fifteenth century at least, has been enormously enriched by German marginalities. To the Greco-Roman tradition they contributed the wholly different traditions of Germany beyond the Roman frontier: the romantic movement, the North European soul; music; the Goethean understanding that colour and light can't be fully and definitively described in

Galilean and Newtonian formulae. And then, more recently, it is on the farther frontier, that of German and Slav, that a great deal of our modern consciousness took its shape. Mozart, Freud, Wittgenstein, Kafka, Wagner, Mann, to take a few at random, are people of the zone whose divide was to be expressed in the Iron Curtain.

The Wall has been for thirty years, that part of the last major European frontier where east and west interpenetrated. That was the curious and special character of Berlin. In the early 1970s I lived for a while in West Berlin, but regularly passed through Checkpoint Charlie to enjoy the rarefied, but real, pleasures of East Berlin. To purchase ten East Marks was a condition of entry – at the rate of one (West) to one (East) mark. It seems very bad value, since the East German mark was all but valueless in the West. But within East Berlin it bought just as much as the West German mark bought in the West.

And East Berlin, in spite of the drabness and the all-pervasive sense of oppression, had some advantages. Beyond the Wall, the rat-race ended. People, equal under oppression to a degree, were slow and nice to one another; old-fashioned courtesies survived. People would talk to you on the street and open their hearts. They were only afraid of the government; not of their friends and neighbours. There was something distasteful, in comparison, in the glitter, the material wealth, the comfort and the competition of West Berlin. But the advantages of living in close community under oppression, like those of the comradeship produced by war, are severely limited.

Another comradeship was consolidated in those years: that of the Germans. Everybody else, almost, had agreed, since early in this century, that they were a bad lot. They had had to face the fact themselves, in the middle of the century, that they had done, or their fellow-countrymen or their parents, relations or friends, had done some pretty bad things. And for this they had been severely punished. And then, by hard work and skill, they had pulled themselves out of the mire and become again a power in the world; a respectable, democratic even liberal, power.

In working-class pubs in Wolfenbüttel and other small places a few miles from the East German border at the end of last summer, when the exodus from the East was beginning, the men at the bar weren't talking about the threat to their jobs as skilled workers flocked out from the East. They were glad their compatriots and comrades were finding freedom. East Germany had long been the hostage beyond the Slav frontier. Nationalism lives.

The demolition of the Wall, like its construction in 1961, is both symbolic and practical. Not just Germany, but Europe, has been changed. We must be prepared to face many nasty manifestations of nationalism, because some old habits will die hard. But these are hiccups in the historical process. What is happening is the demolition of the last significant European frontier. Embrace the Germans. Welcome the Slavs.

32

An American Lineage: The Fishes of Garrison

In 1986 I had a conversation with Hamilton Fish in his apartment on Park Avenue, New York, not far from Hunter College. He was busy, but interrupted his day to talk to me for an hour or two. The project which occupied most of his time then was the publication of materials to prove conclusively to the world, but in particular to the American people, that Franklin Delano Roosevelt had been a fraud, a phoney, a warmonger, a wolf in sheep's clothing, a man quite unworthy to have been president of the United States for one term, not to speak of four. Mr Fish had a male assistant, who came and went several times while we were talking, fully engaged in searching out documents to support his case. In another room a female secretary was dealing with his correspondence and engagements.

Her boss was then ninety-nine years old. He married her the following year, having had no wife for some time (she became his third). He is, alas, no longer with us, having deprived America and the world of the stimulus of one of its most colourful – and upright – characters not long after this final marriage.

Ham Fish had been, among many other things, a US Congressman (a Republican), representing a district in New York State. When I talked to him his son, a middle-aged man, held the same congressional seat. The father gave me of his time because I had been introduced to him by constituents of his son and acqaintances of his in the Hudson River Valley as a writer from Ireland – a country he regarded favourably on grounds which would not have commended it to most American public men of his time and of his stamp: its neutrality in the Second World War. For he was an unreconstructed Isolationist, a survivor of that once powerful group in the Congress which had succeeded, in spite of Woodrow Wilson, in keeping the United States out of the League of Nations and had gone close enough to keeping it out of the Second World War. Leading various committees, delegations and commissions, he had several times met Éamon de Valéra in the 1930s, and greatly admired him.

My reason for going to talk to him, however, had nothing to do with my Irishness and everything to do with his Americanness. Not only had he had an interesting career himself, but his family's political history spanned the two centuries of the American Republic, and extended back into its colonial past. Having got to know the lower Hudson Valley over a number of years previously, I had heard much about the Fishes of Garrison.

Previously unpublished

Garrison is on the left bank of the Hudson, just across the river from West Point. It is a station on the railroad line from Poughkeepsie to Grand Central Station, New York – a train ride to be highly recommended to anyone who enjoys the sight of a majestic mile-wide river, punctuated with places where a history significant in the annals of the world was enacted, and flowing between high bluffs and pleasing, if not stupendous, mountain ranges. A little more than two hundred years ago the Hudson was the main corridor and highway from Canada due south towards the 'Middle Provinces' of British America, and the strategies of the War of the Revolution turned in part on the control of the river passage. Washington, for a crucial period, had his headquarters at Newburgh, on the right bank some miles above West Point and Bear Mountain. The forests along the Hudson and Delaware rivers had been the seat of great native nations, including the Mohawk and the Algonquin, but were penetrated by European invaders and colonists in the seventeenth century. The settlers along the Hudson were Dutch, and this is reflected in many of the river place-names, such as Peekskill and Fishkill. At Fishkill, on the left bank, there is an early-eighteenth-century church, not quite old enough in its present fabric to go back to the Dutch colonial days, but with some funerary tablets inscribed in Dutch. The colony was handed over to the English in the late seventeenth century and was re-named after the king's brother, the duke of York, later James II, becoming New York.

As 'Fish' is a possible Dutch name, I asked my host if that was indeed his family origin. He explained that it was not: their origin was English. His ancestors had first settled in the Bay Colony, but, as he explained it to me, they couldn't stand the authoritarianism of the Puritans who tried to regulate every aspect of the private as well as the public lives of the English colonists; so they moved westward into the Hudson Valley, among the rougher but less intolerant Dutch.

He talked to me about his father. What was remarkable to me, in 1986, was the simple fact that this man's father had served in the administration of Ulysses S. Grant, the general who defeated Robert E. Lee and took his surrender at Appomattox courthouse in 1865 at the end of the Civil War, and later became president of the United States. The father's position in the administration was, admittedly, at as low a level as is possible: he was, the old man told me, an office boy in the department of *his* father, who was Grant's secretary of state.

This was a family that had done the American Republic some service. I was well supplied with information about them on my visit to Park Avenue and had opportunity later to read a good deal more on the subject. The new information did not quite bear out what I had been told; but in a way it explained it. Ham Fish's first recorded colonial ancestor was indeed English: Jonathan Fish, who moved from Lynn, Massachusetts to Sandwich on Cape Cod in 1637. It was not to live among the lubberly and tolerant Dutch of the Hudson Valley that he moved from there, but, not far from New Amsterdam, to Long Island, where, with some others, he founded the settlement of Newtown and was a magistrate. His grandson Jonatahan was town clerk there for fifteen years. This Jonathan's great-grandson Nicholas was born in New York City in 1758 and was studying law when he received the commission of Brigade Major in 1776 in Washington's Continental Army. He fought throughout the War of the Revolution. He was in both battles of Saratoga and commanded a light infantry brigade at Monmouth. At Yorktown, where Lord Cornwallis surrendered and brought the war to an end, he was second in command to Alexander Hamilton, who led the New York and Connecticut men. Through the Yorktown campaign he became a friend of Lafayette as well as Hamilton, and to some extent a protegé of George Washington, who appointed him a supervisor of the revenue. He married Elizabeth Stuyvesant and their son, Hamilton Fish, was born in 1808. This was the grandfather of the Hamilton Fish with whom I conversed in 1986.

Hamilton Fish, born in 1808, was elected to Congress, as a Whig, from the sixth congressional district of New York in 1842, and served a term as congressman. In 1848 he was elected Governor of New York, and he was subsequently elected Senator from New York. Having served his six-year term he travelled to Europe with his family and spent two years there, returning to America to help Lincoln in the presidential campaign of 1860, and in the Civil War he helped undertake measures for the defence of New York, and later was assigned by Lincoln to tend to the grievous needs of Union prisoners of the Confederacy. He returned to Washington in 1869 to take up his post as secretary of state in the Grant administration. Probably his most important achievement in this office was to initiate the *rapprochement* with the United Kingdom that was to be one of the major developments in international affairs towards the end of the century. He exercised a moderating influence on the negotiations with Great Britain concerning the damage done to the Union cause in the Civil War by the *Alabama* and other Confederate ships fitted in British yards during the war. He resisted the pressure within the administration to attempt to force Britain out of Canada and out of the western hemisphere altogether, and wrote in a private letter:

> The two English-speaking progressive liberal governments of the world should not, must not, be divided – better let this question rest for some years even (if that be necessary) than risk failure in another attempt at settlement ... I would not, if I could, impose any humiliating condition on Great Britain. I would not be a party to anything that proposes to threaten her. I believe she is great enough to be just; and I trust that she is wise enough to maintain her own greatness.

His son followed him into politics, as did his grandson, with whom I had my conversation, and his great-grandson. The grandson commanded black troops in the Great War on the Western Front, was author of a bill to bring back the body of the Unknown Soldier of that war to the United States, was chairman of the First Congressional Committee to Investigate Communism, was chairman of the Committee of Three who wrote the Preamble of the American Legion, and was national commander of the American Legion.

A conservative. But a maverick. Before I left him, he presented me with a copy of a letter he had just sent:

Hon. President of the United States
Ronald Reagan
The White House
1600 Pennsylvania Avenue NW
Washington D.C. 20500

Dear Mr President
In view of the fact that the United States invented the fiendish nuclear weapons and used them against Hiroshima and Nagasaki with deady effects, it is our duty to take the lead in abolishing them. The American people believe in the maintenance of peace throughout the world, regardless of party affiliation or race, color and creed.

I request the President of the United States, when he meets with the head of the Soviet Union, to urge the total abolition of all nuclear weapons in every nation within the next two years under effective surpervision ...

The time has come for the American people and the Congress to show some guts in seeking to abolish all nuclear weapons in order to prevent a ghastly and deadly nuclear war, or holocaust that might well destroy civilization.

And the ninety-nine-year-old man also inscribed for me a copy of one of his books execrating the long-dead F.D.R. I came out into the Manhattan sunshine feeling I had visited an American historic monument built of a gritty, idiosyncratic, very American granite.

33

New World Orders

A couple of years ago, as the walls came tumbling down in Eastern Europe, an American professor in a moment of enthusiasm – indeed of triumphalism – ventured the opinion that history had now come to an end. This was so extreme an opinion that it was widely reported at the time, not altogether for its oddity; for with the collapse of the structures of communist State centralism there was widespread in the United States of America a kind of euphoric relief at what was seen primarily as an overwhelming victory for America in the Cold War. That's over. Now it's 'back to normalcy', in the words of an American President spoken after the conclusion of the Great War of 1914–18, the 'war to end war.'

The tendency of American culture is unhistoric: the culture rests on certain powerful and compelling mythic narrations – as, for example, in that tapestry of Western films and yarns that caught the imagination of the whole world for much of the first half of this century. Of course, there are many good historians in America engaged in the task of examining the American past, and endeavouring to do so with some scientific detachment; but such an attitude has not to any great extent been transmitted to the general popular culture of the country, which prefers to direct such energies to the examination of the future.

This is beginning to change; but until recently, popular America has thought of itself as a new order in the world, already established. The professor who suggested that there would be no more history to write, now that the Cold War had ended, was really simply extending to the whole field of international conflict of the past half-century this largely unspoken assumption about America itself: the journey of the ages was over; the destination had already been reached: we're there.

It is not altogether surprising then, that just over a year ago, President Bush, with reference *both* to the collapse in Eastern Europe *and* to the world coalition he was organizing for the war in the Persian Gulf, should refer confidently to the coming into being of a 'New World Order.' He has not really returned to the topic; for he had plainly not thought it through – President Bush is a political opportunist rather than a political philosopher and there is nothing of a Jeffersonian or Lincolnian farsightedness in his strangely erratic statements on matters of general political significance. Besides, his pronouncements on the world

---

Previously unpublished, this summary is based on a lecture given in Kilkenny on 30 January 1992.

at large have become unpopular in his own country: he is much criticized for directing his attention outward and ignoring the depressed and demoralized state of America itself.

Those words are not too exaggerated. The president tried to prop up the morale of his people the other day, in his State of the Union address to the Congress, by boasting again of victory in the Cold War, but I doubt if this attempt will succeed. American public opinion is very uneasy just now and very suspicious of all attempts to cajole the American people with talk of successes abroad. Successes at home are what they are interested in. There is a new isolationism in America. It won't have the same weight as the old isolationism of the 1920s and 1930s – which was strong enough, with the aid of some other forces, to keep the USA out of the League of Nations, for example.

The topic of a New World Order, however, is interesting, especially as seen through American eyes. The United States of America is probably in the early stages of a long slow imperial decline (although this is by no means certain), but the failure of the Eastern power-bloc has left America – for the moment, anyway – as the sole world superpower, in military terms, and also, therefore, in diplomatic influence. Japan and the European Community may be close enough to being, either of them, America's match in economic strength, but with the disintegration of the Soviet Union, there is now no other power, not even China, capable of facing up – in a global struggle – to America's military might. The Americans have learnt, however, both in Korea and in Vietnam, that when a war is localized they may have great difficulty, for reasons outside the sphere of military strength, in bringing their power to bear, and may even lose in the end – as they did in Vietnam nearly twenty years ago. It is largely from the experience of such loss that, since the early 1970s, they have been trying to develop a new system of alignments – a new order – in the world, in which they would no longer be in danger of such an embroilment.

At this point, it is worth bearing in mind that the great global struggle which has now ended – the so-called 'Cold War' – was itself a conflict between two New World Orders, each of which claimed to envisage correctly and beneficially the future of humankind. They were both unlike the new order into which we have entered, the European Community; for the European Community, although its member states have a high level of shared ideology, is not *based* on ideology. It has been highly pragmatic in its development, its purposes and its progress – beginning with the Coal and Steel Authority, whose primary purpose was to place enormous *practical* difficulties in the way of another war between France and Germany – then proceeding to grow through Benelux, the Six, the Nine and so on. There was of course some top-dressing of pseudo-idealism, with vague and cloudy notions about the Europe of Charlemagne and the like, top-dressing on solid practicalities, however.

But political arrangements based on abstract political ideas are another matter. The point about the United States of America, in this context, is that it is a country founded and based not so much on common blood, common ethnic origin, or common history (although all these were involved) as on a common set of ideas. Americans often enough think of their country in this way. Local loyalties of course exist and sometimes are strong, especially in the South (where History looms much larger) but nowadays the overriding loyalty is to the community of America – a very powerful feeling of oneness derived from shared understanding. America in moments of trial becomes a single family because of this shared *ideological* identity. This can cut across the barriers of race and ethnicity, even if usually only for brief periods of crisis. Similarly the now-collapsed Union of Soviet Socialist republics was a state founded on and dedicated to an idea, or rather, an ideology.

The ideas in question are those of freedom, emphasized in the United States, and equality, emphasized in communist theory. Both sides also increasingly frequently invoked the much fuzzier and lazier concept of 'democracy'.

The very notion of a 'new order' stems from the effort which some people have made, down the ages, to examine and understand how people organize themselves in society and how they make rules for this organization. The simplest concept of social order is that people all do what they are told: God tells the king what to do; the king tells his agents and ministers; they tell their servants and clients; husbands tell their wives; parents tell their children; masters tell their slaves. This suits a condition of pre-rational consciousness, pre-self-consciousness, when people had not developed reasoned processes of thought but acted upon impulses communicated to them from outside, or sometimes (as perceived voices, dreams or otherwise) from inside their own heads. It is a model long followed, and may be observed in armies and in religious orders bound to obedience.

The ancient Greeks made serious attempts at a rational understanding of the social order , attempts that went well beyond the rationalizations of pre-rational systems undertaken, for example, by Confucius. Socrates and Plato struggled with the intractable confusion of human affairs, cutting through it with attempts to envisage the essence or ideal of social order. Aristotle carried such rationalizations forward, but continued to find it necessary to distinguish between the 'natures' of citizens and of slaves. It was St Paul who envisaged a 'new man', to be born through Redemption. From this point on, it is Christian teaching that underlies, however deeply and remotely, almost all 'new order' schemes in the West. Such schemes are founded on perceptions of corruption, decay and restoration – not uncharacteristically the restoration of an imagined past, the return to a golden age. They are also founded on the idea, derived from Christian teaching, that we are all equal in the sight of God, each and every one individually and separately loved for our own sake. These ideas have been secularized, often in ways that make them all but unrecognizable.

They have also regularly been evaded; but, although greed for power and wealth overcomes them all the time, they are resilient ideas, and sufficiently strong for lip service to be paid to them. President Bush's preached New World Order sounds like the Peaceable Kingdom, where the lion lies down with the lamb, because he is paying lip service and, to be fair, more than lip service to the ideal of a just world society. But his acted New World Order is different, and not very new. History has not ended.

Mr Bush's government, for example, achieved an extraordinary and almost unprecedented diplomatic success in lining up countries round the world to contribute militarily and financially to the war in the Persian Gulf. But the order which that great effort was intended to restore was not the order of a justly governed world, nor of a peaceful world, but the imperial order imposed by the West which was being disturbed and threatened. Many worthier causes than that of Kuwait have failed to stir the Americans and their clients to such exertions. The imperial power has regularly been directed against populist movements that menace the supplies of oil – as in the case of Dr Moussadek in Iran in the 1950s – and the necessity actually to go to war arose from the American failure to have Saddam Hussein overthrown (assassination would be inevitable) by an army coup, and a compliant dictator installed in his place. The short-term aim of securing the flow of oil on Western terms was achieved, although in a very botched manner. 'Desert Storm' was short and nasty, and quickly died away to an uneasy calm; but it was not a storm in a tea-cup. The world is unstable. History has not come to an end. We will just have to go on living with it.

Index

Act of Appeals (1533), 13
Act of Supremacy (1534), 13
Act of Union (1800), 20, 74
Adams, John, 33
Adams, Henry, 115
Æ [George Russel], 89, 93
Aesthetic Movement, 118
Africa, 20, 21; slaves from, 26; South
    African War, 22; Boers, 134
Age of Reason, *see* Enlightenment
aisling, 50, 53
Aldershot bombing, 174
America, Irish: 217–19 *see also* Colonies;
    United States of America
Antrim, County, 221
Apollinaire, Guillaume, 123, 128
'Apostles, the', 101
Arp, Hans, 127
Arragon, Louis, 127, 128
Art Nouveau, 118, 119
Articles of Cofederation, 31
assassinations, Abraham Lincoln, 132; Tsar
    Alexander II, 133; Sadi Carnot, 133;
    Antonio Canovas, 133; Empress
    Elizabeth of Austria, 133; King
    Umberto of Italy, 133; President
    William McKinley, 133; King Alfonso
    of Spain, 133; José Canalejas, 133;
    Count Stolypin, 134; Sipyagin, 134;
    Plehve, 134; Archduke Ferdinand, 134,
    135
atomic theory, 99–100
'Aughnaboy', 224
Augustine, Saint, 109
Australia, 20, 21, 23
Austria, 202, 236

Baader, Johannes, 129
Bakunin, Michael, 133
Balkans, the, 134

Balla, Giacomo, 121
Ballintubber Abbey, 196
Ballyporeen, 217
baptism of Christ, 214
Barbados, 15
Bargeld, Johannes, 127
Barra, St, 213
Barry, Tom, 84
Baudelaire, Charles, 111
Beck, Col., 236
Belgian Congo, 235
Belfast, 201, 228
Belfast College of Science and Technology,
    228
Belfast High School, 228
Bell, Clive, 101
Bell, J. Bowyer, 84, 163–4, 180
Belloc, Hilaire, 115
Berlin, 201, 204, 234, 236; Berlin Wall, 233,
    236–7
Bermuda, 15–16
Bethmann-Hollweg, Theobald von, 137
    Bindon, Francis, 54
Blaue Reiter, der, 125
Bloody Sunday, 145, 171, 173, 174
Bloomsbury group, 101–2
Bloy, Léon, 115
Boccioni, Umberto, 121
Booth, John Wilkes, 132
Boston, British evacuation of, 53
Brahms, 98
Braque, Georges, 119, 123–24, 125, 130
Breathnach, Breandán, 72
Brendan, St, 213
Breton, André, 127, 128
Brian Bóroimhe, 13–14
Brigit, St, 60
British constitution, 18, 75
Brooke, Rupert, 136
Bunting, Edward, 78